GRAY MATTER
וזאת ליהודה

BY RABBI CHAIM JACHTER
WITH EZRA FRAZER

© Copyright 2000 by Rabbi Howard Jachter, 315 Churchill Road, Teaneck, NJ 07666, USA.

All rights reserved. No part of this publication may be translated, reproduced, stored in a retrieval system or transmitted, **in any form** or by any means, electronic, mechanical, photocopying, recording, or otherwise, without prior permission in writing from the author. Printed in the United States of America by Noble Book Press. The rights of the copyright holder will be strictly enforced.

ISBN 0-9670705-3-8

We wish to thank the following for their support in the publication of this book:

- Congregation Shaarei Ora, the Sephardic Congregation of Teaneck
- Rav Yosef Adler, Congregation Rinat Yisrael
- Rav Kenneth Auman, Young Israel of Flatbush
- Rav Ari Berman, The Jewish Center
- Rav Shmuel Goldin, Congregation Ahavath Torah
- Rav Daniel Korobkin, Kehillat Yavneh of Los Angeles, formerly of Congregation Sons of Israel of Allentown
- Rav Michael Shmidman, Congregation Keter Torah
- Mr. Isaac and Wendy Shulman, Teaneck, New Jersey
- Rav Moshe Snow, Young Israel – Beth El of Borough Park
- Rav Hershel Solnica and the Staff of Torah Academy of Bergen County
- Rav Shmuel and Chana Tokayer, West Orange, New Jersey

בס"ד

Rabbi Ephraim Greenblatt
5556 Barfield Road
Memphis, TN 38120

הרב אפרים גרינבלאט
רב ושו"ב במעמפיס
מחבר שו"ת רבבות אפרים חי"ה

הסכמה

ישיו פ"ס.

הנה ידידי הרב ר' חיים אלעזר שלמה שליט"א שלח לי דבר מסכת סוכה שחיבר לזכות לזכות הרבים, בשם "שלום לעם", ואמרתי גם אני ברצוני לתת ברכה, כברכת התורה שליט"א.

ואמרתי הנה בכגון דא"ל... רצה הקב"ה לזכות את ישראל לפיכך הרבה להם תורה ומצוות, וכאן ראיתי בעל התורה, וכל כן יודע האדם שיבור לו דרך ישרה שיעסוק בתורה שבכתב ושבעל פה, כי רק בכח זה יוכל לזכות ולהבין עם כל ישראל שיהיה זוכה ומזכה את הרבים.

וגם זה כי דברי תורה צריכין חיזוק, ואשרי חלקו של מי שיעסוק בתורה וגם יפיץ אותה לרבים, ואשרי שזוכה לעסוק בתורה ולזכות את הרבים...

ואשרי לו כי אגרת התורה גדולה, כי ואשרי שלומד וילמד אחרים, ויפוצו מעינותיך חוצה.

בסוף בא מעשה ובא לידי דבר זה ויפה השעה הזאת ואקוה שיהיה לו הצלחה בכל מעשה ידיו, ויפוצו מעינותיו חוצה, ויהי רצון שיזכה לכתוב עוד ספרים ולהגדיל תורה ולהאדירה.

וכן הנני מברכו בעה"ח שיזכה להגדיל תורה ולהאדירה וכבר כתב כתב ידו ואותה נפשי ברכה כתורה.

וכאחד נשמח ישמח לבו ותגל נפשו ברבות בניו בנותיו וצאצאיו שיצליח לראות נחת מכל יוצאי חלציו מתוך בריאות ואושר, ויזכה לעשות רצון ד' מתוך שמחה כל רבבות שני עולמות.

בברכה
בכל ברכות דמעלתך אורייתא

בפה מעמפיס יע"א
בכל הכבוד וידידות
כה דברי ידי"ל ואהובי
אוהבו באהבה ובאחדות,

כדבר שלום וכוח וישע רב בכל מילי מב' מלכים
וכ" ומברכו באלפים של ברכה.

Tel: 548-4765

YOUNG ISRAEL OF RIVERDALE
4502 HENRY HUDSON PARKWAY EAST
RIVERDALE, NEW YORK 10471

Mordechai Willig, Rabbi

Table of Contents

Introduction

    Acknowledgments iii
    Dedication vii

Grappling With the Problem of Agunot

    Coercing a Husband to Give a *Get* 3
    The Power of Prenuptial Agreements 8
    Administering Outside Pressure to Give a *Get:*
        Communal Pressure, the New York State
        Get Laws, and Israeli Rabbinical Courts 17
    Hafka'at Kiddushin: Annulment of Marriage 29
    Conditional Marriage 34
    Kiddushei Ta'ut: Marriage Under False Pretenses 40
    Flaws in the Proposal of Rabbi Emanuel Rackman 48

Non-Orthodox Marriages

    The Halachic Status of Civil Marriages 63

    The Halachic Status of Reform Marriages
        Kiddushei Bi'ah and the Presence of Orthodox
            Men in the Audience 69
        Deviations in the Ceremony 73
        The Status of Non-Orthodox Jews Today 78
        Is a *Tinok Shenishbah* Acceptable as a Witness? 83

Modesty

A Husband's Participation in Childbirth ... 93
Women and Leadership Positions ... 99

Monetary Issues

Hasagat Gevul: Economic Competition in
    Jewish Law ... 107
Halachah and Copyright Laws ... 119
The Torah's View of Gambling ... 125

The State of Israel

Exchanging Land for Peace
Hashkafic Considerations ... 135
Halachic Arguments ... 140

The Halachic Status of the Falash Mura ... 145
Should Yeshivah Students Serve in the
    Israeli Army? ... 152

Laws of Shabbat

Laws of Creating an *Eruv*
Defining the Four Domains ... 165
List of Major Cities ... 172
Constructing the *Tzurot Hapetach* ... 181
Issues once the *Eruv* Is Erected ... 192

Milking Cows on *Shabbat*
Using a Non-Jew and Milking to Waste ... 200
Milking in Unusual Manners ... 205
Attaching a Milking Machine Turned Off ... 210

Laws of Holidays

Laws of Holidays

The Second Day of *Yom Tov* for Visitors to Israel 217
May Women Read the *Megillah*? 224
Should One Get Drunk on *Purim*? 234

The *Minhag* of *Kitniyot*
General Overview 239
Ashkenazim Eating with Sephardim 245
Scope of the Practice 250

Biography List 257

Appendix

Introduction

Acknowledgments

When I began teaching as a *rebbe* at the Torah Academy of Bergen County in Teaneck, New Jersey, in 1995, one of my responsibilities was to oversee the production of the Yeshiva's weekly Torah publication called *Kol Torah*. The students and Rabbeim contributed articles each week relating in some way to the *parshat hashavuah*. I wrote a steady article on points of Halachah. This book is a compilation and amplification of some of those Halachah articles. They cover a variety of important halachic issues. Dozens of avid readers have encouraged me to compile the *Kol Torah* essays into book form. I am indebted to these readers for their unwavering support and encouragement. I have striven to present a balanced approach to controversial issues and to educate and inform, so that people should be aware of the varied approaches adopted by great Torah authorities.

I have striven to follow the Gemara (*Chagigah* 3b), which urges Talmud students to "make their ear like an opening to a millstone and acquire an understanding heart to hear those who rule that something is impure and those who rule that something is pure, those who forbid and those who permit, those who disqualify and those who rule that an item is not disqualified." Rashi (*ad. loc.* s.v. *aseih*) explains that "since all of the authorities are sincerely dedicated to *Hashem*, make your ear attentive and learn and know all of the opinions." Familiarizing ourselves with all of the opinions enriches us and enhances our service of *Hashem*.

It is my hope that the book will motivate increased consultation with rabbinical authorities. The greater one's

Gray Matter

knowledge, the greater one's ability to discern when a question should be posed to a halachic authority. Enhanced knowledge facilitates meticulous observance of the Torah.

I thank Ezra Frazer, one of the finest graduates of the Torah Academy of Bergen County, for the countless hours he has invested in bringing this work to fruition. He is a true "*avrech*" - young but wise. His breadth of knowledge, sharp eye, intelligence, language skills, and commitment to excellence has thoroughly transformed this work. I am proud to have co-authored this work with him.

Special thanks to Rachel Frazer, Deborah Wenger, and my sister, Rose Greenman, for carefully reviewing the text for grammar and clarity.

Special thanks to Rav Moshe Rayman for meticulously reviewing the text for accuracy and clarity.

Rav Baruch Simon enhanced the quality of this work with his insightful comments.

I thank Isaac Shulman for his generous support of the production of this work.

I thank my in-laws, Rav Shmuel and Chana Tokayer, for their support of the publication of this work and for their constant support of my varied endeavors.

I thank the entire staff of Torah Academy of Bergen County for their encouragement and support. Most of all, the support of its principal, Rav Yosef Adler, has been indispensable. Rav Adler has contributed immensely to my growth in Torah study and teaching ability. I would also like to thank Rav Adler for raising the necessary funds to finance the printing of this book. Rav Zvi Grumet, the associate principal of the Torah Academy of Bergen County, deserves special thanks for the countless hours spent guiding me the art of teaching with love.

ACKNOWLEDGMENTS

The students at Torah Academy have been a constant source of joy since I joined the staff in 1995. I offer special thanks to the young men who have served with distinction as editors of *Kol Torah*. These young men include Kenneth Banner, Yonah Berman, Meir Dashevsky, Avi Klein, Elisha Olivestone, and Yonatan Schechter. They deserve special credit for their commitment to Torah study, careful observance of mitzvot, and service to the Jewish people. I offer special thanks to Yonah Berman for his assistance in the preparation of this book. His energy and enthusiasm serve as an inspiration.

Avi Klein deserves special thanks for the many hours that he invested in preparing the book for publication. The aesthetic quality of the book is in great measure due to his hard work.

Special mention to Joshua Bender, of blessed memory. Joshua served as the editor of *Kol Torah* in 1995 - 1996 when I joined the Torah Academy staff. Josh introduced me to *Kol Torah* and set a standard of excellence. Josh's contributions to the production of *Kol Torah* have become a permanent component of its success. His presence is to this day discernible in every issue of *Kol Torah*. May his memory serve as a blessing.

My parents, Ben and Shirley Jachter, of blessed memory, were role models of dedication. They selflessly spared no efforts in their support of their children. They raised me to appreciate learning and encouraged me to grow in Torah. I thank my parents for providing an environment for me where I could witness tolerance and the warmth of Torah. May this work serve *l'ilui nishmatam*. A day never passes in which I do not mention them or think of them.

Hashem has brought me the great fortune of studying from outstanding Rebbeim. I had the privilege to study and establish a personal relationship with Rav Yosef Dov Soloveitchik, zt"l, during the last two and a half years that he taught at Yeshiva University. I have also had the privilege of studying and interacting with the following great Torah personalities: Rav Yehuda Amital, Rav J.

GRAY MATTER

David Bleich, Rav Zalman Nechemia Goldberg, Rav Efraim Greenblatt, Rav Aharon Lichtenstein, Rav Melech Schachter, Rav Hershel Schachter, Rav Gedalia Schwartz, Rav Elazar Meyer Teitz, and Rav Mordechai Willig. I thank them all for their patience, time, and efforts that they have devoted to me.

Hashem has privileged me to be married to my wife, Malca. Her wisdom, kindness, warmth, and patience are the joy of my life. She has also made countless contributions and sacrifice to this work in particular and my overall Torah learning in general. May *Hashem* merit us to raise our children, Bracha and Binyamin, in the path of dedication to Torah study, careful observance of mitzvot, and contributions to *klal Yisrael*.

Dedication

The Hebrew title of this work *V'zot L'yehuda* was chosen to honor the memory of my wife Malca's beloved uncle, Rav Yehudah Tokayer, who passed away on 12 Elul 5759. Uncle Yiddy was a very special individual who loved Torah and embodied the essence of T*almud Torah* and *Mitzvot Bein Adam L'chaveiro*. He made people feel comfortable wherever he went. He exhibited great patience, profound insight, and a wonderful sense of humor. He was someone who participated in the community through his formal role as a social worker and informally supported and advised others and acted as a leader in his *shul*. He delivered many *shiurim* both on *Shabbat* and at work. He was able to see *Hashem*'s presence in every aspect of life and was able to transmit that to people around him wherever he was. May this work serve *l'ilui nishmato*.

This work is also dedicated to the memory of my Aunt Mrs. Edith Hersh, who passed away on 20 Tevet 5760. She supported me in all my projects and endeavors throughout the years. I thank her for her generosity and for her many years of helpful advice. She was a woman whose wisdom helped shape who I am today. May this work serve *l'ilui nishmatah*.

GRAPPLING WITH THE
PROBLEM OF AGUNOT

Coercing a Husband to Give a Get

Unfortunately, in the midst of a bitter divorce, a husband might sometimes withhold a *get* (Jewish bill of divorce) from his wife. This chapter discusses when a *beit din* (religious court) may coerce a husband to give his wife a *get* and defines what the Halachah considers coercion. Although coercion generally invalidates a *get*, sometimes a *beit din* **is** halachically permitted to coerce the husband even "with whips."

Talmudic Background

The Mishnah (*Ketubot* 77a) states:

> And these are forced to divorce: one who is afflicted with boils, one afflicted with severe halitosis, one who gathers dog excrement, a copper miner, and a tanner, regardless of whether these blemishes developed before or after the marriage.

According to the accepted view in the Mishnah, a *beit din* does not force the husband to divorce if the woman specifically stated before the marriage that she would tolerate a husband with these defects. The *Shulchan Aruch* (E.H. 154:1) codifies these laws as normative. The Gemara (*ad. loc.*) adds that a *beit din* coerces a husband to give a *get* when his marriage contravenes Halachah, such as the marriage of a *kohein* to a divorcee.

In addition to the cases enumerated in the above Mishnah, where the husband is **forced** (*kofin*) to divorce, there are other cases (e.g. *Ketubot* 70a-71a) where the Mishnah states that a

GRAY MATTER

husband should divorce his wife (*yozti*). In these cases, it is not clear if a *beit din* may force him to do so. Examples of these cases include one who forbids his wife to wear jewelry and one who forbids his wife to visit her father. The *Shulchan Aruch* (E.H. 154:21) first cites *Rishonim* that permit coercing a husband to give a *get* even in a *yotzi* situation. He then cites an opinion that the husband may merely be told that the rabbis require him to give a *get*.[1] If he refuses, he may be called a sinner, but he may not be coerced. The Rama rules in accordance with the latter opinion.

Ma'us Alai

Beyond listing specific cases, the Mishnah does not specify any guiding principles for determining when to coerce a husband. Great debate thus exists among *Rishonim* regarding the ability to coerce a husband to divorce in other cases where the marriage appears doomed.

One extreme position is that of the Rambam (*Hilchot Ishut* 14:8). He rules that whenever a woman claims *ma'us alai* (that she cannot tolerate her husband), the husband can be physically coerced to divorce her. He explains that a woman "is not a captive that she must cohabit with a man whom she hates."

Tosafot (*Ketubot* 63b s.v. *Aval*) cite Rabbeinu Chananeil, Rashi, and Rabbeinu Tam as opposing the Rambam's position. Rabbeinu Tam argues that a woman who claims that her husband is "intolerable" may simply desire to leave her husband for another man. The Mishnah's detailed list of which men are coerced appears to support Rabbeinu Tam's view. It only makes sense to have such a list if most husbands **cannot** be coerced, whereas

---

1. Both these opinions appear in *Tosafot* (*Ketubot* 70a s.v. *Yotzi*) and the Rosh (*Yevamot* 6:11). *Tosafot* believe that the husband may be coerced, and they cite Rabbeinu Chananeil as forbidding coercion. The Rosh rules that we must follow Rabbeinu Chananeil's view in order to avoid any concern of invalidating a *get*.

according to the Rambam, any husband may be coerced if his wife is unhappy. Most authorities accept Rabbeinu Tam's view (*Beit Shmuel* 77:8 and *Chelkat Mechokeik* 77:5).[2]

Coercing a "Rebellious" Husband

Although the Halachah does not follow the Rambam's view, there are certain cases beyond those specifically listed in the Mishnah where some authorities permit forcing the husband to divorce. The *Shulchan Aruch* and Rama (E.H. 154:3) rule that a husband who refuses to support or cohabit with his wife should initially be ordered to do so. If he persists in his refusal, the Halachah considers him "rebellious" and *beit din* may coerce him to give a *get*. In his *Beit Yosef* (E.H. 154 s.v. *Ha'omeir*), the author of the *Shulchan Aruch* explains that the Gemara (*Ketubot* 77a) cites a dispute regarding whether it is better to force such a husband to support his wife or to coerce him to divorce her. While the *Rishonim* debate which view to accept, the *Beit Yosef* cites the Ran and Rambam, who claim that all would permit coercing the husband to divorce once attempts to make him support his wife have failed. In the *Shulchan Aruch*, he extends this ruling to a husband who refuses cohabitation.

Despite the cogency of the *Beit Yosef*'s reasoning, the *Pitchei Teshuvah* (E.H. 154:7) cites the author of the *Shach* (*Gevurat Anashim* 28 and 48) as prohibiting coercion even when the husband refuses support and cohabitation. He argues that perhaps those authorities that rule that the husband should be coerced to **support** his wife would not permit coercing a *get* even when the husband resists the pressure to support her.

In practice, the *Aruch Hashulchan* (E.H. 154:20-21), Rav Yitzchak Elchanan Spektor (*Teshuvot Be'er Yitzchak* 1:10), and

---

2. See, however, *Teshuvot Heichal Yitzchak* (E.H. 1:2) who, while he does not fully adopt the Rambam's position, considers employing it to a limited extent.

GRAY MATTER

Rav Moshe Feinstein (*Teshuvot Igrot Moshe*, E.H. 1:137) all rule in accordance with the *Shulchan Aruch* and Rama and permit forcing such a husband to give a *get*.

Additional Cases that May Warrant Coercion

Beyond those cases that the Gemara specifies, it is difficult to establish what warrants coercion, so disputed cases abound. Examples include a husband who converts out of Judaism but does not prevent his wife from observing *mitzvot*,[3] an epileptic husband[4] (see Rama, E.H. 154:1,5), a husband whose wife committed adultery (see *Teshuvot Heichal Yitzchak*, E.H. 1:1), and a husband whose wife gives a convincing explanation (*amatla mevoreret*) of why she finds him intolerable (*ma'us alai*).[5] A case in the *Shulchan Aruch* (E.H. 154:5) best illustrates the reluctance to coerce when the Gemara does not explicitly mandate it. In this case, a woman claims that her father married her off to a mentally unstable husband because he lacked the financial status to find her anyone better. She says that she thought she could tolerate marriage to this man, but now she finds it intolerable, as he is deranged, and she fears that he will kill her. The *Shulchan Aruch* rules that such a man cannot be coerced to give a *get*, "for we only coerce those whom the Rabbis have mentioned."[6]

Executing the Coercion

Even when coercion is mandated, the Mishnah (*Gittin* 88b) states that it is only valid when done under the auspices of a Jewish (rabbinical) court. If non-Jews force the husband, the *get*

---

3. If the husband obstructs his wife's observance of *mitzvot*, such as if he prevents her from keeping the laws of family purity or feeds her non-kosher food, all agree that he may be coerced to give a *get* (Rama, E.H. 154:1).
4. For a discussion of epilepsy in Halachah, see *Techumin* (14:352-365).
5. For a summary of the debate on this issue, see *Teshuvot Yabia Omer* (vol. 3, E.H. 18).
6. Of course, the *Aruch Hashulchan* (E.H. 154:11) notes that the woman is not required to continue living with such a husband.

is unacceptable. Nevertheless, the Mishnah does permit a non-Jew to administer the actual coercion, provided that he orders the husband to "do what the Jews are telling you to do." *Rishonim* and *Acharonim* debate how explicitly the non-Jew must link his actions to the *beit din*'s ruling.[7]

The parameters of acceptable non-Jewish involvement in coercion are critical in many situations today. For example, it is common for couples (before or after marriage) to sign binding arbitration agreements that submit any divorce proceedings to the jurisdiction of a particular rabbinical court. If the *beit din* subsequently rules that the husband may be coerced to give a *get*, it is halachically acceptable for a civil court to enforce the *beit din*'s ruling. Although the civil court system is implementing the coercion, it is merely ordering the husband to obey the *beit din*. On the other hand, if the judge orders a husband to give a *get* absent the instructions of a *beit din*, the subsequent *get* is very problematic.

Conclusion

The Halachah does not always permit coercing a husband to give a *get*. As *Tosafot* (*Ketubot* 70a s.v. *Yotzi*) write, "No man can be coerced to divorce until clear proof [to permit this] is found." Accordingly, coercion must be used sparingly and only under eminent rabbinical guidance.

---

7. See Rav Tzvi Gartner's *Kefiyah B'get* 14.

The Power of Prenuptial Agreements

Prenuptial agreements are fast becoming an increasingly common phenomenon at Orthodox weddings. This chapter addresses the prenuptial agreement formulated by Rav Mordechai Willig, in cooperation with two Israeli authorities, Rav Zalman Nechemia Goldberg and Rav Chaim Zimbalist.

Introduction

The need for a halachically valid prenuptial agreement is well documented. Often, a spouse withholds a *get* (Jewish divorce document) as leverage in seeking money or child custody, or simply to inflict pain on an estranged partner. As a member of the Beth Din of Elizabeth since 1993, this author has witnessed many situations in which both women and men have suffered at the hands of recalcitrant spouses. Twice, a recalcitrant husband agreed to give a *get* only because he had signed a proper prenuptial agreement. Other rabbis and laymen report similar experiences.

The Problem of Coercion

Formulating a halachically sound agreement is far from simple. One cannot simply sign an agreement to give or receive a *get* in case of a civil divorce. Such an agreement is not halachically valid, because it is a *kinyan devarim*, a commitment merely to perform an action, and lacks any monetary consideration.[1]

---

1. See Rambam (*Hilchot Mechirah* 5:14), *Biur Hagra* (*Even Ha'ezer* 134:12), and *Beit Shmuel* (E.H. 134:7). The Tel Aviv Rabbinical Court has twice refused

THE POWER OF PRENUPTIAL AGREEMENTS

Furthermore, a husband must give a *get* without coercion. If a man is wrongly coerced to give his wife a *get*, the *get* is not valid, and the couple remains married.[2] Accordingly, a rabbinical court may not coerce a husband to give his wife a *get* even if he promised to do so before their marriage. In addition, Rabbeinu Gershom instituted that a wife's consent is necessary in a *get* proceeding (Rama, *Even Ha'ezer* 119:6). In fact, Rav Akiva Eiger (*Even Ha'ezer* 119:4) cites the opinion of the Maharam of Mintz that, following Rabbeinu Gershom's enactment, a woman who is coerced to accept a *get* is not divorced.[3] Therefore, a prenuptial agreement must be formulated in a way that does not inappropriately coerce either party to participate in the *get* procedure.

The Problem of Monetary Penalty

One possible formulation obligates whichever party refuses to take part in a *get* ceremony to pay a set sum of money to the aggrieved spouse on a daily basis. Such an agreement goes beyond a mere *kinyan devarim*, as it includes a monetary commitment. Nevertheless, this agreement remains halachically questionable, because it may constitute improper coercion to participate in a *get*. Nearly all authorities consider financial pressure to be coercion and only permit its use when Halachah permits coercion.[4]

Rishonim debate the Halachah regarding one who gives a *get* only for fear of paying a fine imposed upon himself (see *Beit Yosef*, E.H.134). The Maharik rules that the husband is giving the *get* of his own free will, because he voluntarily agreed to pay this

---

to enforce this type of commitment by a husband to give a *get* (*Piskei Din Rabbaniyim* 8:179 and 8:358-361).

2. Rambam, *Hilchot Geirushin* 2:20 and *Shulchan Aruch*, *Even Ha'ezer* 134:7-8. We discuss this topic at greater length in the chapter entitled "Coercing a Husband to Give a *Get*."

3. Also see *Teshuvot Noda Biy'hudah* (*Even Ha'ezer* 1:75), *Aruch Hashulchan* (E.H. 119:16), and Rav Yehuda Amital's article in *Daf Kesher* (1:141-142).

4. See *Kefiyah B'get* (Chapters 95-100) for a thorough discussion of the status of financial coercion.

monetary penalty. The Rashba, on the other hand, asserts that this constitutes coercion. The Rama (E.H. 134:5) cites, as a normative compromise approach, that initially (*lechatchilah*) the penalty should be eliminated before the husband gives the *get*. However, if the husband already gave a *get* to his wife out of fear of monetary penalty (*bedi'eved*), the *get* is considered acceptable.[5]

Due to the controversy surrounding it, halachic authorities have not endorsed an agreement that includes a self-imposed monetary penalty. In fact, this author saw Rav Zalman Nechemia Goldberg (in 1993, as a member of the Jerusalem Rabbinate District Court) refuse to perform a *get* for a couple with a separation agreement that penalized the husband for withholding a *get*.

Binding Arbitration Agreements

Despite the potential pitfalls, at least two ways of constructing a halachically acceptable prenuptial agreement do exist.[6] The first is a binding arbitration agreement in which husband and wife bind themselves to the jurisdiction of a particular *beit din*. This agreement requires a recalcitrant party to obey the ruling of the chosen *beit din*,[7] and a secular court would presumably enforce the *beit din*'s ruling. This agreement is halachically acceptable because it does not coerce either side to give or receive a *get*. The couple does not agree to participate in a *get* ceremony; rather, they merely agree to obey the ruling of a

---

5. See *Taz* (E.H. 134:6), Gra (E.H. 134:14), and *Chazon Ish* (E.H. 99:5), who endorse the Rama's decision, and *Pitchei Teshuvah* (E.H. 134:10) and *Aruch Hashulchan* (E.H. 134:26-29) for a critique of this ruling from *Teshuvot Mishkenot Yaakov* (38). Also, see *Pitchei Teshuvah* (E.H. 50:8).
6. For a discussion of two alternative formulations, see Rav J. David Bleich's *Bintivot Hahalacha* pp. 3-20 and *Contemporary Halakhic Problems* 3:329-343.
7. The agreement requires specifying the *beit din* to be used, because a New York court (Pal v. Pal, 45 A.D.2d at 739, 356 N.Y.S.2d at 673) has ruled that the secular courts may not convene a *beit din* on behalf of the parties. See Rav J. David Bleich's discussion of this point in *The Journal of Halacha and Contemporary Society* (p. 38) and Rav Willig's essay in *The Prenuptial Agreement: Halakhic and Pastoral Considerations* (pp. 29-35).

THE POWER OF PRENUPTIAL AGREEMENTS

particular *beit din.* Rav J. David Bleich drafted an example of such an agreement (*The Journal of Halacha and Contemporary Society* 7:25-41). In fact, Rav Moshe Feinstein (*Teshuvot Igrot Moshe, Even Ha'ezer* 4:107) finds no halachic problems with this type of document. This agreement empowers a *beit din* by making it likely that a civil court will enforce its ruling. For example, if a *beit din* rules that a husband must give a *get,* the wife may petition the civil court to force him to honor the arbitration agreement that he signed. This coercion is halachically acceptable, as the civil court merely enforces the ruling of the *beit din,* and the *beit din* may sometimes coerce a man to give a *get.*[8]

A Financial Arrangement for Separation

Rabbis Goldberg, Willig, and Zimbalist added a financial agreement to supplement the binding arbitration agreement.[9] It is based on an agreement formulated by the famed Rav Yaakov of Lissa to provide financial motivation for giving a *get,* but in a manner that does not constitute coercion (*Torat Gittin* 134:4 s.v. *Kenasot;* cited in *Pitchei Teshuvah* 134:9).[10] The husband waives

---

8. In limited instances, Halachah permits a *beit din* to physically coerce a man to give a *get;* see *Ketubot* (77a), *Gittin* (88b), and *Shulchan Aruch* (*Even Ha'ezer* 134:7 and 154). Physical coercion is illegal according to United States law, but American courts can compel a husband to obey the *beit din* when he has signed a binding arbitration agreement. While Halachah never permits civil courts to independently coerce a husband to give a *get,* it does permit civil courts to enforce the rulings of a proper *beit din* (*Shulchan Aruch,* E.H. 134:9; *Beit Shmuel* 134:15). For further discussion of the interface between halachic prenuptial agreements and American law, see Rav Yitzchak (Irving) Breitowitz's *Between Religious and Civil Law: The Plight of the Agunah in American Society* (pp. 77-162).
9. Rav Willig notes that a husband who feels uneasy with the financial agreement should still sign a binding arbitration agreement. Nonetheless, Rav Willig stresses that there is a "substantial advantage" to signing a prenuptial agreement with the financial component (*The Prenuptial Agreement: Halakhic and Pastoral Considerations,* pp. 34-35).
10. Rav Yaakov of Lissa's document differs slightly from the current prenuptial agreement in one notable way. Couples signed his agreement as

his halachic rights to his wife's earnings (*ma'asei yadayim*) while maintaining his obligation to support her. The man is thus motivated to give a *get* in order to release himself from his financial obligation to his estranged wife. This is not coercion because the husband's financial obligations are a result of the marriage and are **not** a punishment for withholding a *get*. Therefore, he gives a *get* out of dissatisfaction with his marriage and not because of outside coercion. Concerns of invalidating a *get* only arise when a financial penalty is **directly linked** to the *get* (see next chapter).

Based on Rav Yaakov of Lissa's idea, the three contemporary rabbis devised a prenuptial agreement for use today. The husband agrees to pay $100 per day[11] to support his wife in case they do not maintain domestic residence.[12] This obligation remains in effect for the duration of the halachic marriage. In addition, the husband waives his rights to the *ma'asei yadayim* of his wife. The document carefully avoids linking the husband's support obligation to his giving a *get*.

The wife cannot sign a parallel agreement, obligating herself to support her husband after separation, as the Halachah

---

part of the divorce settlement, whereas couples sign the current agreement before the marriage. This does not appear to impact the efficacy of the prenuptial agreement, as the time of its signing is irrelevant.

11. This sum can vary depending on the couple's financial status and geographical location. For instance, Rav Yaakov Kermaier (of Hong Kong) told this author in 1998 that $300 a day was necessary for daily support in Hong Kong, due to the high cost of living. Such an amount would likely invalidate a prenuptial agreement in New York, except for unusually wealthy people.

12. As a possible alternative, Rav Elazar Meyer Teitz has suggested that the obligation commence after the completion of a civil divorce. This formulation would allow for reconciliation after the separation without any financial pressure. Additionally, it could help prevent an unscrupulous wife from separating without a *get* in order to collect money from her husband. Rav Teitz's suggestion is not viewed as linking the financial agreement to the *get*, because the civil divorce is halachically insignificant.

THE POWER OF PRENUPTIAL AGREEMENTS

does not require a woman to support her husband. The husband is protected in most instances by the binding arbitration agreement, as *batei din* are more willing to rule that a wife must receive a *get* than to rule that a husband must give a *get*. The husband's consent is biblically mandated, whereas requiring the wife's consent was instituted much later by Rabbeinu Gershom. Since *dayanim* are extremely hesitant in forcing a husband to give a *get*, it is more important that a financial incentive be given to the husband to participate in a *get*.

One potential danger of this agreement is that an unscrupulous wife may refuse to accept the *get* in order to collect more money. The husband is protected from this by a clause that ends the monetary obligation if the wife refuses to follow a ruling or recommendation of the specified *beit din*.[13]

Avoiding Asmachta

Another possible problem with a prenuptial agreement is *asmachta*. This term refers to a financial obligation that someone accepts out of the mistaken belief that he will never have to pay it.[14] The Halachah invalidates any agreement deemed to constitute *asmachta*. The clauses "*mei'achshav*" (that the obligation begins as of the signing of the agreement) and "*kanu beveit din chashuv*" (that the husband accepts the obligation in an esteemed *beit din*) have been added to overcome this problem. By beginning the obligation immediately, the husband shows that he takes the obligation seriously and accepts that he might

---

13. Rav Aryeh David Klapper of Boston has suggested adding the following clause to further protect husbands from unscrupulous wives: "Furthermore, the sum shall be deemed forfeit unless Bride actually notifies Groom in writing on the first day of the weekly period that she intends to collect the sum. Said written notification must include her notarized signature." Rav Basil Herring of the Orthodox Caucus told this author that the Caucus is currently attempting to further refine the prenuptial agreement.
14. We discuss the issue of *asmachta* at greater length in the chapter entitled "The Torah's View of Gambling."

actually have to pay it (*Shulchan Aruch, Choshen Mishpat* 207:14-15). The effect of declaring that the agreement was made before an esteemed *beit din* is beyond the scope of our discussion.[15] Although an esteemed *beit din* is not necessarily present at every wedding, the Rama (C.M. 207:15) rules that the husband's acceptance **as if** such a *beit din* is present suffices (*hoda'at ba'al din kemei'ah eidim dami*).[16]

Rav Hershel Schachter has told this author another reason why this prenuptial agreement is not an *asmachta*. The problem of *asmachta* only arises when one commits to an **exorbitant** sum, which he undoubtedly does not plan on paying. In this case, however, the husband is agreeing to pay a **reasonable** sum for supporting his wife.[17]

This type of document is not a new idea. As mentioned earlier, Rav Yaakov of Lissa proposed a similar agreement. In fact, in medieval times the communities of Shum (Speyers,

---

15. See *Encyclopedia Talmudit* (2:111-112) for a review of the different theories.
16. The *Nachalat Shivah* (23) presents a *shetar chatzi zachar* (document to grant a daughter inheritance) in which *mei'achshav* is employed to avoid a problem of *asmachta*. In fact, Rav Zalman Nechemia Goldberg told this author that this formula is accepted by the *Ketzot* (281:6), the *Netivot* (281:9), and the *Chatam Sofer (Teshuvot,* C.M. 144). Both Rav Feivel Cohen (*Kuntress Midor L'dor* pp. 13-14 in the Hebrew section) and Rav Yaakov Blau (*Pitchei Choshen* 8:175 note 5) use "*kanu beveit din chashuv*" to avoid a problem of *asmachta* in their respective versions of a *shetar chatzi zachar*. See, however, *Bintivot Hahalachah* 1:21-31. Rav Zalman Nechemia suggested to this author that even if one considers his and Rav Willig's prenuptial agreement to constitute an *asmachta,* the agreement would not create a problem of an improperly coerced *get*. He explained the document carefully avoids linking the husband's support obligation to his giving of a *get*.
17. See *Bava Metzia* (104a), *Tosafot (Bava Metzia* 66a s.v. *Uminyumei*), and *Shulchan Aruch* (C.M. 207:15). Even when the money is punitive, not all authorities consider small monetary penalties to be coercion (see *Pitchei Teshuvah*, E.H. 134:11, and *Teshuvot Heichal Yitzchak*, E.H. 1:1:52).

THE POWER OF PRENUPTIAL AGREEMENTS

Worms, and Mayence) used a similar prenuptial agreement, which is published in the *Nachalat Shivah* (Chapter 9) and in unabridged versions of the *Kitzur Shulchan Aruch*. Rav Zalman Nechemia Goldberg argues that the communal practices of Shum have not elapsed, further eliminating the problem of *asmachta*.[18]

The prenuptial agreement formulated by the three contemporary rabbis has obtained the support of many *dayanim* who are highly regarded as experts in the laws of *gittin*. Rav Willig serves on the Beth Din of America (affiliated with the Orthodox Union and Rabbinical Council of America). Rav Goldberg and Rav Zimbalist both currently serve as members of the Israeli Chief Rabbinate's *Beit Din Hagadol*. They have also served for many years on the District Rabbinical Courts of Jerusalem and Tel Aviv respectively. In these capacities, they have dealt with thousands of divorce cases. Their document has also earned the written approval of additional *dayanim* (printed in *The Prenuptial Agreement: Halakhic and Pastoral Considerations* pp. 19-20). These authorities include Rav Ovadia Yosef, Rav Yitzchak Liebes (head of the Beth Din of the Igud Harabonim of America), and Rav Gedalia Schwartz (head of the Beth Din of America). Rav Hershel Schachter and Rav Elazar Meyer Teitz (head of the Beth Din of Elizabeth, New Jersey) have told this author that they also approve of the prenuptial agreement. In addition, in December 1999 eleven *Rashei Yeshivah* of Yeshiva University signed a letter distributed to all members of the Rabbinical Council of America "strongly urg[ing] all officiating rabbis to counsel and encourage marrying couples to sign such an agreement."

Conclusion

Being involved as a *dayan* in instances of *igun* often makes this author wish that everyone would sign a halachically sound prenuptial agreement. We have too often encountered

---

18. A communal enactment might not constitute an *asmachta* (*Tosafot, Bava Metzia 66a* s.v. *Uminyumei*; Biur Hagra, C.M. 207:57; and *Techukah Leyisrael Al Pi Hatorah* 3:208).

situations in which such an agreement might have prevented a situation of *igun*. Furthermore, **people must be careful to avoid tampering with the precise formulation of the approved prenuptial agreement, as the slightest changes in its language can invalidate it.** This author has witnessed actual cases in which attorneys and rabbis without extensive training in the laws of *gittin* formulated prenuptial agreements. These agreements were unenforceable because they did not properly address the issues outlined above. It is also important from the perspective of both Halachah and civil law that the couple understand the content of the prenuptial agreement that it will sign.[19] Experience teaches that the rabbi, husband, and wife should each keep a copy of the agreement. In addition, the Beth Din of America stores signed prenuptial agreements as a service to the community.

A review of the classic responsa literature reveals that there were few incidents of a vindictive spouse spitefully withholding a *get* before the twentieth century. The proliferation of this phenomenon seems unique to the modern era. There is hopeful news, though, as surveys and anecdotal evidence indicate that a proper prenuptial agreement is being used in many of the weddings conducted in the Orthodox community. If utilized properly, this agreement has the potential to render this type of *igun* a rarity, as it was throughout most of Jewish history. One may obtain copies of the agreement on the Internet at www.orthodoxcaucus.org.[20] We hope that all couples will sign the agreement when they marry, but they will never need to use it.

---

19. See *Teshuvot Yabia Omer* (vol. 3, E.H.13), *Bintivot Hahalachah* (1:24-25, note 4), and *The Prenuptial Agreement: Halakhic and Pastoral Considerations* (p. 42).
20. Attractive copies of Rav Willig's prenuptial agreement are available for purchase from the Orthodox Caucus at 124 Cedarhurst Avenue, Cedarhurst, NY 11516. The Orthodox Caucus played a major role in the facilitation of the development of the prenuptial and its dissemination to the Jewish community.

Administering Outside Pressure to Give a Get: Communal Pressure, the New York State Get Laws, and Israeli Rabbinical Courts

This chapter discusses the possibility of imposing various outside pressures to bring about the giving of a *get*. In an earlier chapter, we discussed when a *beit din* may coerce a husband to give a *get*. Since the Halachah restricts the situations in which a husband can be coerced, it is important to develop measures that fall short of coercion, yet push the husband to give a *get*.

Communal Sanctions

Even when a *beit din* may not coerce a husband to give a *get*, attempts must be made to convince him not to unfairly withhold a *get*. Rav Yosef Eliyahu Henkin (*Eidut Leyisrael* 46) writes that "one who withholds a *get* because of unjust monetary demands is a thief" and compares such behavior to murder. Rav Yaakov Kaminetsky (in a letter printed in the beginning of Rav Tzvi Gartner's *Kefiyah B'get*) derides men who unfairly withhold *gittin* as "oppressors" and urges helping their wives.[1] The Rama describes one possible way to help obtain a *get* without coercion (E.H. 154:21):

> [In] any situation where the Halachah does not permit the husband to be coerced with whips [to give a *get*], the husband may not be excommunicated. Nevertheless, [the *beit din*] can

---

1. This attitude appears to be rooted in a ruling of Rabbeinu Yerucham (*Sefer Mei'sharim* 23:8).

issue a decree that all Jews must withhold any favors from the recalcitrant spouse and refrain from engaging in business with him, circumcising his sons, burying his deceased relatives, and any other sanction which *beit din* wishes short of excommunication.

Rabbeinu Tam initiated these sanctions, so they are known as *harchakot d'Rabbeinu Tam*. The halachic basis for these sanctions is that a man cannot be **coerced** to give a *get*, but **withdrawing favors** from him is allowed. Coercion refers specifically to threatening a husband with physical harm or with having his property taken away. Here, no harm is done; rather, things that might have been bestowed are withheld.[2]

Not all authorities agree with Rabbeinu Tam and the Rama. The author of the *Shach* (*Gevurot Anashim* 72, cited by *Pitchei Teshuvah*, E.H. 154:30) believes that these sanctions **are** coercive. The *Chazon Ish* (E.H. 108:12) rules in accordance with the *Shach*'s strict view. On the other hand, the *Aruch Hashulchan* (E.H. 154:63) rules in accordance with Rabbeinu Tam and the Rama that these sanctions do not constitute coercion. This is also the view of Rav Bezalel Ashkenazi (*Teshuvot* 6 and 19), the Maharam Lublin (*Teshuvot* 1), the *Eliah Rabbah* (13), and Rav Yitzchak Herzog (*Techukah Leyisrael Al Pi Hatorah* 3:202,209 and *Teshuvot Heichal Yitzchak* E.H 1:1).[3] It also seems to be the view of Rav Moshe Feinstein (*Teshuvot Igrot Moshe*, E.H. 1:137).

---

2. There are also other theories of why *harchakot d'Rabbeinu Tam* do not constitute coercion. See Rav Tzvi Gartner's *Kefiyah B'get* (118:3-4).

3. Rav Herzog even suggests that placing someone in American prison does not constitute coercion, noting that the classical coercion described in rabbinical sources is flogging, and being imprisoned in America is not as bad as being flogged. However, Rav Moshe Feinstein (*Teshuvot Igrot Moshe*, E.H. 1:137 and 4:106) and Rav Shlomo Zalman Auerbach (*Moriah* 19:1-2:61) both implicitly reject Rav Herzog's view. It should be noted that Rav Herzog suggested this extraordinary leniency only in a case that also involved several other lenient factors.

Administering Outside Pressure to Give a Get

Moreover, a student of this author suggests that the *Shach*'s argument does not apply today. He argues that imposing *harchakot d'Rabbeinu Tam* in the *Shach*'s time (seventeenth-century Poland) was as severe as excommunication (*nidui*).[4] During that period, Jews depended on each other for earning a livelihood. However, **sanctions** in our communities certainly have less impact than **excommunication** in previous generations, due to our lack of communal unity. Thus, it is likely that even the *Shach* would not object to imposing *harchakot d'Rabbeinu Tam* in our communities. However, it is possible that they remain coercive according to the *Shach* in a cohesive Chassidic community.

In practice, many *batei din* adopt a compromise approach. They impose *harchakot d'Rabbeinu Tam* only when the wife unilaterally decides to end the marriage (*to'enet ma'us alai*) and provides a reasonable basis (*amatla mevoreret*) for her actions (see *Birurim B'hilchot Hareiyah*, p.243). In such a case, many authorities permit full coercion of a husband to give a *get* (see *Teshuvot Yabia Omer*, vol. 3, E.H.18). Thus, a double doubt (*safeik s'feika*) exists regarding the permissibility of *harchakot d'Rabbeinu Tam*. First, It may be that *harchakot d'Rabbeinu Tam* are not coercive. Second, perhaps if a woman has an *amatla mevoreret* for her claim of *ma'us alai*, then the Halachah permits coercion.

Accordingly, a *beit din* may impose strict sanctions on many recalcitrant spouses. An example of implementing these sanctions appears recorded in Rav Ovadia Yosef's *Teshuvot Yabia Omer* (vol. 7, E.H. 23) and Rav Eliezer Waldenberg's

---

4. The excommunication described by the *Shulchan Aruch* (*Yoreh De'ah* 3:34) is more severe than *harchakot d'Rabbeinu Tam*. It precludes counting the excommunicated person in a *minyan* or eating with him and prohibits him from washing his clothes, wearing leather shoes, or cutting his hair. As we have cited from the Rama, excommunicating a recalcitrant husband in this manner for refusing to give a *get* constitutes coercion.

GRAY MATTER

Teshuvot Tzitz Eliezer (17:51). Rav Ovadia and Rav Waldenberg present a decision of the *Beit Din Hagadol* of the State of Israel where they, along with Rav Yitzchak Kulitz, imposed *harchakot d'Rabbeinu Tam* on a recalcitrant husband. The husband yielded shortly afterwards and gave his wife a *get*. Such sanctions have also been imposed by the Va'ad Harabbanim of Riverdale and have proven successful in prodding the recalcitrant spouse to participate in a *get* ceremony.

It should also be noted that a spouse who is summoned to *beit din* and fails to respond can be issued a *seiruv*, which states that the spouse is in contempt of *beit din*. In such a situation, all agree that the spouse can be excommunicated and banned from entering a synagogue (*Shulchan Aruch* and Rama, *Yoreh De'ah* 334:11,43). The spouse is being coerced to appear in *beit din*, not to participate in a *get* ceremony.

1983 New York State Get Law

A helpful tool in obtaining a *get* from a difficult spouse is the 1983 New York State *Get* Law (Domestic Relations Law 253). This law calls for the judge in a civil court to withhold a civil divorce until the party who filed for divorce[5] removes all barriers to remarriage (i.e., gives a *get*). Rav Moshe Feinstein (*Teshuvot Igrot Moshe*, E.H. 4:106) and Rav Yosef Eliyahu Henkin (letter printed in *Techukah Leyisrael Al Pi Hatorah* 3:206)[6] rule that this law is not considered coercion of the husband to give a *get*. Rav Yitzchak Breitowitz (*Between Civil and Religious Law*, p. 203 note 599) cites several other prominent rabbis who also approve of this law.[7]

---

5. This law withholds a civil divorce only from the **plaintiff**.
6. Rav Henkin wrote his letter in 1954, when the Union of Orthodox Rabbis of the United States and Canada first proposed this law. New York State did not enact this law until 1983, ten years after Rav Henkin's death.
7. These authorities include Rav Yaakov Kaminetsky, Rav Moshe Stern, Rav Shimon Schwab, Rav Yechezkel Roth, and Rav David Cohen.

ADMINISTERING OUTSIDE PRESSURE TO GIVE A GET

This law is not coercive, as it in no way punishes the husband. He merely gives a *get* in exchange for a civil divorce. Rav J. David Bleich (*Bintivot Hahalachah* 1:37) explains that, according to civil law, one does not have a "right" to a civil divorce. Rather, it is a privilege bestowed on a citizen by the court. Withholding a civil divorce until the husband gives his wife a *get* is the equivalent of not giving the husband a gift until he gives a *get*.

This "*Get* Law," enacted in New York State, has proven effective in motivating some recalcitrant spouses to give a *get*. In light of its moderate success in New York, we should consider lobbying to pass such legislation in all jurisdictions where Jews live.[8] Interestingly, Rav Asher Ehrentreu (a member of the administration of Israeli rabbinical courts) related to this author that he persuaded a judge in a former Soviet republic to withhold a civil divorce until the husband gave his wife a *get*.

The Controversial 1992 New York State Get Law

Despite its many successes, the 1983 *Get* Law has not facilitated the resolution of all cases of *igun* in New York State. If a husband feels so determined to harm his wife that he does not mind foregoing a civil divorce, this law will not pressure him. Furthermore, if the spouse who is listed as the defendant withholds a *get*, the plaintiff cannot use this law to his or her benefit. Consequently, some felt the need to enact additional legislation to help obtain *gittin* from recalcitrant spouses.

Rav Moshe Feinstein (*Teshuvot Igrot Moshe*, E.H. 4:106) further clarifies precisely what constitutes coercion. He explains that if the judge **fines** a husband for failing to give a *get*, this constitutes illicit coercion and invalidates a *get*. If, however, the civil judge, wanting the husband to give a *get*, makes the husband

---

8. Rav Yitzchak Breitowitz (*Between Civil and Religious Law*, pp.181-182) mentions that attempts in several states to pass similar legislation have been unsuccessful. He discusses at length the American legal issues surrounding such laws (pp.179-202).

pay his wife a great deal of **financial support** (*demei mezonot*), the *get* is undoubtedly valid in Rav Moshe's opinion. Since no **formal** link exists between the alimony order and the giving of the *get*, the judge's order is not considered coercive (see *Pitchei Teshuvah*, E.H.134:11, and 154:4). However, a *get* issued on the heels of a fine imposed by a judge for failure to give a *get* is invalid, since the judge's formally links the fine to the *get*.[9]

This issue is the crux of the debate concerning the halachic validity of the 1992 New York state law. This law (DRL 236B) states that a judge shall consider the effect of either side's refusal to remove barriers to remarriage (in other words, to give or receive a *get*) when dividing the couple's property and establishing the sum of alimony.

This law can be read as a financial **penalty** imposed on the husband for his refusal to give a *get*. According to such a reading, a husband who gives a *get* to avoid the ramifications of this law is considered coerced, and the *get* is invalid. Alternatively, one may interpret the law not as a penalty but as a provision for a recalcitrant husband to provide his wife with **monetary support**. Indeed, Rav Kenneth Auman told this author that he asked two judges how they interpreted this law, and each judge responded by offering one of the two possible interpretations. Rav Tzvi Gartner (*Tradition* 32:3:93) cites two actual court cases that highlight this problem. In the first case, a New York judge used the *get* law to penalize a recalcitrant spouse for only belatedly participating in a *get* ceremony. In the second case, the same judge ruled that the *get* law merely "addresses the parties' status as they come before the court and how that status will affect their economic futures."

---

9. This is how Rav Zalman Nechemia Goldberg explained Rav Moshe's responsum to this author. It may be, however, that Rav Moshe requires not only that there be no **formal** linkage between the *get* and payment, but also that the **substantive** reason for the payment be to support the wife and not to fine the husband. This difference is critical, should a judge decided to obligate the husband to "support" his wife by paying a sum that is well above the cost of living. Rav Yitzchak Breitowitz (*Between Civil and Religious Law*, p. 137) presents several possibilities of how to understand Rav Moshe's ruling.

Administering Outside Pressure to Give a Get

Considering that the *get* law's vagueness is its obvious flaw, Rav Zalman Nechemia Goldberg told this author that the solution to this problem is simple. The law must be amended so that it will unambiguously be a support provision, making its implementation halachically valid according to Rav Feinstein's ruling.

However, this solution is not as easy as it seems. When a civil court judge awards financial support in the form of alimony, Rav Moshe permits performing a *get* even if the alimony was not warranted according to Halachah. However, halachic authorities hotly debate this matter. Many of them disagree with Rav Moshe and believe that any monetary obligation that a *beit din* would not impose constitutes coercion to give a *get*. For example, they believe that if the judge raises the alimony of a recalcitrant husband (which the judge will reduce if the husband gives a *get*), he is coercing the husband to give a *get*. Indeed, both Rav Shlomo Zalman Auerbach and Rav Yosef Shalom Eliashiv (*Moriah* 19:1-2:58-61) rule that the 1992 New York State *Get* Law is halachically unacceptable and urge its immediate repeal. Rav Eliashiv clearly indicates that he considers the monetary payments imposed by the court on the husband to constitute coercion.[10]

Israeli Rabbinical Courts

In Israel, rabbinical courts have the power to issue certain punishments against men who deny their wives *gittin*.[11] In cases where absolute coercion is warranted, they can sentence a recalcitrant husband to jail. Even when coercion is not warranted,

---

10. For further discussion and debate of the 1992 law, see *Teshuvot Beit Avi* (5:169), *The Journal of Halacha and Contemporary Society* 27:5-34), *Moriah* (19:1-2:53-57), *Between Civil and Religious Law* (pp. 209-238), and *Tradition* (32:3:91-95). *Teshuvot Igrot Moshe* (E.H. 3:44) is often quoted in defense of this law.
11. See Rav Yitzchak Breitowitz's *Between Civil and Religious Law* (pp. 168-177) for a review of the attempts by the State of Israel's secular courts to curtail these powers.

GRAY MATTER

they have certain powers, such as preventing the husband from leaving the country, which some *dayanim* practice.[12] The following case illustrates another potential tool of *batei din* in Israel even when they do not fully coerce - the power to deny a prisoner parole. Rav Shlomo Dichovsky, one of the *dayanim* who adjudicated the case, describes it in detail in *Techumin* (1:248-254).

After a year of marriage, the wife sued for a *get*, charging that her husband had been sentenced to four years in jail for theft and drug charges. The *beit din* ruled that the husband "must" ("*chayav*") give a *get*. *Chayav* is the modern Israeli *beit din* term for the Talmud's *yotzi*. In such a case, there is a dispute regarding the permissibility of coercing the husband to give a *get* (see our opening chapter). According to the accepted practice, *beit din* may impose *harchakot d'Rabbeinu Tam* on such a husband, but he cannot be coerced to give a *get*. At the conclusion of the court hearing, the husband cursed and spat at the *dayanim* and was promptly returned to jail.

The *beit din* faced an interesting option for pressuring the husband. The policy in Israeli jails is that a third of a prisoner's sentence is removed for good behavior. The *beit din* could threaten to recommend that the parole board deny the prisoner early release due to his misbehavior in *beit din*, unless he gave his wife a *get*. If he gave a *get*, the *beit din* would recommend early release. Since Halachah does not permit coercing this man to give a *get*, the question is how to define such a recommendation. One could argue that it constitutes coercion, as it is a punishment of imprisonment for withholding a *get*. Alternatively, perhaps the *beit din* is merely offering to do the husband a favor and forgive the husband for his misbehavior if he gives his wife a *get*. Denying the husband a favor is not considered coercion (see *Igrot Moshe*, E.H. 4:106).

---

12. For a discussion of whether preventing a husband from leaving the country constitutes coercion, see *Kefiyah B'get* (Chapter 76) and Techumin 15:224-225.

Administering Outside Pressure to Give a Get

Removing an Unjust Penalty

The Rivash (*Teshuvot* 127) rules that if the coercive element is not directly linked to the *get*, the *get* is unquestionably valid. For example, if a man was imprisoned for abandoning his wife and gave her a *get* to secure his release, the *get* is undoubtedly valid. He was imprisoned to motivate him to return to his wife, not to give a *get*. Although giving a *get* obtained his release, the cause of his continued imprisonment was not his refusal to give a *get*. The Rivash (132) issues a similar ruling regarding a man who was imprisoned for violating a communal edict forbidding weddings without the presence of ten men at the ceremony. The man gave a *get* to secure his release from prison. The Rivash rules that the *get* is unquestionably valid, as the imprisonment was not imposed for refusing to give a *get*.

The Rivash's responsa would seem to justify offering the husband an early release only if he gives a *get*. The husband was imprisoned for drugs, and his ongoing imprisonment is due to the drug crimes and the inappropriate behavior displayed toward the *dayanim*. However, the *Tashbetz* (1:1) and Ra'anach (*Teshuvot* 63) disagree about applying the Rivash's ruling if the coercive element was imposed unjustly. The Ra'anach permits such a *get*, while the *Tashbetz* rules that it is questionable if a *get* given under such circumstances is valid.

The question of whether to rule in accordance with the *Tashbetz* or the Ra'anach is unresolved. The *Aruch Hashulchan* (E.H.4:106) rules in accordance with the *Tashbetz*, whereas Rav Moshe Feinstein (*Teshuvot Igrot Moshe*, E.H. 4:106) seems to rule in accordance with Ra'anach.[13]

In the Israeli case under discussion, the husband was imprisoned for reasons that had nothing to do with the *get*. Securing his release by giving a *get* is certainly not coercive

---

13. For an in-depth discussion of this issue, see *Pitchei Teshuvah* (E.H.134:11).

according to the Ra'anach. According to the *Tashbetz*, however, this should depend upon whether Halachah permits imprisoning someone for theft and drug charges. Nonetheless, Rav Dichovsky claims that even the *Tashbetz* would permit denying parole to this husband. He explains that even the *Tashbetz* only prohibits threatening to now punish the husband for another charge if he does not give a *get*. On the other hand, if the husband was already punished for the other charge without any connection to the *get*, Rav Dichovsky claims that all opinions would permit denying him parole.

Rav Dichovsky's Ruling

Rav Dichovsky rules that the *beit din* can recommend to the parole board to deny the husband parole due to two considerations. First, the *beit din* is not in the position to imprison the husband. It is merely recommending the withholding of a favor, parole, from the husband. The Maharik (*Teshuvot* 133) rules (citing Rabbeinu Tam) that withholding a favor does not constitute coercion.

Furthermore, the *Chelkat Yoav* (*Dinei Oness*, section five) rules that if one is in a *yotzi* situation, where the rabbis require him to give a *get*, his complete free will is not required for the *get* to be valid. Even if the husband only has free will according to a minimal definition, the *get* is acceptable, for he must give it.

Thus, since in this case the husband was obligated to give a *get*, it is acceptable for him to give a *get* even if he does so because of pressure to secure his early release from prison.

There is one potential problem with Rav Dichovsky's position. The Mabit (*Teshuvot* 2:138) does not even permit putting indirect pressure on a husband if the pressure is so great that he has no choice but to give a *get*.[14] Accordingly, perhaps

---

14. The Mabit does not permit using indirect coercion to give a *get* even if the coercive factor is halachically legitimate.

a jail sentence is so severe that it essentially leaves the husband no choice but to give a *get*.[15] Nonetheless, Rav Dichovsky did not concern himself with this responsum of the Mabit, because the Mabit seemingly contradicts himself elsewhere (1:22). In that responsum, he rules that a man who was imprisoned for being a heretic may be denied release from prison until he gives a *get*. The *Simchat Kohein* (vol. 3, E.H. 9) suggests a resolution to the contradiction. He claims that even the Mabit permits pressuring the husband with other punishments if the *dayanim* sincerely desire to punish the husband for his other offenses. The Mabit's strict ruling only relates to situations where the *dayanim* pursue the unrelated charges in a veiled attempt to obtain a *get*. Since Rav Dichovsky and his colleagues sincerely wished to punish the husband for cursing and spitting at them, they were not merely orchestrating his punishment as a ploy to obtain a *get*.

Objections to Rav Dichovsky

The other two rabbis who heard the case with Rav Dichovsky rejected his approach (*Piskei Din Rabbaniyim* 11:300-308). They explained that in the aforementioned responsa, the prison authorities were indifferent to the performance of a *get*. Accordingly, even if a *beit din* would work to free the husband in return for giving a *get*, the prison authorities themselves made no such linkage. The prison authorities never stated that they would release the man for giving a *get*. In Israel, however, the government officials will notify the husband that his early release is in return for giving a *get*.

---

15. Rav Yitzchak Breitowitz (*Between Civil and Religious Law*, p. 82) points out that the Mabit's responsum does not apply to financial pressure in the United States. Although forcing a husband to pay an excessive sum seemingly leaves him no plausible option other than to give a *get*, Rav Breitowitz argues that the husband could always default on the money. One who defaults on a debt in America does not receive particularly harsh punishments, so the choice between giving a *get* or facing the penalties for defaulting on financial obligations is a legitimate choice.

Conclusion

Harchakot d'Rabbeinu Tam and the 1983 New York State *Get* Law are effective means to motivate recalcitrant husbands to give a *get*. However, as long as the 1992 law is mired in controversy, it cannot be used as an effective tool against recalcitrant spouses. A *beit din* cannot supervise a *get* whose halachic acceptability is in doubt. Nonetheless, many individuals have pointed out to this author that virtually all rabbinical courts administer *gittin* on behalf of New York State residents when there is no indication that the husband is motivated to give the *get* by the 1992 law.[16] In Israel, *batei din* enjoy legal powers that sometimes enable them to put greater pressure on a recalcitrant husband, although *batei din* must judge each case independently.

---

16. For further discussion of this point, see *Between Civil and Religious Law*, pp. 213-214 note 633. The rulings of the Netziv (*Teshuvot Meishiv Davar* 4:46), Rav Yitzchak Elchanan Spektor (*Teshuvot Be'er Yitzchak*, E.H. 10:8), and the *Chazon Ish* (E.H. 99:2), are often cited in defense of this practice. See, however, *Bintivot Hahalachah* 1:38-54.

Hafka'at Kiddushin: Annulment of Marriage

The Talmudic concept of *hafka'at kiddushin*, annulling a marriage, often arises in discussions about how to help *agunot*, although its practical applications virtually do not exist.

The Basis for Hafka'at Kiddushin

The notion that *Chazal* can annul a marriage appears six times in the Gemara.[1] There are two categories of *hafka'at kiddushin*. One is where the rabbis declare a marriage void due to the unethical behavior involved (see *Tosafot, Yevamot* 110a s.v. *Lefichach*). For example, the Gemara in *Yevamot* (110a) and *Bava Batra* (48b) describes a husband who physically coerced a woman into consenting to marry him. While such a marriage should technically take effect, the rabbis annul it in response to the man's improper conduct.

The second category consists of cases where the original marriage contained no problems, but a problem arose when the husband attempted to send his wife a *get*. For example, the Gemara (*Ketubot* 3a) addresses a husband who embarked on a long journey. Before leaving, he gave his wife a *get* and stipulated that it would only take effect if he did not return within thirty days. The husband made every effort to return home on time, but he was unable to fulfill the condition due to circumstances entirely beyond his control (*oneis*). Since the husband had a legitimate excuse for not returning, the *get* was biblically invalid.

---

1. *Yevamot* 90b, *Yevamot* 110a, *Ketubot* 3a, *Gittin* 33a, *Gittin* 73a, and *Bava Batra* 48b.

GRAY MATTER

Nevertheless, *Chazal* effected the *get* through the mechanism of *hafka'at kiddushin*. In such a situation, it is unclear if the marriage is nullified retroactively[2] or if the rabbis merely render the *get* effective despite the husband's initial wishes.[3]

In *Gittin* 73a, the Gemara speaks of a dangerously ill individual (*shechiv meira*) who divorced his wife and subsequently regained his health. Technically, his recovery invalidates the *get*, as the husband clearly gave the *get* under the assumption that he would die shortly. If he would recover, it was understood that the *get* would be invalid. Nevertheless, *Chazal* validate the *get* by employing *hafka'at kiddushin*.

The Gemara explains that *hafka'at kiddushin* works because "everyone gets married according to the will of the Rabbis." In other words, every marriage contains an implicit condition that *Chazal* must accept it. Accordingly, *Chazal* may veto a marriage if one contracts it in an unethical manner. Similarly, *Chazal* may effect a divorce even when the *get* is invalid on a biblical level. *Tosafot* (*Ketubot* 3a s.v. *Adaata* and *Gittin* 33a s.v. *Kol*) note that we explicitly authorize *Chazal* in this manner, as the groom states that he is marrying his wife "according to the laws of Moses and Israel" ("*kedat Moshe veyisrael*").

Practical Implementation

At first glance, the power to annul marriages seems like the ideal solution to the *agunah* problem. However, there are major obstacles to its implementation today. First, the basis for it is that husbands declare at their weddings that the Rabbis must consent

---

2. This is the opinion of the Ri (*Tosafot, Gittin* 33a s.v. *Ve'afk'inhu*), as he indicates that such a *get* retroactively exonerates a woman who receives it after committing adultery.
3. The Rashba (*Teshuvot* 1:1162 and commentary to *Ketubot* 3a), for example, explains that *hafka'at kiddushin* only serves as a threat in these cases. The Rabbis' assertion that the marriage will be annulled forces the husband to accept the *get*'s validity, lest his married life be rendered cohabitation outside of marriage. Also see *P'nei Yehoshua* (*Ketubot* 3a).

HAFKA'AT KIDDUSHIN: ANNULMENT OF MARRIAGE

to the marriage. Accordingly, only a central, recognized rabbinical court, such as the *Sanhedrin*, may implement *hafka'at kiddushin*, but no such *beit din* exists today. As Rav Yitzchak Herzog writes (*Techukah Leyisrael Al Pi Hatorah* 1:76), *hafka'at kiddushin* may someday become an option if one *beit din* is accepted by everyone, "but in the present situation there is nothing to discuss."

Another major problem exists with implementing *hafka'at kiddushin* today. The Gemara records many objectionable marriages that are binding, indicating that the Rabbis do not annul them. For example, *Chazal* do not annul the marriage of a *kohein* and a divorcee, although such a marriage is explicitly prohibited by the Torah (*Vayikra* 21:7).[4] While criteria presumably exist to determine when marriages may be annulled, the Gemara never articulates them. The Rashba (*Ketubot* 3a) provides some insight:

> One may ask why a woman should remain an *agunah* if her husband was lost in a body of water without finite boundaries (*mayim she'ein lahem sof*). Let the Rabbis annul the marriage! The answer is that the Rabbis do not annul a marriage unless the man has handed his wife a [rabbinically acceptable] *get*.

This, of course, gives only partial criteria. When a couple marries in a proper manner, the marriage can end only in a *get*. However, there are objectionable marriage ceremonies that *Chazal* invalidate through *hafka'at kiddushin* without requiring a *get*, whereas other equally objectionable ceremonies remain untouched by *Chazal*. *Chazal* annul a marriage ceremony in which the wife was forced to consent, yet refrain from annulling the marriage of a *kohein* and a divorcee. Elsewhere (*Teshuvot* 1:1185), the Rashba addresses this issue:

> We do not say that whenever a husband entered a marriage in an unethical manner the rabbis

---

4. See *Teshuvot Binyamin Ze'ev* (106) for a list of objectionable marriages where *Chazal* do not invoke *hafka'at kiddushin*.

annulled the marriage. Rather, we believe that only in those specific instances in which *Chazal* state that the marriage is annulled do we actually annul the marriage.

The Rashba cites the case of someone who appointed another man as his agent to marry a certain woman (*Kiddushin* 58b). The agent, instead of contracting the marriage on behalf of his friend, married the woman himself. The Gemara states that the "marriage is valid despite his unethical behavior." The Rashba concludes that only in those cases specifically mentioned by *Chazal* is the marriage annulled. While some attempts have been made to define criteria for implementing *hafka'at kiddushin*,[5] the overwhelming majority of *Rishonim* agree that it may only be applied where the Gemara invokes it.[6] Indeed, the Rambam makes no mention of *hafka'at kiddushin* in the entire *Mishneh Torah*. The Radach (*Teshuvot* 19) explains that *Chazal* considered *hafka'at kiddushin* a last resort, to be employed only out of great desperation (*machmat dochak gadol*). In certain specific cases, *Chazal* used it, but we may not extrapolate to other cases.

The *Beit Yosef* (*Even Ha'ezer* 28) and Rama (E.H. 28:21) clearly affirm that we do not invoke *hafka'at kiddushin* when it is not specifically employed by the Gemara. The Rama writes:

> A community that institutes a policy, accepted by the entire community, that anyone who marries in the absence of ten men will have his marriage invalidated must nevertheless be strict and require a *get* [in this circumstance].

---

5. See Maharam of Rothenberg (cited by Mordechai, *Kiddushin* 522) and Radbaz (*Teshuvot* 1:42).
6. *Teshuvot Binyamin Ze'ev* (106), Rivash (*Teshuvot* 399), Radach (*Teshuvot* 19), Maharik (*Teshuvot* 84), Re'em (*Teshuvot* 14), *Tashbetz* (2:5), *Yachin Uvoaz* (2:20) and *Beit Yosef* (*Teshuvot, Dinei Kiddushin* 6 and 10). The Raavan (cited in *Teshuvot Seridei Eish* 3:25 and *Teshuvot Tzitz Eliezer* 1:26:4) even prohibits applying *hafka'at kiddushin* today to cases mentioned in the Gemara, but most *Rishonim* do not appear to go so far.

HAFKA'AT KIDDUSHIN: ANNULMENT OF MARRIAGE

The Vilna Gaon (*Biur HaGra*, E.H. 28:57) explains that this situation appears analogous to the case described in *Yevamot* (110a). In both cases, a marriage ceremony was conducted in an improper manner. One might have thus thought that one who violates his community's policy has his marriage declared null and void. Nonetheless, we do not declare the marriage invalid, as we restrict the application of *hafka'at kiddushin* to the situations that the Gemara specified. Indeed, the *Acharonim* universally reject applying *hafka'at kiddushin* to new situations.[7]

Conclusion

Rav David Tzvi Hoffman (*Melameid Leho'il* 3:51) states what has emerged as the consensus Orthodox view on this topic. He writes, "No God-fearing rabbi will state that rabbis today are empowered to perform *hafkaat kiddushin* in the absence of a *Sanhedrin* [a central rabbinate accepted as authoritative by all Jews -H.J.]." For a lengthier discussion of *hafka'at kiddushin*, see Ezra Frazer's article in Yeshivat Har Etzion's *Alei Etzion* (8:97-130).

---

7. Mabit (*Teshuvot* 1:206), Maharit (*Teshuvot, Even Ha'ezer* 2:39), Chacham Tzvi (*Teshuvot* 124), *Avnei Miluim* (28:58), *Biur HaGra* (*Even Ha'ezer* 28:56-57), and *Melamed Leho'il* (3:22,51). An even lengthier list of *Acharonim* who reject any application of *hafkaat kiddushin* to a communal enactment appears in *Otzar Haposkim* (vol. 10, 28:112:1). Also see *Seifer Ein Tenai Benisu'in*, which includes the signatures of more than 400 *Acharonim* against a proposed "solution" to the *agunah* problem that included *hafka'at kiddushin*. While the proposal contained other flaws, the application of *hafka'at kiddushin* was a primary reason given for their vehement opposition to the plan. Among the signatories are Rav Yisrael Meir HaKohen, Rav Chaim Soloveitchik, Rav Chaim Ozer Grodzinski, Rav Yechiel Michel Epstein, Rav Tzvi Pesach Frank, Rav Malkiel Tannenbaum, Rav Shimon Shkopp, and Rav Elya (Pruzhner) Feinstein.

Conditional Marriage

Some French rabbis in the late nineteenth and early twentieth centuries suggested instituting a condition to every Jewish marriage in order to solve the *agunah* problem. The condition would abrogate the marriage retroactively in case of civil divorce. The proposal was immediately rejected by Rav Yitzchak Elchanan Spektor, and all the eminent halachic authorities of the following years spurned any mention of reviving it. In the next generation, both Rav Yosef Eliyahu Henkin (*Kol Kitvei Harav Henkin* 2:129) and Rav Yitzchak Herzog (*Techukah Leyisrael Al Pi Hatorah* 1:76) affirmed that the entire Orthodox rabbinate rejected the proposal.

The Proposal of the French Rabbis

The introduction of civil marriage and divorce in nineteenth-century France created a major challenge for the Jewish community. Jews now enjoyed the option of divorcing without performing a *get*. This reality, coupled with the diminishing authority of rabbis, lead to situations of *igun* and *mamzeirut*. As a possible solution, some rabbis in France suggested including a provision in all marriages that if the couple divorced civilly, the marriage would be retroactively annulled. This idea was entertained in 1885 and 1893, and Rav Yehudah Lubetzky, a rabbi in Paris during that period, succeeded in thwarting the plan both times. In 1907, a group of French rabbis resolved to implement conditional marriages. Rav Lubetzky collected the letters of over 400 eminent rabbis against conditional marriages and succeeded in repealing the resolution.

This solution was based on an established procedure cited by the Rama (*Even Ha'ezer* 157:4). The procedure, as presented

CONDITIONAL MARRIAGE

by the Rama, is intended to resolve a halachic dilemma faced by Jews since medieval times when a family has only two sons, one of whom has abandoned Judaism for another faith. If the remaining brother dies without any children, his widow requires *chalitzah* (see *Devarim* 25:4-10) from her apostate brother-in-law. Having abandoned Judaism, he would likely refuse to participate in such a ceremony, preventing the widow from ever remarrying.

To solve this problem, the Rama recommends contracting the marriage on condition that it would be retroactively nullified if the husband dies childless.[1] The *Taz* (E.H.157:1) cites his father-in-law, the *Bach*, who permitted employing such a condition if the whereabouts of the husband's only brother are unknown. Similarly, most authorities accept the ruling of the *Nachalat Shivah* (Laws of *Chalitzah* 22:8) that this arrangement can also be made when the groom's only brother is mentally incompetent (*cheireish* or *shoteh*), for they, too, cannot perform *chalitzah*.[2]

Indeed, Rav Yehuda Amital told this author that he has performed two wedding ceremonies in this manner when the groom's only brother was mentally incompetent. Due to the complexities of properly formulating the necessary condition, a Rav may perform this type of ceremony only with the approval and guidance of an eminent halachic authority. Rav Amital acted with the approval and guidance of Rav Moshe Feinstein.

Problems with the Rama's Leniency

Nearly all halachic authorities of the time[3] rejected the proposal to make all marriages contingent upon not ending in civil

---

1. Rav David Tzvi Hoffman (*Teshuvot Melameid Leho'il* 3:51) also suggests using this condition when concern exists that the husband's brother will extort a large sum of money in return for performing *chalitzah*.
2. See *Aruch Hashulchan* (E.H. 157:15), *Pitchei Teshuvah* (E.H.157:9), and *Teshuvot Igrot Moshe* (E.H.1:147).
3. See, for example, *Teshuvot Tzafnat Pa'anei'ach* (37), *Teshuvot Or Samei'ach* (*Likutei Teshuvot* 10), *Teshuvot Melameid Leho'il* (3:22), and *Teshuvot Tzitz Eliezer* (1:27).

divorce. An entire book, *Ein Tenai Benisu'in*, was published in 1930, collecting the letters that hundreds of the previous decades' halachic authorities sent Rav Lubetzky against the proposal. They rejected the proposal both on technical halachic grounds and on public policy grounds.

The halachic problems are indeed formidable even in the Rama's case. Some authorities (see *Pitchei Teshuvah*, E.H.157:8, and *Sh'eilat Yaavetz* 2:15) reject the Rama's ruling regarding an apostate brother-in-law for two reasons. They argue that the condition, by circumventing *chalitzah*, contravenes a Torah commandment (*matneh al mah shekatuv batorah*). Whenever a non-monetary condition conflicts with a Torah law, the condition is void and the transaction is effective (see *Ketubot* 56a). In this case, the marriage should be effective, and the condition that cancels the marriage if the husband dies childless should be void.

Additionally, the Gemara (*Yevamot* 94b and *Ketubot* 72b-74a) seems to teach that only the betrothal component of marriage (*kiddushin*)[4] can be entered conditionally. The *nisu'in* component of marriage (after which the husband and wife begin living together), on the other hand, cannot be entered conditionally (*ein tenai benisu'in*). The reason for this is the rule of "*ein adam oseh be'ilato be'ilat zenut*," one does not want his sexual relations to be considered by Halachah as outside the context of marriage. Thus, one will waive any conditions made before marital relations, fearing that failure to meet the conditions will nullify the marriage and turn the couple's marital relations into premarital relations. Accordingly, once the couple engages in marital relations, any conditions made before the *kiddushin* no longer apply.

In spite of these problems, such great authorities as the *Noda Biy'hudah* (E.H.56), the *Chatam Sofer* (vol. 1, E.H.110-111),

---

4. In today's weddings, the groom performs *kiddushin* when he gives the bride a ring or, in some Sephardic circles, a coin.

CONDITIONAL MARRIAGE

and the *Aruch Hashulchan* (E.H.157:15-17) defend the Rama's ruling. Regarding the condition's conflict with the laws of *chalitzah*, they rule that the condition is not void unless one contracts the marriage on condition that the laws of *chalitzah* **do not apply** to it. However, the Rama suggested a condition that retroactively nullifies the marriage if the man dies childless. This condition **sidesteps** the institution of *chalitzah*, without directly contravening it, by rendering the "widow" a woman who never married. In such a case, the laws of *chalitzah* truly do not apply. Thus, the Rama's condition is not *matneh al mah shekatuv batorah*.

Avoiding the problem of *ein adam oseh be'ilato be'ilat zenut* is more challenging, but this, too, is possible. *Tosafot* (*Yevamot* 94b s.v. *Ela*) teach that it is not **impossible** to enter *nisu'in* conditionally; it is merely highly unusual. Thus, for example, if the couple declares before engaging in marital relations (with witnesses standing behind the wall) that the marital relations should not void the prior conditions, the conditions remain (see *Beit Shmuel* 157:6 and *Aruch Hashulchan*, E.H. 157:17).

Moreover, marital relations cancel prior conditions only when it is reasonably likely that the conditions will not be fulfilled. The risk of retroactively rendering the couple's relations premarital is thus great. The Halachah assumes that the couple intends to nullify the condition upon commencing cohabitation in order to avert this risk. However, in the Rama's case, the *Noda Biy'hudah* and *Aruch Hashulchan* emphasize, the chances that the marriage will be retroactively nullified are relatively small. Most couples have children, so the issue of *chalitzah* will probably never arise. Should the husband develop a terminal illness before having children, he will make every effort to give his wife a *get* before dying, to guarantee that their marital relations do not retroactively become promiscuous. Accordingly, in the Rama's case, marital relations do not cancel the condition, as the risk of *be'ilat zenut* is miniscule.

GRAY MATTER

Rejections of the Proposal of Conditional Marriage

Halachic authorities unanimously rule that the Rama's case cannot serve as a precedent for contracting **all** marriages on condition that no civil divorce will be issued. Unlike *chalitzah*, the risk of civil divorce is considerable, so marital relations cancel the conditions. Additionally, we can be more lenient in trying to avoid the requirement of *chalitzah* than in trying to avoid *gittin*, for remarrying without a *get*, by contrast to remarrying without *chalitzah*, is a capital sin. Thus, one cannot extrapolate a lenient ruling regarding *chalitzah* to the area of *gittin*. Moreover, it is exceedingly impractical to conduct every wedding in such a cumbersome and immodest fashion. Telling witnesses (from behind a wall) immediately before cohabitation that a prior condition stands can be tolerated in rare instances, but it cannot become standard procedure.

Rav David Tzvi Hoffman (*Teshuvot Melameid Leho'il* 3:22) outlines additional reasons to reject this proposal. He notes that the laws of formulating conditions are complex, so many rabbis do not know them. One must formulate the conditions in a precise manner (*tenai kaful, hein kodem lelav, tenai kodem lemaaseh*, etc.), and one could easily make a mistake.

The Rama's case sidestepped the requirement of *chalitzah* in a number of rare instances. The French proposal would eliminate the entire institution of *gittin*. Rav Hoffman expresses great concern that making every marriage conditional would weaken the institution of marriage, the backbone of the Jewish community. If every couple would know that its marriage could be retroactively undone at any time, then anyone tempted to cheat on a spouse could do so without a guilty conscience. He or she would be able to file for a civil divorce, thereby retroactively canceling the marriage and avoiding the sin of adultery. We must not weaken the entire institution of marriage in order to solve the difficulties a tiny percentage of people encounter.

Conclusion

All major halachic authorities have rejected instituting a condition in every marriage to annul it retroactively when a civil divorce is given. Rabbis who signed letters in *Ein Tenai Benisu'in* against this proposal include Rav Yitzchak Elchanan Spektor, Rav Chaim Ozer Grodzinski, Rav Chaim Soloveitchik, Rav Yisrael Meir Kagan, Rav Yechiel Michel Epstein, Rav Meir Simcha of Dvinsk, Rav Malkiel Tannenbaum, Rav Tzvi Pesach Frank, and Israeli Chief Rabbis Avraham Yitzchak Kook and Ben-Zion Uzziel.

Kiddushei Ta'ut: Marriage Under False Pretenses

In dealing with *agunah* situations, it is very important to determine the halachic status of marriages where a husband discovers a major defect in his wife, or vice versa, only after they have married.

Talmudic Background

The Gemara discusses the halachic validity of a marriage in which the husband discovers defects in his wife that existed before the marriage. The Mishnah (*Ketubot* 72b) describes a marriage in which the couple articulated no special conditions. After the wedding, the man discovered preexisting physical defects (*mumin*) in the woman and now wishes to divorce her. The Mishnah teaches that, in such a case, a *get* is required to terminate the marriage, but the husband is not required to pay the *ketubah* (which is usually paid when a couple divorces). The Gemara adds that the man is exempt from paying the *ketubah* only if the defect is one that most people would find intolerable.

Tosafot (*ad. locum* s.v. *Al*) explain that the *get* in this case is required merely out of doubt.[1] The Halachah does not rule unequivocally that the marriage is invalid because it was entered on a fraudulent basis (*kiddushei ta'ut*). Rather, since the man might have entered the marriage despite the woman's defects, one cannot conclude with certainty that the marriage constitutes *kiddushei ta'ut*. Thus, a *get* is required for the woman to remarry.

---

1. *Tosafot* are unsure whether this *get* is required on a biblical or a rabbinical level.

KIDDUSHEI TA'UT: MARRIAGE UNDER FALSE PRETENSES

The husband is not required to pay the *ketubah*, as one is never forced to pay a doubtful monetary obligation. His exemption from payment results from the halachic principle of *hamotzi mei'chaveiro alav haraayah*, "The burden of proof rests upon the individual who demands the money from his peer" (*Bava Kama* 46a).

The Case of an Ailonit

Tosafot (ad. loc. s.v. *Al*; *Yevamot* 2b s.v. *O*, and *Gittin* 46b s.v. *Hamotzi*) point out a seeming contradiction between the aforementioned Mishnah in *Ketubot* and the Mishnah in *Yevamot* (2b). In *Yevamot*, the Mishnah indicates that if the husband discovered a major defect after the wedding, no *get* is required to dissolve the marriage. Presumably, this is because the husband entered the marriage on a fraudulent basis. The Mishnah addresses a case where the woman turns out to be an *ailonit*, a woman who is sterile and devoid of feminine characteristics.[2]

In order to distinguish between the two cases, *Tosafot* suggest that being an *ailonit* is an unusually severe defect. If a particular woman is undoubtedly found to be an *ailonit*, the marriage is considered invalid and no *get* is required. If the defect is less severe, the marriage may nevertheless be valid, so a *get* is required. The Rosh (*Ketubot* 7:10) explains that being an *ailonit* is an unusually serious defect because the primary reason for marriage is to produce children.

The Talmud contains no explicit textual proof for *Tosafot*'s conclusion. Accordingly, many *Rishonim* even require a *get* (albeit only rabbinically) for an *ailonit*, fearing that perhaps her husband would have married her regardless.[3] Rabbeinu Tam, who maintains the latter view, infers his position from another Mishnah (*Ketubot* 100b). It states that an *ailonit* is not entitled to a

---

2. See *Encyclopedia Talmudit* (1:523-528) for a review of her halachic status.
3. *Nimukei Yosef* (*Yevamot* 1a in the pages of the Rif, s.v. *O Nimtze'u*, quoting Rabbeinu Tam), *Maggid Mishnah* (*Hilchot Ishut* 4:10), and Rambam (according to the *Lechem Mishneh ad. loc.*). For an explanation of this opinion, see *Chazon Ish* (E.H. 79:16).

41

GRAY MATTER

ketubah payment, implying that she does nonetheless require a *get*. Indeed, the Mishnah in *Gittin* (46b) specifically addresses the case of one who gives his wife a *get* because she is an *ailonit*! *Tosafot* respond that the woman discussed in this particular Mishnah is merely a *safek ailonit*, one whose status as an *ailonit* is in doubt. *Tosafot*, however, cite no Talmudic texts to support this contention.

The *Beit Shmuel* (39:15) cites *Tosafot*'s opinion that no *get* is required if the wife was discovered to undoubtedly be an *ailonit*. However, he also cites Rabbeinu Tam's view (44:7) that a *get* is nevertheless required rabbinically. The *Aruch Hashulchan* (E.H. 44:5) rules in accordance with Rabbeinu Tam to require a *get*.

Belated Objections

The *Chelkat Mechokeik* (39:9) and the *Beit Shmuel* (39:7,16) both note that only if a man complains **immediately** about a problem is his claim of *kiddushei ta'ut* considered. If, however, he fails to complain about the problem immediately, explains the *Beit Shmuel*, the absence of a complaint constitutes acceptance of the defect. Even if the husband complains later about the defect, the marriage is **undoubtedly valid**. The *Aruch Hashulchan* (E.H. 39:13) also notes that if the couple continues to cohabit as a normal married couple, the marriage is certainly valid despite the defect.[4] He notes that remaining together indicates that the husband considers the defect insignificant.

---

4. Regarding a nonobservant couple, where that the couple might cohabit even without being halachically married, see *Teshuvot Igrot Moshe* (E.H. 4:13). He suggests that such a couple's continued cohabitation might not disqualify a claim of *kiddushei ta'ut*. His case involved *mamzeirut*, which is more lenient than remarrying without a *get*, and there were other lenient considerations involved, so it is unclear how Rav Moshe would rule in the situation that we are discussing. Regarding observant women, Rav Moshe (E.H. 4:113) clearly writes that the couple must cease cohabitation upon the defect's discovery, or else "it is difficult to invalidate the marriage."

KIDDUSHEI TA'UT: MARRIAGE UNDER FALSE PRETENSES

Defects in the Husband

The Gemara, *Rishonim*, and *Shulchan Aruch* discuss only the case of a man who finds a defect in his new wife. They do not explicitly address the case of a woman who finds a severe defect in her husband, but the *Acharonim* discuss this issue at length.[5]

One view among the *Acharonim* is that of the *Aruch Hashulchan* (E.H.44:10) and the *Chazon Ish* (E.H.69:23). These two authorities rule that even if a woman discovers an extremely severe flaw in her new husband, such as that his male organs are missing or damaged, the marriage is nevertheless valid. They base this ruling on the Gemara's phrase, "*nicha lah b'chol d'hu*," that a woman will settle for any companion (*Yevamot* 118b and *Bava Kama* 111a). The Gemara cites Reish Lakish's remark, "*Tav l'meitav tan du mil'meitav armelo*," that a woman feels it is better to be together with another (even with a "very low quality" partner) than to be alone.

This passage in the Gemara does not mean that all women will settle for a marginal husband. Rather, Rav Moshe Feinstein (*Teshuvot Igrot Moshe*, E.H.4:113) explains that some women have this attitude, so we must be concerned that any particular wife belongs to the significant minority of women who would accept any man as a husband. Thus, as long as she did not expressly stipulate at the wedding ceremony that she marries this man on condition that he has no defects, the marriage is valid. There is no implicit condition that she would not marry someone with a severe defect. Accordingly, the marriage is valid even if the woman finds an extremely severe defect in the husband. It appears from the *Aruch Hashulchan* and *Chazon Ish* that the woman requires a *get* on a **biblical** level.

---

5. The *Otzar Haposkim* (Chapter 39) presents a detailed review of the halachic debate on this issue.

GRAY MATTER

Distinguishing Between Defects

Some authorities take a more lenient approach regarding a woman who finds defects in her husband. Both Rav Yitzchak Elchanan Spektor (*Teshuvot Be'er Yitzchak* 4:3) and the *Beit Halevi* (3:3) rule that if a woman discovers a severe defect in her husband, such as impotence, she requires a *get* only on a **rabbinical** level. The distinction between biblical and rabbinical levels becomes significant if other lenient considerations exist, such as when a witness to the wedding ceremony might have been invalid or when the husband disappeared and might be dead. Between the other considerations and the lighter status of rabbinical prohibitions, a rabbi might rule leniently and permit the woman to remarry in such a case. Rav Chaim Ozer Grodzinski (*Teshuvot Acheizer* 1:27), for example, combined other lenient considerations with the possibility of *kiddushei ta'ut*, in a case where it seems clear that he would not have permitted the woman to remarry solely based on *kiddushei ta'ut*.

These authorities believe that one should not interpret the phrase "*nicha lah b'chol d'hu*" as meaning that a woman will literally marry "any" man. Rather, there are some men who are actually considered less than *kol d'hu* (minimal). For example, an impotent man is not even a minimally acceptable husband, for it is obvious that nearly all women would never knowingly marry such a man.[6]

Nevertheless, both the *Beit Halevi* and Rav Yitzchak Elchanan believe that the wife of an impotent man does require a *get* on a rabbinical level if no other lenient consideration exists. The *Beit Halevi* writes, "There is absolutely no room to say that she does not need a *get*, for even if a man finds a severe defect in a woman, a *get* is rabbinically required." Similarly, Rav Yitzchak

---

6. The Maharam of Rothenburg (cited in Mordechai, *Yevamot* 29, and *Teshuvot Maimoniyot Hashayachot L'seifer Nashim* 29) also suggests that *tav l'meitav tan du mil'meitav armelo* and *nicha lah b'chol d'hu* do not apply to extreme cases, such as a man who converted to another religion. Regarding the Maharam's willingness to rely on his suggestion in practice, see *Teshuvot Mahari Mintz* (12).

KIDDUSHEI TA'UT: MARRIAGE UNDER FALSE PRETENSES

Elchanan argues that *Chazal* were concerned with the highly unlikely possibility that perhaps the woman would have tolerated marrying an impotent man. He cites as a precedent *Chazal*'s refusal to permit a woman to remarry if her husband drowned in a body of water without finite boundaries (*mayim she'ein lahem sof*), although it is extremely unlikely that her husband is still alive.

Rav Moshe Feinstein's Extraordinary Ruling

Rav Moshe Feinstein (*Teshuvot Igrot Moshe*, E.H. 1:79) disagrees will all of the aforementioned authorities and argues that if a woman discovers a severe defect in her husband, she does not require a *get*. Rav Moshe writes that one should make all efforts to obtain a *get*, but a lenient ruling may be given if these efforts fail. He reasons that some defects are so severe that, clearly, no woman would have married this man.[7] For example, Rav Moshe takes issue with Rav Yitzchak Elchanan and argues that no woman would marry an impotent man. Thus, just as a man who mistakenly marries an *ailonit* does not require a *get*, so too a woman who marries an impotent man does not require a *get*. Rav Moshe takes this exceedingly bold argument[8] one step further, asserting that even Rabbeinu Tam would not require a *get* for a woman to remarry upon discovering a severe preexisting defect in her husband. As we have mentioned above, Rabbeinu Tam rules demands a *get* to dissolve the marriage if a man discovers that his wife is an *ailonit*. Rav Moshe argues that only a man might agree to marry a woman with a severe defect, because his ability to give a *get* assures him a relatively easy halachic exit from the marriage. However, it is obvious to all, Rav Moshe claims, that no woman would marry a man with a severe defect. She would never risk being unable to tolerate the man's problem, because she knows that she has no simple halachic mechanism to escape from the marriage.

---

7. See *Teshuvot Chavot Yair* (221) and *Teshuvot Maharsham* (3:16) for approaches that resemble Rav Moshe's, although they hesitate to implement them in practice.
8. It is bold because, as Rav Yosef Henkin notes (*Peirushei Ibra*, p. 43), it lacks any textual basis in the classical sources.

45

GRAY MATTER

Limitations on Rav Moshe's Ruling

Rav Moshe suggested applying this ruling in five actual cases. They involved an impotent man (*Teshuvot Igrot Moshe*, E.H. 1:79), a man who concealed that he had been institutionalized prior to the marriage (E.H. 1:80), a man who concealed that he vehemently opposed having children and later forced his wife to abort a fetus (E.H. 4:13),[9] a man who concealed that he was a practicing homosexual prior to the marriage (E.H. 4:113), and a man who concealed that he converted to another religion (E.H. 4:83). In the last case, however, Rav Moshe hesitated to permit the woman to remarry without a *get*, as she did not observe Torah law. It must be clear beyond the shadow of a doubt that the woman never would have married such a man. However, since this woman did not practice Judaism seriously, Rav Moshe questioned whether we can assume that she would never marry an apostate.

Similarly, Rav Yitzchak Herzog (*Teshuvot Heichal Yizchak*, E.H. 2:25) appears to fundamentally accept Rav Moshe's premise. Nonetheless, Rav Herzog did not permit a Sephardic sixteen-year-old girl to remarry without a *get* after she married a man in his forties whom she thought was significantly younger. Although the girl had been deceived, Rav Herzog explained that one could not state unequivocally that a sixteen-year-old girl in such a community would never marry a man in his forties.[10]

---

9. It should be noted that in this responsum, Rav Moshe does not address the woman's ability to remarry; rather, he addresses the status of her children from a second marriage as *mamzeirim*. The prohibition of *mamzeirut* is lighter, so it is more common for authorities to rule leniently regarding it than regarding the woman's ability to remarry. Furthermore, the marriage under discussion was performed by a Conservative rabbi, so this created additional grounds for leniency (see *Techumin* 18:84-91).

10. The Rama (E.H. 42:4) notes that we do not rule in matters of marriage based on assumptions (*umdenot*). The *Aruch Hashulchan* (E.H. 42:8) claims that this principle even applies to undocumented information that appears obvious (*umdena demuchach*), while the *Chazon Ish* (E.H. 52:3) permits basing

KIDDUSHEI TA'UT: MARRIAGE UNDER FALSE PRETENSES

Rav Moshe issued his ruling about an impotent husband in 1951 and his ruling about an institutionalized husband in 1955. The present availability of psychiatric drugs allows for treating many psychiatric illnesses and casts doubt upon whether he would have ruled this way today. Similarly, impotence can be treated and cured in most cases today. It is thus unclear if a woman today would undoubtedly refuse to marry a man with either of these ailments. Even some homosexuals, with the help of psychotherapy, can lead a healthy married life.

Moreover, Rav Moshe did not rely on the woman's testimony alone to verify the husband's impotence and mental illness. Rather, the rabbis involved in the case examined the medical records of the husbands, and the doctors even testified that they unsuccessfully tried to cure one husband's impotence. In today's society, it is highly unlikely that such information would be forthcoming from medical officials.

Conclusion

It is extremely difficult to permit either partner in a marriage to remarry solely based upon *kiddushei ta'ut*. Every effort should be made to obtain a *get* even when major defects are discovered in either spouse. For a defect to be considered as grounds for *kiddushei ta'ut*, it must be clear beyond the shadow of a doubt that virtually no one would marry a person with the defect. Moreover, the defect must already be in existence before the marriage.[11]

---

a ruling on obvious information. The rulings of Rav Moshe and Rav Herzog appear to make similar assumptions to the *Chazon Ish*.
11. This requirement is not unique to marriage. In every business transaction, the consumer can renege on a deal by claiming that he bought defective merchandise only if the defect existed before the sale. Otherwise, every consumer who had bad luck with his product could undo the deal. For example, anyone who bought a stock could undo the purchase if the stock plummeted, and every rancher could undo the purchase of a cow if the cow died in his possession. For a discussion of this principle, see *Tosafot* (*Bava Kama* 110b s.v. *De'adaata* and *Ketubot* 47b s.v. *Shelo*).

Flaws in the Proposal of Rabbi Emanuel Rackman

An advertisement appeared in the *Jewish Week* (August 28, 1998) presenting the procedures for annulling a marriage based on *kiddushei ta'ut* (see previous chapter). The advertisement added that these principles guide the practice of the *Beit Din Zedek LiBaiayot Agunot,* which Rabbis Emanuel Rackman and Moses Morgenstern operate.[1] Shortly afterwards, Rabbi Rackman distributed a letter to the membership of the Rabbinical Council of America (dated December 14, 1998) defending the principles outlined in the advertisement. In this chapter, we explain why virtually all Orthodox rabbis reject these procedures (see, for example, Appendix).

Abuse of Kiddushei Ta'ut

In the previous chapter, we discussed Rav Moshe Feinstein's position that a woman may remarry without a *get* (based on the principle of *kiddushei ta'ut*) if she documents that her husband had such serious defects that no woman would knowingly marry him. We concluded our discussion by noting that the defect must have existed before marriage, such that the woman married the husband only because he concealed the defect from her. Rabbi Rackman seeks to apply Rav Moshe's ruling even further. Rabbi Rackman argues that if a husband abused his wife during the course of the marriage, his actions indicate that at the time of the wedding he "had the seeds" of an

---

1. After publication of the advertisement, it was reported that Rabbis Rackman and Morgenstern split from one another.

FLAWS IN THE PROPOSAL OF RABBI EMANUEL RACKMAN

"abuser personality." Since no woman wants to marry an abuser, the marriage is nullified on the grounds of "*kiddushei ta'ut*." Similarly, a husband who withholds a *get* undoubtedly had a sadistic personality already at the time of marriage.

Rabbi Rackman's suggestion contains numerous flaws. First, the mere fact that a man has an "abuser personality" by no means ensures that he will actually abuse his wife. Although some in the field of psychology believe in determinism, the Rambam (*Hilchot Teshuvah* 5:1) writes that belief in free will is a central element of the halachic worldview. Furthermore, husbands who ultimately abuse may have shown aggressive and controlling tendencies before their marriage, but they did not display any **guarantees** that they would abuse their wives. Many men who exhibit aggressive and controlling tendencies never end up abusing their wives. Thus, the criterion for *kiddushei ta'ut*, that no woman would ever agree to marry a man with these tendencies, has not been met. Often, a woman marries a man with some negative character traits, feeling that he is a good person overall and hoping that these negative traits will not manifest themselves in her husband in their worst form. *Tosafot* (*Ketubot* 70a s.v. *Yotzi*) write that we may not coerce a husband to give a get without "clear proof" that it is permissible; surely, we require clear proof to void the marriage with no *get*.[2] Certainly, the *Jewish Week* advertisement's assertion that (emphasis added) "in **every** case" of *igun* that they had seen, "the latent defects of the husband gave rise to such abusive behavior as to render them unfit to be husbands" is quite an extraordinary finding.

Rav Dr. Abraham Twerski (*The Shame Borne in Silence: Spouse Abuse in the Jewish Community*, pp. 16-18) writes the following regarding the character traits that lead to an abusive husband (emphasis added):

---

2. Interestingly, when the *Shulchan Aruch* (E.H. 154:3) discusses the propriety of coercing a physically abusive husband to give a *get*, he does not mention the option of declaring the marriage null and void.

One of the weakest areas in human psychology is prediction of behavior. Psychiatrists are often asked to testify in court about a given person's potential for violent behavior. The track record of success in predicting behavior is nothing to write home about. The correlation of psychological profiles with actual occurrence or absence of subsequent violence is rather low, and the "hunch" of a non-professional is probably of equal reliability....

There are, however, at least some behavioral clues, which are red flags. Mind you, they are not **predictors** of abuse, but they do indicate higher risk.... **A man may have one or more of these traits or warning signs and not turn out to be an abuser.** All we are saying is that any of these traits increase the risk of potentially abusive and controlling behavior.

Rabbi Rackman's suggestion is especially problematic in light of psychotherapies that empower a person to control his anger. A woman who discovers that her husband has a bad temper will likely advise him to see a psychologist before she will regret ever having married him. If this temper later deteriorates into spouse abuse, the marriage remains binding. As Rav Yosef Dov Soloveitchik (cited by Rav Hershel Schachter in *Beit Yitzchak* 29:232) explained (in rejecting Rabbi Rackman's proposal), this situation parallels a businessman who purchased a volatile stock out of hope that its price would rise. Even if the stock's value eventually plummets, he cannot go back to the seller and demand a refund. Just as business entails some level of gambling, so too, in marriage one takes risks (see *Tosafot, Bava Kama* 110a s.v. *De'adaata*). The Beth Din of America summed up this argument well (in a letter to all Rabbinical Council of America members, decrying the actions of Rabbis Rackman and Morgenstern): "Potential psychological tendencies do not create '*kiddushei ta'ut*,' since they may remain undeveloped."

FLAWS IN THE PROPOSAL OF RABBI EMANUEL RACKMAN

Even if Rabbi Rackman's idea were acceptable in theory, its implementation contains a significant practical problem. It is often very difficult to formally produce incontrovertible evidence that someone physically abused his spouse (see Rama, E.H. 154:3). Proving that someone had an abuser personality is even more difficult, if not impossible. Similarly, it is exceedingly difficult to prove that one who denies his wife a *get* had a sadistic personality at the time of marriage. At the very least, the *dayanim* must see psychological records documenting these tendencies from before the marriage. In Rav Moshe's responsa regarding impotent and institutionalized husbands, official medical records proved the women's claims. On the other hand, *The Jerusalem Report* (August 3, 1998) disclosed that Rabbi Moses Morgenstern issues his rulings merely based on the woman's word, undoubtedly an unacceptable practice.[3] Rabbis can rarely obtain private medical files in today's litigious society, for doctors do not generally release these records to clergy with the same ease that they may have done in Rav Moshe's time.

Lack of Coercion as Grounds for Annulment

The *Jewish Week* advertisement proceeds to present a second argument for annulling marriages without a *get*. In previous generations, a *beit din* could coerce a recalcitrant husband,[4] whereas today violent coercion is illegal and punishable in the United States. Thus, whenever a cruel husband denied a *get* to his wife, she may claim that had she known that coercion was not possible, she would not have married him.

---

3. See, for example, *Teshuvot Noda Biy'hudah* (vol. 1, E.H. 54), cited in *Pitchei Teshuvah* (E.H. 157:9).

4. The *Jewish Week* advertisement correctly notes that coercion is sometimes a viable option, but the advertisement misleadingly presents the Rambam's view as normative. In fact, virtually all later authorities reject the Rambam's criteria for when a *beit din* may coerce a husband. For the parameters of when Halachah permits coercing a husband to give a *get*, see our opening chapter, "Coercing a Husband to Give a *Get*."

GRAY MATTER

This argument bears the same fundamental flaw as the previous one. For consideration as grounds for *kidushei ta'ut*, a problem must be so great at the time of marriage that, without a doubt, no woman would get married in such a situation. Regarding ignorance of the impracticality of coercion, this logic simply does not hold true. It has been known for years that American law prohibits physically coercing husbands to give *gittin*, yet thousands of Jewish couples marry every year. Each woman, while she obviously does not expect at her wedding that she will someday suffer as an *agunah*, may recognize that a tiny percentage of marriages unravel into *igun*. Despite this risk, she marries with the belief that she and her husband will live a happy life together. If things later go wrong, Rav Soloveitchik's analogy to a stock consumer again applies.

No one denies the potential existence of **individual** women who would never marry if they understood the risks of *igun*. However, we can only entertain the possibility of *kiddushei ta'ut* when virtually **all** women would never marry. In the cases addressed by Rav Moshe, not only did the women immediately leave their husbands, but almost any woman would leave a husband with defects such as homosexuality. In Rabbi Rackman's case, all married women in America, including those who are happily married, live under the potential threat of *igun*. How many of them immediately abandon their husbands upon discovery of the fact that this threat exists? According to Rabbi Rackman's logic, Jewish marriage does not exist in the United States, as every woman married her husband only out of ignorance of the dangers of *igun*.

Misunderstanding Marriage

The *Jewish Week* advertisement continues by presenting a third reason to treat marriages as *kiddushei ta'ut*. It argues "that many women if informed would in no way agree to the *kinyan*/acquisition nature of *kiddushin*/marriage." The advertisement explains that no woman wishes for her husband to have "title to the wife's body." Consequently, if women understood the true nature of Jewish marriage, they would not agree to marry according to Halachah.

The advertisement mistakenly portrays Orthodox marriage in an extremely negative light in order to prove that no woman would agree to such a marriage. As Rav J. David Bleich (*Tradition* 33:1:115-116) has commented, "The sole right of which the bride is divested is the capacity to contract a marriage with any other male.... [The advertisement's] description of halakhic marriage is grossly overstated. The husband does not acquire 'title to the wife's body.' A wife is not a slave. The husband acquires a servitude rather than title to her body - an extremely important legal distinction." The Rashba (*Kiddushin* 6b s.v. *Iy Neima*) explicitly writes that the husband "does not actually own her body." Rav Bleich notes that his female students, including those who are not Orthodox, willingly marry according to Jewish law even after he has taught them the true technical meaning of the ceremony.

Furthermore, one can engage in a halachic transaction even without comprehending the precise theory of the transaction ceremony. As long as a consumer fundamentally understands that he is buying or selling something, the transaction takes effect. Would Rabbi Rackman annul every business transaction if either side were not well versed in tractates *Bava Metzia* and *Bava Batra* and their many commentaries?

Even if Rabbi Rackman were correct about the theory of marriage, one major problem with his argument remains. The fact that many halachically knowledgeable women marry under Orthodox auspices proves that not all women consider a halachic ceremony intolerable. If Rabbi Rackman were correct, every woman should leave her husband upon learning of the halachic meaning of marriage. According to Rabbi Rackman, every unlearned married woman is currently living in sin, as she was married under false pretenses and continues to cohabit with her husband.

GRAY MATTER

One final difficulty prevents virtually any application of *kiddushei ta'ut*. The *Chelkat Mechokeik* (39:9) and the *Beit Shmuel* (39:7,16) both note that we only consider claims of *kiddushei ta'ut* when the spouse lodged a complaint is **immediately**. If, however, he or she failed to complain about the problem immediately, the absence of a complaint constitutes acceptance of the defect. Even if the husband or wife complains later about the defect, the marriage is **undoubtedly valid**. The *Aruch Hashulchan* (E.H. 39:13) also notes that if the couple continues to cohabit as a normal married couple, the marriage certainly takes effect despite the defect. Remaining together indicates that the spouse considers the defect insignificant.

Other Claims of the Jewish Week Advertisement

The advertisement also contains much critical misinformation about *agunah*-related issues. It states that "a single witness, circumstantial evidence, and hearsay" are all admissible proof to free an *agunah*. The authors of the advertisement apparently confused the meaning of the term *agunah* in different contexts. The *agunah* who may remarry based on questionable evidence is a woman whose husband is presumed dead without clear evidence of the death. The Halachah permits the woman to remarry only with some proof of his death, but the lighter forms of evidence delineated in the advertisement suffice. The Rambam (*Hilchot Geirushin* 13:29) explains that the husband's life or death is a fact that can often be proven even without witnesses. Although the Halachah nonetheless requires some sort of testimony, its relaxes the standards. Whereas we usually require two witnesses, to guarantee that neither is lying, here we assume that a witness will not lie about something that may be determined even without him. The Ra'avad (*ibid.*) adds that we are lenient about the testimony to free an *agunah* because we trust the woman to thoroughly research her husband's death before remarriage. Thus, even if a *beit din* permits the woman to remarry based on shaky evidence,

FLAWS IN THE PROPOSAL OF RABBI EMANUEL RACKMAN

she will presumably not do so without independently verifying her husband's death.

The *Jewish Week* advertisement refers to a totally different type of women as *agunot*. These women's husbands are alive and well but deny them *gittin*. The advertisement applies the above passage from the Rambam to them, presumably to permit verifying the claims of these *agunot* with flimsy evidence. However, the Rambam's logic does not apply to these women, because the details of divorce cases, such as whether a husband abused his wife, are not easily discovered. A *beit din* thus cannot rule on these matters without clear documentation or testimony. As we have already noted, Rav Moshe Feinstein checked medical records before accepting that a husband was impotent or institutionalized and thus invalidating the marriage. Rabbi Moses Morgenstern, on the other hand, has reportedly issued annulments without investigating the claims of the women involved (*The Jerusalem Report*, August 3, 1998).

The advertisement claims that "fear of *mamzeirut* is an illusion." In other words, the advertisers deny that the children of a woman who remarries without a *get* are *mamzeirim* (progeny of a forbidden union whom the Torah forbids to marry natural-born Jews). Of course, the advertisers recognize that the status of a *mamzeir* appears explicitly in the Gemara (*Yevamot* 49a), but they cite a responsum of the Maharsham (1:9, cited by the advertisers simply as 9) as a basis for averting this problem. The Maharsham suggests that a first husband may save his ex-wife's second marriage from being adultery (if she remarried without a *get*) by giving her a *get* that retroactively annuls the first marriage.

The advertisement ignores several major problems with implementing such a *get*. The Maharsham never actually performed such a *get* and noted that it is fraught with halachic problems. He only suggested it as a theoretical possibility ("*lahalachah velo lema'aseh*"). His hesitancy is particularly relevant when one considers that many other halachic authorities

55

discuss the Maharsham's suggestion, and they almost unanimously reject it.[5] Rav Shlomo Zalman Auerbach (*Minchat Shlomo* 1:76) lists six flaws in the Maharsham's idea and flatly rejects its practical implementation.

The most startling part of the advertisement's reference to the Maharsham is that his idea bears no relevance to the situations addressed by the advertisement. The Maharsham dealt with how the first husband can help his remarried ex-wife by doing certain things in the *get* procedure, while the advertisement addresses husbands who refuse to cooperate with the *beit din* or the wife in performing a *get*. Rabbi Rackman later clarified that the advertisers merely wished to demonstrate from the Maharsham's responsum that rabbis always find a way to free potential *mamzeirim* from *mamzeirut*. If this was their intention, they apparently failed to notice that the Maharsham, after writing that a retroactive *get* was not feasible in his case, concludes his responsum by writing that he sees no realistic way to permit the *mamzeir* in question.

Writing a Get Against the Husband's Will

According to press reports, Rabbi Morgenstern also grants a *get* on behalf of recalcitrant husbands.[6] Rav Herzog, known for his extraordinary leniency on *agunah* issues, wrote that he would not even dream of doing such a thing (*Teshuvot Heichal Yitzchak*, E.H. 2:64:3-4). A husband must issue the *get* of his own free will, so a *get* is not valid unless the husband orders the scribe to write the *get* and witnesses to sign it (Mishnah, *Gittin* 71b). Regarding

---

5. See *Tzitz Eliezer* (15:58) and *Minchat Yitzchak* (2:66:32). On the other hand, see *Heichal Yitzchak* (E.H. 2:19). For a thorough discussion and rejection of the Maharsham's proposal, see Rav David Lau's essay in *Techumin* (17:251-271).

6. Rabbi Moses Morgenstern has distanced himself from the *Jewish Week* advertisement. Instead, he claims to rely on other factors that he has not published (to this author's knowledge).

FLAWS IN THE PROPOSAL OF RABBI EMANUEL RACKMAN

the practice of writing a *get* on behalf of a recalcitrant husband, Rav Hershel Schachter (*Be'ikvei Hatzon* 30:14) writes:

> And behold, in our time, one man has arisen who considers himself a Torah scholar... and he added that even if the husband specifically declared not to give his wife a *get*, we can give it as a "benefit" (*zachin*) against his will, since it is purely beneficial [for the recalcitrant husband].... It is obvious that even if we understood like the [extraordinarily lenient view of] Rav [Eliyahu] of Lublin, of whom the *Heichal Yitzchak* wrote that God forbid should one rule in accordance with his opinion, nonetheless, supplying the husband's consent on the grounds that [the *get*] is beneficial for him, when the husband openly declares to the contrary, is unspeakable. It is clearly against the Halachah, and that self-proclaimed Torah scholar's idea was not accepted.

Rav Feinstein's Explicit Rejection of the Proposal

Rav Moshe Feinstein (*Teshuvot Igrot Moshe Even Haezer* 1:53) was presented with the following tragic question. A husband had refused to give a *get* to his wife and the woman subsequently remarried in a civil ceremony and had a child with her second husband. A rabbi proposed to Rav Moshe that perhaps the child is not a *mamzer* because the couple engaged in intense fights and the husband was incarcerated immediately following the first marriage. The rabbi proposed that the first marriage should be considered invalid because had she known that the husband would engage in such serious misbehavior she never would have married him. Rav Feinstein entirely rejects this proposal and ruled that the child is certainly a *mamzer*. Rav Feinstein writes that the proposal is "certainly incorrect because any problem that arises subsequent to the marriage cannot serve as a reason to view the marriage as having been entered on a fraudulent basis." This husband cruelly withheld a *get* from his wife and yet Rav Moshe did not consider this as a basis to invalidate the marriage even to spare the child from the stigma of *mamzeirut*.

Conclusion

We have presented a brief summary of why the Orthodox rabbinate has rejected the ideas and actions of Rabbis Rackman and Morgenstern. A much lengthier treatment appears in Rav J. David Bleich's essay in *Tradition* (33:1:90-128). Rav Bleich concludes his discussion (p. 128) by noting that he ordinarily does not discuss material that does not merit serious consideration, but he feels a need to address the *Jewish Week* advertisement due to the publicity it received. Regarding this book, too, the reader should not erroneously think that refuting the proposals of Rabbi's Rackman and Morgenstern indicates a minimal amount of respect for their proposals. While their dedication to helping *agunot* is noble, their distortion of halachic sources is troubling, regardless of whether it stems from honest mistakes or deliberate manipulation of texts.

Let us hope that the women "freed" by Rabbis Rackman and Morgenstern will not choose to have children until they receive valid *gittin* from their husbands, as virtually the entire Orthodox rabbinate would consider their children to be *mamzeirim*. The rabbis of many prominent Modern Orthodox communities in the New York area jointly signed a letter stating their refusal to recognize the annulments of Rabbis Rackman and Morgenstern (printed in *The Jewish Press* June 5, 1998 and reprinted in Appendix). Indeed, every major Orthodox rabbinical organization has rejected the actions of Rabbis Rackman and Morgenstern, including the Beth Din of America (Orthodox Union and Rabbinical Council of America), the Israeli Chief Rabbinate, Agudath Israel, and the Eidah Chareidit Badatz. Rav Ovadia Yosef even repealed the ordination of a man whom he once ordained after the man participated in several of Rabbi Morgenstern's annulments (*The Jerusalem Report*, August 3, 1998).

FLAWS IN THE PROPOSAL OF RABBI EMANUEL RACKMAN

Both the rabbinical and lay communities must unite to fight the tragedy of *agunot* and the danger of invalid annulments. We must convince *agunot* to avoid this "court" and help them receive universally accepted *gittin*. A prescription for greatly reducing incidence of *igun* is universal usage of a halachically acceptable prenuptial agreement, severe social sanctions against recalcitrant spouses, and activist *batei din*.

We will conclude by citing from a speech delivered by Rav Yosef Dov Soloveitchik to the Rabbinical Council of America, in response to Rabbi Rackman's proposal:[7]

> I have to discharge a duty. Believe me, I do it with much sadness in my heart. You know I never criticize anybody; I have never attacked anybody. But today... I feel it is my duty to make the following statement....
>
> I also was told that it was recommended that the method of *afka'inhu rabanan lekiddushin mineih* [to annul marriages] be introduced.... Do you expect to survive as Orthodox rabbis? Do you expect to carry on the *mesorah* under such circumstances? Chaos will replace Torah. I hope that those gathered here will join me in objecting to such discussion at a rabbinical convention. I cannot imagine a Republican National Convention or Democratic National Convention where a symposium would be held as to whether communism should replace democracy in the United States.

---

7. A relevant piece of the Rav's speech appears in *The Journal of Halacha and Contemporary Society* (9:140-141). The Rav's students cite his adamant opposition to Rabbi Rackman's proposal regarding *kiddushei ta'ut* in *Hamevaser* (38:2) and *Beit Yitzchak* (29:232).

NON-ORTHODOX MARRIAGES

The Halachic Status of Civil Marriages

One of the most serious problems confronting American Jewry as a community is the possible validity of non-Orthodox marriages.[1] As a practicing *dayan* on the Beth Din of Elizabeth, this author has encountered numerous situations in which this issue came to the fore. It is protocol among all *batei din* to require a *get* even if the couple was married only civilly. However, when certain situations arise, a *get* is either difficult to obtain or insufficient. One example is when a man refuses to grant a *get* to his wife even after the couple has received a civil divorce. If it can be determined that the couple's marriage lacked halachic validity, the woman is permitted to remarry without a *get*. Another regrettably common situation is *mamzeirut*, where a woman conceived a child before she received a *get* from her former husband. A child conceived during a halachically adulterous relationship is a *mamzeir* and may not marry a natural-born Jew (see *Shulchan Aruch, Even Ha'ezer* 4).[2] In these situations, we cannot simply "play it safe" and assume the validity of the civil marriage at the *agunah*'s or *mamzeir*'s expense, so the marriage's halachic status must be determined.

---

1. For summaries of the halachic status of civil marriages see *Techumin* (2:255-263), *Otzar Haposkim* (vol. 10, 26:6:3-5) and Rav Gedaliah Felder's *Nachalat Tzvi* (2:296-328).
2. Even if the woman were to receive a *get* from her first husband, it would not help the children who were already conceived through an extramarital relationship (see *Minchat Shlomo* 1:76).

GRAY MATTER

Talmudic Background

The Mishnah (*Kiddushin* 2a) teaches that a Jewish marriage, *kiddushin*, can be created through "money, written contract, or sexual relations." Civil marriage ceremonies lack religious significance, so their halachic validity could come only from the couple's subsequent cohabitation.

The Mishnah (*Gittin* 81a) speaks of a divorced couple who sleeps alone in an inn. *Beit Hillel* believes that the couple is remarried by virtue of the cohabitation. The Gemara explains that *Beit Hillel's* opinion is predicated on two key principles. First, although no one saw a sexual act, we view the witnesses who saw the couple enter the room as if they saw such an act (*hein hein eidei yichud hein hein eidei bi'ah*). Upon establishing that the couple engaged in sexual relations, *Beit Hillel* applies the rule of *ein adam oseh be'ilato be'ilat zenut* (one does not normally engage in sexual activity outside of marriage). The man thus wants his encounter in the inn to constitute an act of *kiddushin*, lest it be deemed illicit. The halachic issue concerning civil marriage depends on whether the principles of *ein adam odeh be'ilato be'ilat zenut* and *hein hein eidei yichud hein hein eidei bi'ah* apply to a civilly married couple.

Rishonim and Shulchan Aruch - Catholic Weddings

The question of civil marriage did not emerge until the nineteenth century, as the institution did not exist until then. However, *Rishonim* dealt with a similar problem, the halachic status of Jews who married in a Catholic ceremony and lived together. The Rivash (*Teshuvot* 6) wrote a landmark responsum on this issue, presenting two major arguments why Jews married in a Catholic ceremony are **not** married according to Halachah. He notes that a couple who chooses to marry in a Catholic ceremony demonstrates that it does not wish to be married according to Torah law. Furthermore, the Rivash asserts that the Talmudic rule of *ein adam oseh be'ilato be'ilat zenut* does not apply to those who do not observe the laws of family purity. If a

THE HALACHIC STATUS OF CIVIL MARRIAGES

man and woman engage in sexual relations when she is a *nidah* (a sin punishable by *kareit*, spiritual excision), they undoubtedly do not object to sexual contact outside the context of marriage (a weaker prohibition).[3] The *Terumat Hadeshen* (209), Radbaz (1:351), and *Mishneh Lamelech* (*Hilchot Geirushin* 10:18) agree with the Rivash. Indeed, the Rambam (*Hilchot Ishut* 7:23) writes that the rule of *ein adam oseh be'ilato be'ilat zenut* only applies to those who are "kosher" (proper) among the people of Israel.

Both the *Shulchan Aruch* (*Even Ha'ezer* 149:6) and the Rama (E.H. 26:1) accept the Rivash's lenient ruling. The *Shulchan Aruch* writes, "[Regarding] a man and woman who were forcibly converted and later married in a Catholic ceremony, even though everyone [Jewish] sees them entering their home alone... no *kiddushin* exist between this man and woman."

Contemporary Rulings

These rulings serve as precedents for the overwhelming majority of authorities, who rule that civil marriages are not halachically binding. Rav Moshe Feinstein (*Teshuvot Igrot Moshe, Even Ha'ezer* 75) articulates this view:

> If the people who had only civil marriage are halachically observant, the couple requires a *get*

---

3. Rav Yitzchak Herzog (*Teshuvot Heichal Yizchak* E.H. 2:31:3) notes that this assumption is not always true. While halachically sensitive Jews recognize that having relations with a *nidah* is more severe than engaging in sexual relations outside of marriage, this may not always be true of secular Jews. As Rav Herzog writes, a secular Jew may be unable to imagine the severity and importance of family purity, yet he will realize that living together out of wedlock is a "corruption of serious human morality." Nevertheless, Rav Herzog himself rules that civil marriages are not halachically binding, for reasons that we shall see later in this chapter. Regrettably, it is doubtful that Rav Herzog's assessment of the secular Jews of his time applies to non-Orthodox Jews today, when much of Western society no longer views premarital sex as corrupt and amoral (see *Aseih Lecha Rav* 8:72).

because of the rule *ein adam oseh be'ilato be'ilat zenut*. If it is possible, one should obtain a *get* even for those couples who are not halachically observant, as is the generally accepted rabbinical practice. However, if it is impossible to obtain a *get* and the woman would otherwise remain an *agunah*, one may rely on the lenient ruling of the Rivash.

The main proponent of the dissenting view is Rav Yosef Eliyahu Henkin (*Perushei Ibra*, Chapters 3-5). He argues that if the couple intends to be married, then every sexual act should be viewed as an act of *kiddushin*. Rav Henkin vigorously argues that a couple need not intend to marry according to Jewish law for *kiddushin* to take effect. The Halachah considers *kiddushin* to be created when a couple engages in marital relations and intends to have a permanent monogamous relationship.

The overwhelming majority of halachic authorities reject Rav Henkin's position. Rav Meshulam Roth (*Teshuvot Kol Mevaser* 22) writes, "Virtually all of the great halachic authorities of the previous generation agree that a couple which was married only in a civil ceremony essentially does not require a *get*."

Rav Avraham Shapiro (*Teshuvot Devar Avraham* 3:29) vigorously disputes Rav Henkin's arguments. He notes that the rulings of the Rivash, *Terumat Hadeshen*, Radbaz, *Shulchan Aruch*, and Rama seem to contradict Rav Henkin's assertions. Furthermore, a couple is not halachically married if the man and woman do not intend to marry according to **Torah law**.

This argument revolves around the question of what creates *kiddushin*. Is it intent for a permanent monogamous relationship or for marriage according to Jewish law? Indeed, many of those espousing the lenient view refer to the *Shaagat Aryeh*'s opinion (cited in *Teshuvot Beit Ephraim*, E.H. 42) that the rule of *hein hein eidei yichud hein hein eidei bi'ah* does not apply

THE HALACHIC STATUS OF CIVIL MARRIAGES

to unlearned people[4] who are unaware that *kiddushin* can be created through marital relations. We apparently do not consider the couple's general interest in a marriage relationship halachically significant as long as there is no interest in marrying according to Halachah.[5] This assertion is echoed by Rav Yitzchak Herzog (*Teshuvot Heichal Yitzchak* E.H. 2:31:3-4), who further notes that the sexual relations of a couple who mistakenly believes it had a halachic ceremony do not effect a marriage (*Ketubot* 73b). Why, he argues, should a secular couple who mistakenly believes that it does not need a religious ceremony be treated any differently?

Exceptions

There are a couple of possible exceptions to the consensus regarding civil marriage. One is the case discussed by Israel's late Sephardic Chief Rabbi, Rav Ben-Zion Uzziel (*Teshuvot Mishpetei Uzziel*, E.H. 29). Rav Uzziel writes that if a couple lived in a country where Jewish wedding rituals were forbidden, we should be concerned that the rule of *ein adam oseh be'ilato be'ilat zenut* applies. After all, it could well be that the couple desired a halachic marriage, so, in the absence of any other ceremony, it had sexual relations for the purpose of marriage.

Another possible exception is a non-observant couple who married civilly and later became more observant. Although the couple initially did not marry according to Halachah, one could argue that once the couple increasingly observes *mitzvot*, it wants to be halachically married. Its continued sexual relations effect this marriage based on the principle of *ein adam oseh be'ilato be'ilat zenut*. If a previously non-Orthodox couple finds itself in such a situation and wishes to ensure that it is married halachically, a competent rabbi must be consulted.

---

4. It appears from the responsum that the **witnesses** must know that marital relations can contract a marriage, although it is not entirely clear if he requires them or the couple to know this.
5. See, however, *Teshuvot Or Samei'ach* (*Likutei Teshuvot* 10).

Conclusion

The overwhelming majority of halachic authorities believe that civil marriages are not halachically binding. They include Rav Chaim Ozer Grodzinski (*Teshuvot Achiezer* 4:50), Rav David Tzvi Hoffman (*Teshuvot Melameid Leho'il* 3:20), Rav Yechiel Yaakov Weinberg (*Teshuvot Seridei Eish* 3:22), Rav Yitzchak Isaac Herzog (*Teshuvot Heichal Yitzchak*, E.H. 2:30-31), Rav Yaakov Breisch (*Teshuvot Chelkat Yaakov* 1:1), Rav Shlomo Zalman Auerbach (*Teshuvot Minchat Shlomo* 3:100) and Dayan Y.Y. Weisz (*Teshuvot Minchat Yitzchak* 3:125). Furthermore, today there may be yet another reason to rule that civil marriages are not halachically valid. Rav Henkin based his stringent view on *ein adam oseh be'ilato be'ilat zenut*. Rav Chaim David Halevi argues that, unfortunately, this principle no longer holds true in many Western countries (*Aseih Lecha Rav* 8:72). In practice, Rav Shiloh Raphael writes (*Techumin* 7:284), "In case of *igun*, all *batei din* in Israel permit the woman [married only in a civil ceremony] to remarry without a *get*. Nevertheless, the accepted practice is to try to arrange a *get*, if at all possible, even if only a civil ceremony took place." Obviously, since this is a complex area of Halachah, a rabbi of eminent stature must be sought when confronting the situations that we have discussed.

The Halachic Status of Reform Marriages
Part I: Kiddushei Bi'ah and Orthodox Males in the Audience

Having addressed the status of civil marriages in the previous chapter, we now shift our attention to a related issue, the halachic view of Reform weddings.

Contracting a Marriage Through Relations

Rav Moshe Feinstein (*Teshuvot Igrot Moshe, Even Ha'ezer* 1:76) suggests that even those authorities who deem civil marriage halachically binding (see previous chapter) would agree that a couple married by a Reform rabbi is not halachically married. He bases his argument on the Gemara's discussion of a groom who gave his bride an object worth less than a *perutah*,[1] after which he consummated the marriage (*Ketubot* 73b). One opinion believes that the couple is married, for we assume that people realize *kiddushin* require an object worth a *perutah*. Since the couple understands that its formal marriage ceremony is not valid, it opts to create *kiddushin* through sexual relations.

The other opinion asserts that people generally do not know that the ring must be worth at least a *perutah*, so the couple does not realize that its wedding ceremony did not conform to Halachah. Hence, the man and woman do not intend to create *kiddushin* with their sexual relations, because they believe that their sexual relations are already sanctioned by their wedding ceremony and do not require anything more.

---

1. The money or object given for the purpose of marriage must be worth at least a *perutah* (an ancient coin); see *Kiddushin* 2a.

GRAY MATTER

The *Shulchan Aruch* (*Even Ha'ezer* 31:9) rules that the couple is halachically married when the ring used in the wedding ceremony was worth less than a *perutah*. The Rama adds that the couple is married only if it realizes that the wedding ceremony lacked halachic validity and that *kiddushin* must thus be created by sexual relations. However, if it believes that the marriage ceremony was valid, the couple is **not** married even after engaging in sexual relations.

Rav Moshe and the Maharsham (*Teshuvot* 2:101) write that those who ask a Reform rabbi to marry them erroneously believe that the Reform ceremony constitutes *kiddushin*, so they do not intend to create *kiddushin* later through sexual relations. Accordingly, the only way for a Reform wedding to take effect would be if the Reform ceremony itself were halachically valid. We will now outline the issues surrounding a Reform wedding ceremony.

Male Orthodox Jews in the Audience

Jewish law requires the presence of two male qualified witnesses in order for a wedding ceremony to have halachic validity. The presence of witnesses for *kiddushin* and *gittin* is required to render the action halachically significant, and not merely to provide evidence after the fact. Consequently, even a videocassette of the wedding cannot substitute for the presence of qualified witnesses at the ceremony.

The *Shulchan Aruch* (*Choshen Mishpat*, 33-35) delineates who the Halachah considers a qualified witness. Anyone who is known to have violated a monetary crime, regardless of its punishment, or a negative Torah prohibition punishable by *malkot* (lashes) or death, such as desecrating *Shabbat*, is disqualified on a Torah level. Thus, one who is known to cheat in business, drive on *Shabbat*, or eat non-kosher food cannot serve as a witness for *kiddushin*. In addition, any first or second-degree relative of the bride, groom, or other witness is invalid.[2]

---

2. The Rama (C.M. 33:2) claims that the Rambam considers maternal

THE HALACHIC STATUS OF REFORM MARRIAGES PART I

Accordingly, Rav Moshe writes:

> It appears correct to me that a marriage ceremony conducted by a Reform rabbi has no halachic validity if a thorough investigation demonstrates that two qualified witnesses did not see the groom hand the bride the ring and recite *"harei at mekudashet li"* (the wedding formula, "Behold you are married to me...").

The Chatam Sofer's Ruling

The *Chatam Sofer* (*Teshuvot* 100, cited by *Pitchei Teshuvah*, E.H. 42:11) poses a potentially serious challenge to Rav Moshe's ruling. In the *Chatam Sofer*'s case, a rabbi performed a wedding, and two men were designated as witnesses of the *kiddushin*. A few weeks later, the rabbi discovered that one of the witnesses was a relative of the bride.

The *Chatam Sofer* rules that the marriage was valid despite the fact that one of the designated witnesses was disqualified. He explains that anyone present at the wedding could potentially serve as a witness (assuming he was not invalid for any other reason), and even people who did not see the delivery of the ring to the bride still knew that the transfer occurred. This knowledge fits the halachic category of *anan sahadei*, knowledge that is equivalent to seeing the transfer itself (see *Shevuot* 33b-34a). This concept resembles last chapter's rule of *hein hein eidei yichud hein hein eidei bi'ah*.

The *Chatam Sofer*'s ruling could limit Rav Moshe's leniency to cases when no valid witnesses attended the wedding ceremony.

---

relatives invalid witnesses only on a rabbinical level. Accordingly, observant maternal relatives who saw the wedding ceremony take place could make the wedding valid on a biblical level. On the other hand, the *Shach* (C.M. 33:7) offers a different interpretation of the Rambam's words and argues that even the Rambam invalidates maternal relatives on a biblical level.

GRAY MATTER

However, Rav Moshe asserts that the *Chatam Sofer*'s ruling does not apply to a wedding conducted by a Reform rabbi, as it requires the officiating rabbi to be both well versed in Halachah and punctilious about all halachic details related to marriage. Only in such a situation can those at the wedding presume that a halachically valid ceremony took place. However, if the men in the audience are not certain that the *kiddushin* were conducted strictly in accordance with Halachah, they cannot serve as witnesses without watching the ring's delivery with their own eyes.[3]

Conclusion: Criticism and Acceptance of Rav Moshe

Despite Rav Moshe's claim that even Rav Yosef Eliyahu Henkin, who believes that civil marriages are binding, will agree that Reform marriages are not binding, Rav Henkin rules otherwise (*Teshuvot Ibra* 2:76). He vehemently attacks Rav Moshe's ruling and depicts its implementation as "a sin." Although some great rabbis dispute Rav Moshe's lenient ruling, many agree with it. As we have noted, the Maharsham articulates a similar view to that of Rav Moshe. In addition, Rav Eliezer Waldenberg (*Teshuvot Tzitz Eliezer* 8:37) accepts Rav Moshe's analysis and ruling. He seeks to demonstrate that many great authorities disagree with the aforementioned ruling of the *Chatam Sofer*. Moreover, he agrees with Rav Moshe that the *Chatam Sofer*'s ruling does not apply to a wedding ceremony conducted by a Reform rabbi. It should be emphasized, though, that even Rav Moshe urged that all efforts be made to administer a *get* on behalf of a divorced couple even if it was married in a Reform ceremony.

---

3. Dayan Y.Y. Weisz (*Minchat Yitzchak* 2:66) does not appear to agree with Rav Moshe's claim. Dayan Weisz believes that even in a situation, such as a Reform wedding, where the audience has its doubts as to the validity of the marriage, everyone in the audience knows that a potentially valid ceremony took place. Accordingly, if there are Orthodox non-relatives in the audience during the wedding ceremony, there is a *safeik* (doubt) as to the marriage's validity. Rav Shlomo Zalman Auerbach (*Minchat Shlomo* 3:100) rejects this approach. If there are no valid witnesses in the audience, even Dayan Weisz accepts Rav Moshe's lenient ruling (at least regarding *mamzeirut*).

The Halachic Status of Reform Marriages
Part II: Deviations in the Ceremony

Rav Moshe Feinstein wrote several responsa about the halachic status of Reform wedding ceremonies, including a 1970 responsum where he examines several of their problematic parts (*Teshuvot Igrot Moshe, Even Ha'ezer* 3:25). In addition to the lack of valid witnesses, which we have addressed in the previous chapter, Rav Moshe argues that Reform marriages also lack halachic validity for other reasons:

> They do not perform an act of *kiddushin*. Rather he merely responds "yes" to the rabbi's question, "Do you wish to take this woman as your wife?"... These are not words of *kiddushin* [such as the required phrase, "Behold you are betrothed to me with this ring"]; rather, these words express consent to joining in marriage. [The man and woman] subsequently exchange rings as an expression of their marriage, which they believe to have been contracted already by answering "yes."

The Double Ring Ceremony

In the above responsum, Rav Moshe suggests that double ring ceremonies raise concern about how the couple understood the wedding procedures:

> Even though he gives her a ring, she also gives him a ring, which demonstrates that his giving her a ring was merely a present in honor of their marriage, and there is no act of *kiddushin*.

GRAY MATTER

Dayan Aryeh Grossnass (*Teshuvot Lev Aryeh* 31) presents a similar approach. It should be noted that there are many variations of the double ring ceremony, and they might have different halachic standings.

Disagreement with Rav Feinstein

Many great rabbis disagree with this assertion of Rav Moshe. Both Rav Zalman Nechemia Goldberg and Rav Hershel Schachter expressed their opinions to this author that once the groom gives the bride a ring, they are married. Whatever happens after the delivery of the ring is irrelevant in their view.[1]

The Gemara (*Nedarim* 87a) seems to support Rav Goldberg and Rav Schachter's view. The Gemara states that one may retract even a formal statement (such as testimony in *beit din*) as long as the retraction occurs immediately after the statement (*toch kedei dibur*). However, this rule does not apply to four areas of Halachah - cursing our Creator (God forbid), idolatry, *kiddushin*, and *gittin*. Accordingly, once *kiddushin* have taken effect, one cannot retract them (except with a *get* or death). Thus, once the groom gives the bride a ring, the bride's giving the groom a second ring should be irrelevant.

Defense of Rav Feinstein's Ruling

Nonetheless, one may suggest a defense of Rav Moshe's ruling. Rav Chaim Soloveitchik (commentary to Rambam's *Hilchot Chalitzah* 4:16) explains that a couple does not become married merely by the ritual performance of *kiddushin*. Rather, *da'at*, intention, is necessary to create the marriage. Accordingly, the couple must have *da'at* that giving the ring creates the *kiddushin*; without intention, the *kiddushin* cannot take effect. Since the statement of vows and the double ring ceremony confuse the couple's *da'at*, the marriage is not effective.

---

1. Nonetheless, both these authorities disapprove of conducting a double ring ceremony, its effectiveness notwithstanding (see *Teshuvot Igrot Moshe*, E.H. 3:18).

THE HALACHIC STATUS OF REFORM MARRIAGES PART II

Moreover, in videos of Reform weddings that this author has seen, the rabbi typically declares at the conclusion of the *chuppah*, "I now pronounce you man and wife in the eyes of man and in the eyes of God." Women who participated in these ceremonies have told this author that they thought they were married according to Jewish tradition when the rabbis made this declaration.

The Rama (E.H. 42:1) writes, "Regarding *kiddushin* we do not use assumptions or [circumstantial] proofs to establish that a [man or] woman did not intend to be married." It would thus seem that we cannot assume that the couple did not intend to be married at the right time in the ceremony. Nevertheless, there is still room to invalidate Reform weddings. This is because the basis for the Rama's ruling (as explained by Rav Yechezkel Landau, *Teshuvot Noda Biyhudah* 1:59, cited by *Pitchei Teshuvah*, E.H. 42:3) is that unarticulated thoughts have no halachic significance (*devarim sheb'leiv einam devarim*). However, in the case of the Reform double ring ceremony, the circumstances clearly indicate a lack of *da'at*. The groom and bride demonstrate with their actions that they do not want the groom's delivery of the ring to effect *kiddushin*. In fact, *Tosafot* (*Kiddushin* 49b s.v. *Devarim*) write that when the individual's intentions are obvious, they do indeed have halachic standing. The *Chazon Ish* (E.H. 52:3) also writes that even the Rama would invalidate a marriage if it is blatantly obvious that the couple did not intend to marry halachically (see *Techumin* 18:92-99).

Indeed, it is common in observant communities for a man to present an engagement ring to his fiancée, yet we do not believe that the couple is thereby married (see Rama, E.H. 45:2). This is because they clearly **do not** intend to create *kiddushin* with the engagement ring.

Limitations of Rav Feinstein's Ruling

Rav Moshe's ruling probably does not apply to every case of a double ring ceremony. This author saw on video a traditional Conservative rabbi conduct a double ring ceremony. The rabbi told the groom to give the ring as an expression of marriage and subsequently told the bride to give him a ring as a pledge of her love. He seemed to be attempting to distinguish between the groom's delivery of the ring (which creates *kiddushin*) and the bride's handing the groom a ring.

Although Rav Moshe strongly disapproves of such a ceremony (*Teshuvot Igrot Moshe*, E.H. 3:18), he probably would believe that this form of a double ring ceremony does not invalidate the wedding. In this case, no concrete evidence exists that the couple does not wish to create *kiddushin* with the delivery of the ring from the groom to the bride.

Ownership of the Ring

Rav Moshe (*Teshuvot Igrot Moshe*, E.H. 1:76) further notes that the groom often does not own the ring at Reform weddings.[2] If the ring belonged to the bride (or anyone else) before the ceremony, the *kiddushin* are not valid.

Rav Zalman Nechemia Goldberg expressed his disagreement Rav Moshe to this author. He referred to a ruling of the Rosh (*Kiddushin* 1:20, codified in *Shulchan Aruch*, E.H. 28:19) that if one borrows a ring and informs the lender that he wishes to use it for *kiddushin*, the *kiddushin* are valid. Although the ring was borrowed, the lender intends to give the ring as a present (and not merely a loan) to the groom so that the *kiddushin* can take effect. Similarly, the groom intends to acquire the ring in order to properly implement the *kiddushin*.[3]

However, one may respond that the Rosh's ruling applies only to those who know that the wedding ring must belong to the groom. Rav Moshe states this explicitly in *Teshuvot Igrot Moshe* (E.H. 1:90).

---

2. It is vitally important that the groom own the ring to be used for *kiddushin*; see *Shulchan Aruch* E.H. 28. In fact, it is common practice for the officiating rabbi to ask the groom at the time of *kiddushin* if the ring belongs to him; see *Beit Shmuel* 28:49.

3. See *Teshuvot Beit Yitzchak* (1:104) for an application of this ruling.

The Halachic Status of Reform Marriages Part II

In fact, the *Mishnah Berurah* (649:15) seems to support Rav Moshe's contention. He rules that one who uses a borrowed *lulav* does not fulfill the *mitzvah* on the first day of *Sukkot* (the first two days in the Diaspora) unless the lender knows that the borrower must halachically acquire it. Otherwise, we assume that the lender gave the *lulav* as a loan and not as a present.

Conclusion

We must try our hardest to assure that divorcing couples who were married in a Reform Jewish ceremony receive a valid *get*. Only when a spouse refuses to participate in a *get* ceremony, or when possible *mamzeirut* exists, do some rabbinical courts consider relying on Rav Moshe Feinstein and the authorities who agree with him to invalidate a Reform wedding ceremony.

The Halachic Status of Reform Marriages
Part III: The Status of Non-Orthodox Jews Today

In most non-Orthodox wedding ceremonies, the designated witnesses are themselves non-Orthodox Jews. Determining their halachic status is thus critical for ascertaining the status of the weddings that they witness.

The Status of Tinok Shenishbah

The Talmud (*Shabbat* 68b) discusses the laws of a *tinok shenishbah*, one who is unaware of the laws of *Shabbat* because he was abducted as a baby and raised among gentiles. The Gemara rules that if such an individual desecrates *Shabbat*, he is nonetheless regarded as an inadvertent sinner. Accordingly, we do not view one who was raised among non-Jews as a deliberate sinner, for he never realizes the problems with his actions.

Does the same apply to a Jew who is raised among non-observant Jews? Logically, he should be treated the same way, for he also does not understand what *mitzvot* are or why he should keep them. In fact, the Rambam (*Hilchot Mamrim* 3:1-3), when he codifies the harsh actions that the Halachah prescribes for a known *apikores* (someone who rejects one of the pillars of traditional Jewish thought), limits their application as follows:

> This rule applies only to one who has consciously rejected belief in the Oral Law on his own thoughts and reasoning, such as Tzadok, Baytus (both of whom started sects that rejected parts of our Oral Law), or their followers. However, children and

grandchildren of those who go astray... who were born to Karaites and were raised with these tenets, such a person is like a *tinok shenishbah...* He is like one who was coerced [to violate *mitzvot*]. Although he heard as an adult that he is Jewish and saw practicing traditional Jews, he is still like one who is coerced, since he was raised on mistaken beliefs. It is therefore appropriate to try to influence them to return to traditional Jewish observance and beliefs and draw them with pleasant engagement until they return to a Torah life.[1]

Applications to Modern Jewry

In modern times, we have seen a lamentable rise in the number of non-observant Jews, many of whom are raised this way from infancy. Is such a Jew considered a *tinok shenishbah*? In the early nineteenth century, Rav Yaakov Etlinger (*Teshuvot Binyan Tzion Hachadashot* 23) wrote the following about the Jews of his time:

> It is difficult for me to issue a ruling regarding contemporary non-observant Jews. We see that the majority of the Jewish community is no longer observant and *Shabbat* desecration has become the norm. It is possible that these people should be considered as ones who think what they are doing is permissible, and as such they are *karov lemeizid*, falling short of being considered deliberate transgressors (see *Makkot* 7b). In addition, many of them recite *kiddush* and later engage in *Shabbat* desecration. Thus, they do not deny that God is the Creator. The children of these people, who are ignorant of the laws of *Shabbat* and are merely emulating their parents, should be regarded as *tinokot shenishbu*.

---

1. For a discussion of the Rambam's attitude towards Karaites, see Professor Gerald Blidstein's essay in *Techumin* (8:501-510).

GRAY MATTER

Several decades later, Rav David Tzvi Hoffman echoed Rav Etlinger's view of secular Jews (*Melameid Leho'il* 1:29):

> The *Binyan Tzion* [wrote] that *Shabbat* desecrators in our time are somewhat like *tinokot shenishbu*, because most Jews in our land unfortunately are *Shabbat* desecrators, and it is not their intention to deny our basic beliefs.

Rav Kook

Rav Avraham Yitzchak Kook (*Igrot Hareiyah* 1:4) adopts a similar approach regarding non-observant Jews of the early twentieth century (translated by Rav Dr. Norman Lamm in *Jewish Tradition and the Non-Traditional Jew*):

> The Tosafists remark on *Sanhedrin* 26b (s.v. *Hechashud*) that someone suspected of performing an act of sexual immorality because he was seized by passion is not disqualified as a witness, because "his passion coerced him"....
>
> Similarly, we may say that the "[secular] spirit of the times" acts as an evil intellectual temptress who seduces the young men of the age with her charm and her sorcery. They are truly "coerced," and God forbid that we should judge them as willful heretics.[2]

Chazon Ish

The *Chazon Ish* (*Yoreh Deah* 2:16),[3] in his famous remarks regarding *moridin velo ma'alin* (the Halachah that

---

2. For a thorough discussion of the circumstances when one's desires may be deemed a coercive force, see Prof. Nachum Rackover's essay in *Techumin* (18:197-209).
3. See Rav Mayer Twersky's discussion of these comments of the *Chazon Ish* in *Tradition* (30:4:92).

mandates throwing certain grievous sinners and heretics into deep pits and leaving them to die), appears to concur with Rav Kook:

> It would appear that this Halachah is only operative when Divine providence is clearly evident, as it was when miracles were commonplace and the *bat kol* (heavenly voice) was functional, and the righteous individuals of the generation were under special Divine providence discernable to all. In those times, heretics perversely provoked themselves to the pursuit of pleasure and anarchy and in those times excising evil people constituted protection of the world because all knew that inciting the people of the generation would bring calamity to the world; it would bring pestilence and war and famine. But now, in an era during which God's providence is concealed and the masses are bereft of faith, orchestrating the death of sinners does not repair the breach in the wall of religion, but enlarges it because the masses will view such actions as destructive and violent, God forbid, and since our sole purpose is to be constructive, this Halachah [of *moridin*] is not operative at a time when it does not yield constructive results, and it is incumbent upon us to attract the masses to Torah through love and to position them so that they can experience the radiance of Torah to the best of our ability (translated by Rav Mayer Twersky, *Tradition* 30:4:92).

He adds (*Yoreh Deah* 2:28):

> The *Hagahot Maimoniyot* wrote that one may not hate the heretic until he has disregarded rebuke. At the end of the work *Ahavat Chessed*, the author cites Rav Yaakov Molin to the effect that we must love the sinner. He also quotes the Maharam of Lublin to show that we must consider the sinners as

those who have not yet been rebuked, for we no longer know how to rebuke properly (see *Arachin* 16b), and hence one must treat them as transgressors under duress. As a result, we cannot exempt these sinners from [standard Jewish] obligations, such as *yibum* and other *halachot* (translation by Rav Dr. Norman Lamm).

It is important to note that both Rav Kook and the *Chazon Ish* go even further than Rav Etlinger and Rav Hoffman. The latter speak of children whose parents gave them little Jewish education, so these children grew up with neither knowledge nor faith. Rav Kook and the *Chazon Ish*, however, describe mitigating factors for even those who received some Orthodox education but nonetheless went astray. These people are victims of the "spirit of the times" and the lack of noticeable Divine providence. On the other hand, the context of the *Chazon Ish*'s remarks must also be noted. In the first paragraph cited, he is writing about the life and death matter of *moridin velo ma'alin*. In the second paragraph he concludes by applying his concept to "*yibum* and other *halachot*," but it is unclear how broad a range of *halachot* this statement covers.[4]

Conclusion

It is appears from our citations (*Shabbat* 68b, Rambam, *Binyan Tzion*, *Melameid Leho'il*, Rav Kook, and *Chazon Ish*) that many halachic authorities view most non-Orthodox Jews today as *tinokot shenishbu*.[5] See *Teshuvot Minchat Elazar* (1:74) for a dissenting view.[6]

---

4. Regarding the status of a *tinok shenishbah* who touches wine, the *Binyan Tzion* permitted the wine in case of need, but he encouraged refraining from drinking it if possible. For a summary of this issue, see *Nishmat Avraham* (*Yoreh Deah* 124:1).
5. For a discussion of halachic attitudes towards non-Orthodox Jews, see *Jewish Tradition and the Nontraditional Jew*, edited by Rav J. J. Schachter.
6. Also see *Teshuvot Igrot Moshe* (E.H. 4:59).

The Halachic Status of Reform Marriages
Part IV: Is a Tinok Shenishbah Acceptable as a Witness?

In the previous section, we established that most authorities consider non-observant Jews today to be *tinokot shenishbu*. We will now discuss the ramification of this for non-Orthodox marriages, the acceptability of a *tinok shenishbah* as a witness. The rulings of Rav Moshe Feinstein, Rav Waldenberg, Maharsham, Rav Aryeh Grossnass, Rav Tzvi Pesach Frank, Rav Yitzchak Herzog, and Rav Chaim David Halevi to invalidate Reform marriages all assume that the non-Orthodox Jews present at the ceremony cannot serve as witnesses.[1] Others, however, question that assumption.

This issue has tremendous ramifications regarding the unity and well-being of the Jewish people. A halachic ruling to accept a *tinok shenishbah* as a witness essentially means that many marriages conducted by non-Orthodox rabbis have halachic validity, resulting in a massive *mamzeirut* problem. In 1996, Dr. Yitzchak Skolnik, director of the Kayama Organization, reported that statistics indicated that merely fifteen percent of divorced Jewish couples performed a *get*. As we know, the children born to a woman who has remarried without a *get* are *mamzeirim* if the woman's first marriage was halachically valid.

---

1. Rav Yosef Shalom Eliashiv appears to agree with these authorities, at least in case of potential *mamzeirut*. Rav Hershel Solnica reports that Rav Eliashiv ruled that a woman whose mother had remarried without the benefit of a *get* was not a *mamzeret* since two observant Jews were not present at the mother's first marriage.

GRAY MATTER

Sanhedrin 26b - The Gravediggers' Case

In general, anyone designated by the Halachah as a *rasha* (sinner) cannot serve as a witness (*Shemot* 23:1). Thus, anyone who commits a sin punishable by *malkot* (lashes) cannot serve as a witness (as the Torah refers to one who is punished by *malkot* as a *rasha*, in *Devarim* 25:2). Similarly, deliberately violating a Torah law that is punishable by *kareit* or death disqualifies one as a witness. In addition, one who engages in theft or other monetary offenses and one who does not believe in the thirteen basic beliefs of Judaism cannot serve as witnesses. Nonetheless, the Gemara (*Sanhedrin* 26b) recounts:

> A certain group of gravediggers used to bury the dead on the first day of *Shavuot* [in violation of Halachah]. Rav Papa excommunicated them and disqualified them from serving as witnesses. Rav Huna, the son of Rav Yehoshua, declared that these gravediggers were valid witnesses [despite their violating Torah law]. Rav Papa challenged Rav Yehoshua, "But aren't they *resha'im* [sinners who are invalid witnesses]?" He responded that they think they are performing a *mitzvah*. He retorted, "But did we not excommunicate them!" Rav Yehoshua answered that the gravediggers think they were excommunicated to serve as atonement for their actions.

Apparently, a sinner is deemed a *rasha* only when he sins knowingly. On the other hand, if the individual does not realize that he is sinning, as was the situation with the gravediggers, he may still be accepted as a witness. In fact, the *Shulchan Aruch* (*Choshen Mishpat* 34:3) codifies the gravediggers' case as normative. The Rama thereupon quotes from the Rivash (*Teshuvot* 311) that "the same exception applies to anyone who appears to have sinned due to a mistake."

THE HALACHIC STATUS OF REFORM MARRIAGES PART IV

Later Applications of the Gravediggers' Case

Rav Akiva Eiger (*Teshuvot* 96, cited by *Pitchei Teshuvah*, E.H. 42:18) was asked about the validity of a wedding where the witnesses shaved with razors. At first glance, the wedding would appear not to be valid, as shaving with a razor is punishable by *malkot* and should disqualify the witnesses.[2] Rav Eiger, however, forbade the woman to remarry without receiving a *get*, since "so many people violate the rule forbidding shaving with a razor that the parties in question do not think they are truly violating a serious prohibition."[3]

Furthermore, Rav Chaim Ozer Grodzinski (*Teshuvot Achiezer* 3:25) ruled that witnesses who signed a *get* in South Africa were acceptable witnesses, despite the fact that they kept their shops open on *Shabbat* (although they did not do *melachah*). Rav Chaim Ozer explained that the people in South Africa were accustomed to keeping their stores open on *Shabbat*, so they did not believe that they were violating *Shabbat*.[4]

Non-Observant Jews - Rav Aharon Walkin vs. Rav Moshe Feinstein

Rav Akiva Eiger and Rav Chaim Ozer discuss the status of individuals who, while being lax in specific areas, are generally committed to observance of Halachah. What if someone observes virtually no *mitzvot*? We are speaking not of those people who have **rejected** the halachic belief system and lifestyle. Rather, we are speaking of people raised in non-observant homes

---

2. Shaving with a razor violates a biblical commandment (see *Vayikra* 19:27). Regarding electric shavers, there is much greater room for leniency (see Rav Shabtai Rappaport's essay in *Techumin* (13:200-208) and Aharon Frazer's article, available at http://www.yucs.org/~frazers/imshefer.html).
3. Due to the current availability of electric shavers, Rav Eiger's ruling presumably no longer applies, as otherwise observant men rarely shave with razors.
4. For an explanation of the prohibition involved in opening a store on *Shabbat*, see Rav Chaim Ozer's responsum.

who mistakenly believe that one can be a "good Jew" without observing Halachah, and those who keep Halachah are merely "fundamentalists" or are going beyond the call of duty.

Rav Aharon Walkin (*Teshuvot Zekan Aharon* 1:74) rules that one may accept testimony from a non-observant Jew. He addresses a situation in which a woman in an Eastern European community received a letter from members of the Argentine Jewish community reporting the death of her husband. At that time, hardly any members of the Argentine Jewish community observed Halachah. Rav Walkin nonetheless accepted their testimony, asserting that one only ceases to be a valid witness if he realizes that his sins will invalidate him. If ignorant Jews do not realize that desecrating *Shabbat* will deprive them of their ability to testify, they remain acceptable witnesses. Rav Walkin cites a similar comment of the *Sema* (34:57) as a precedent for his ruling.[5] Rav Herzog (*Techukah Leyisrael Al Pi Hatorah* 3:232-233, 238-239) raises this possibility as well.[6]

Rav Moshe Feinstein (*Teshuvot Igrot Moshe Even Ha'ezer* 1:82, 4:32:7, and 4:60) argues that even a *tinok shenishbah* is

---

5. Rav Walkin does not claim that permission to testify is inherent within the status of a *tinok shenishbah*. Rather, he rules that this permission results from ignorance of how one invalidates himself as a witness. In practice, though, there is almost no difference, for those who are raised without knowledge of *mitzvot* generally do not realize that failing to observe *mitzvot* invalidates one's testimony.

6. It is important to note that in a case of potential *mamzeriut*, Rav Herzog, along with Rav Tzvi Pesach Frank, ruled that a Reform marriage was invalid due to the absence of valid witnesses (see *Teshuvot Lev Aryeh* 31, addendum to the responsum). It thus appears that Rav Herzog's comments in *Techukah Leyisrael Al Pi Hatorah* were not meant as an absolute ruling to permit the testimony of non-observant Jews, but merely as a theoretical suggestion. Rav Ovadia Yosef (*Yabia Omer* vol. 8, E.H. 18) also accepts the testimony of a *tinok shenishbah* to prove that a woman is a widow. He indicates, however, that he is only being lenient because *Chazal* were very lenient about accepting testimony to let a widow remarry.

THE HALACHIC STATUS OF REFORM MARRIAGES PART IV

disqualified from serving as a witness. Indeed, it is not difficult to distinguish between a non-observant Jew, who does not view himself as bound by Halachah, and the gravediggers (and their later parallels), who were committed to the halachic system but mistakenly violated some of its rules (see *Teshuvot Minchat Yitzchak* 2:66). Moreover, it seems exceedingly clear from the *Shulchan Aruch* (*Choshen Mishpat* 34:17) that unless one is committed to keeping *mitzvot*, he cannot serve as a witness. For further explanation of why even a *tinok shenishbah* is unfit to serve as a witness, see the comments of Rav Avigdor Neventzall (quoted in *Techumin* 13:420), and Rav Avraham Sherman (*Techumin* 18:250).

These authorities would most likely advise treating a *tinok shenishbah* with respect and love, as we cited last chapter from Rav Kook and the *Chazon Ish*. Nevertheless, until he returns to a life of halachic observance, he cannot serve as a witness.

The Karaites' Status

Rav Zalman Nechemia Goldberg suggested to this author what he considers a clear proof that a *tinok shenishbah* can serve as a witness. The Rama (E.H. 4:37) writes that we may not marry Karaites or their descendants, as they are possibly (*safeik*) *mamzeirim*.[7] The concern is that the Karaites' marriages are valid, while their divorces are not. Rav Zalman Nechemia reasoned that if a *tinok shenishbah* is not a valid witness, then why would the Rama be concerned about the validity of the Karaites' marriages? As we have previously cited, the Rambam explicitly states that the second generation of Karaites is treated like *tinokot shenishbu*. It would thus appear that the Rama considers a *tinok shenishbah* to be a valid witness.[8]

---

7. See *Kiddushin* (74a-76a) for a similar ban on marrying Samaritans.
8. The halachic literature concerning the acceptability of Samaritans as witnesses might support Rav Zalman Nechemia's assertion. See *Gittin* 10, *Tosafot* (*Gittin* 10b s.v. *Iy Lav*), Rambam (*Hilchot Avadim* 6:6), and *Teshuvot Machaneh Chaim* (1:34) cited by the *Otzar Mefarshei Hatalmud* (*Gittin* 1:492).

GRAY MATTER

This author replied to Rav Goldberg that the Radbaz (*Teshuvot* 1:73, 2:796, and 4:219) rules that the Karaites are not *mamzeirim*, because their *kiddushin* are invalid. The Radbaz clearly writes that Karaites are unfit to serve as witnesses. Even if we were to reject the Radbaz and accept the Rama's ruling, we may distinguish between it and Rav Moshe's ruling. The Rama addresses an entire community, whereas Rav Moshe addresses individual cases. In the latter situation, one is usually able to investigate thoroughly if two valid witnesses saw the delivery of the ring from the groom to the bride. In the former case, the Rama addresses the status of all Karaites, who had existed for hundreds of years by his time. Regarding the Karaites, it is possible that valid witnesses saw the delivery of the ring at some of their weddings, thereby rendering those ceremonies halachically valid (as occurs at a number of non-Orthodox weddings).[9] Over the years, if women in such marriages remarried without *gittin*, their children from the new marriages were *mamzeirim*. Over the centuries, this likely occurred repeatedly, creating a situation of collective *safeik mamzeirut* for the Karaite community. However, the Rama might agree with Rav

---

Rav Moshe Feinstein (*Teshuvot Igrot Moshe*, E.H. 4:59) distinguishes between Karaites and contemporary non-observant Jews. Rav Moshe's explanation of why the Karaites might be acceptable as witnesses is somewhat similar to the *Chazon Ish*'s (*Yoreh Deah* 2:18) explanation of why Samaritans might be acceptable as witnesses.

9. The historical background surrounding the Rama's source is unclear. The ban on marrying Karaites first appears in a responsum of questionable authorship (cited by the Mabit, *Teshuvot* 1:38). This responsum states that the Karaites' marriages are halachically binding "either through *kesef* [giving a ring, or other valued object] or *bi'ah* [marital relations]." The Radbaz argues that the responsum makes several problematic assumptions, and he therefore permits marrying Karaites. In his attempt to understand the responsum, the Radbaz argues that the only possible way for Karaites to have valid marriages is if Rabbanites (the medieval forerunners of Orthodox Jews) attended their wedding. For a treatment of the history and halachic status of Karaite wedding ceremonies, see Michael Corinaldi's *Hama'amad Ha'ishi Shel Hakara'im* (pp. 34-142).

THE HALACHIC STATUS OF REFORM MARRIAGES PART IV

Moshe's approach regarding a specific wedding, if a thorough investigation reveals that no valid witnesses saw the groom give the bride a ring.

An Actual Case

When this author spent a month observing the Jerusalem Beit Din in Tammuz 5753, an interesting case came before it. A young couple sought a marriage license,[10] but the woman's mother had been previously married and never received a *get*. The woman presented a document from a prominent Rav (Rav Reuven Feinstein, Rav Moshe's son) stating that she was not a *mamzeret*, because her mother's marriage was a Reform ceremony that no valid witnesses attended.

Rav Zalman Nechemia Goldberg was uncertain how to rule, as he believed that a *tinok shenishbah* is an acceptable witness. Finally, he consulted his eminent father-in-law, Rav Shlomo Zalman Auerbach, who ruled that the *beit din* should authorize the woman to receive a marriage license in light of Rav Feinstein's ruling.[11]

Conclusion

One should make great efforts to ensure that a divorcing couple receives a valid *get* even if it did not marry in an Orthodox ceremony. In case of *igun*, where a man (or woman) is not cooperating in giving a *get*, an eminent rabbi should be consulted for ruling in the matter.

---

10. Matters of personal status are under the exclusive control of the Orthodox Rabbinate in Israel.
11. It is unclear to this author if Rav Shlomo Zalman ruled leniently because he agreed with Rav Moshe's leniency (at least in case of *mamzeirut*), or if he disagreed with Rav Moshe, but he did not wish to impose his own stringent view on a woman who was already permitted to remarry by an eminent halachic authority.

Postscript

The status of Conservative marriages is quite a complex topic. See this author's Hebrew essay in *Techumin* (18:84-91). More information regarding this issue can be found in *Teshuvot Igrot Moshe* (E.H. 1:135, 4:13, 4:46, and 4:78). The reason for the complexity of this issue is the extremely wide range of practices and beliefs among Conservative rabbis and lay individuals.

Modesty

A Husband's Participation in Childbirth

Many women appreciate their husbands' presence during childbirth, and many couples jointly learn techniques such as Lamaze breathing and the Bradley method. From a halachic perspective, the husband's involvement depends upon when the expectant mother become a *nidah*, at which time she may have no physical contact with her husband.

Breaking of the Water

Rav Feivel Cohen (*Badei Hashulchan* 194:30) writes that when a woman's water breaks, she becomes a *nidah*.[1] Rav Cohen does not cite a textual source for this ruling, but he writes (*Tziyunim* 48) that "this is the accepted protocol among halachic authorities."

In reality, not all authorities agree with his assertion. Dr. Avraham S. Avraham (*Nishmat Avraham, Yoreh De'ah* 194:1) cites Rav Shlomo Zalman Auerbach and Rav Yehoshua Neuwirth, who both rule that after her water breaks, a woman may perform a *bedikah* (internal examination). If she finds no blood, she is not a *nidah*. Rav Mordechai Willig stated (in a lecture at Yeshiva University) that he believes the latter opinion to be more persuasive. He explained that the breaking of the water is not associated with a flow of blood, and no classical source definitively states that a woman is a *nidah* at this point. Rav Ovadia Yosef (*Taharat Habayit* 2:53-54) also rules leniently. Expectant parents should consult their rabbi concerning which opinion to follow.

---

1. If there is a great need for her husband to assist his wife at this time, Rav Cohen rules that one may rely on the opinions that she is not yet a *nidah*.

GRAY MATTER

Labor

Acharonim debate whether a woman automatically becomes a *nidah* during labor. The *Shulchan Aruch* (*Yoreh De'ah* 194) does not state that once a woman is in labor, she acquires the status of a *nidah*. However, he does rule (194:1-2) that a *yoledet* (a woman who **has given** birth) has the status of a *nidah* even if she did not see any blood (a highly unlikely occurrence), based on the Gemara's principle (according to the accepted view) that the uterus cannot open without the release of some blood (see *Nidah* 21a-b).

In his discussion of violating *Shabbat* to save lives, the *Shulchan Aruch* (*Orach Chaim* 330:3, based on *Shabbat* 129a) permits violating *Shabbat* to assist a woman with childbirth. He rules that a woman is considered a *yoledet* (and has the status of a dangerously ill patient) "from the time when she sits on the birthing stool, or from the time that blood comes forth, or from the time that her friends have to support her arms and hold her up since she cannot walk."

The *Acharonim* debate if just as a woman is considered a dangerously ill person at the onset of labor, she is also considered a *nidah* at the onset of labor. The *Badei Hashulchan* (194, *Biurim* s.v. *Mipnei*) in his summary and analysis of the dispute, cites the *Sidrei Taharah*, who notes that the Gemara (*ibid.*) mentions the uterus opening when a woman is in labor. Applying the aforementioned rule that the uterus does not open without releasing at least some blood, the *Sidrei Taharah* claims that a woman in labor is considered a *nidah* even without actually seeing blood.

Other *Acharonim*, including the *Noda Biy'hudah* and *Beit Meir* (both cited by the *Badei Hashulchan*), disagree. They argue that the aforementioned rule only applies when something is **released** from the uterus. In such a situation, the Halachah assumes blood to be released along with the object that emanates from the uterus. If, however, the uterus does not release anything, its opening alone does not automatically render the woman a *nidah*.

A Husband's Participation in Childbirth

Rav Moshe Feinstein (*Teshuvot Igrot Moshe, Yoreh De'ah* 2:75) rules that one should follow the *Sidrei Taharah*'s strict opinion. Rav Feivel Cohen (*Badei Hashulchan ibid.*) rules that, if the woman needs her husband's help to alleviate her pain,[2] the lenient approach may be followed. He argues that no early authorities mention that a woman who is in labor is automatically a *nidah*. Nonetheless, as has already been mentioned, Rav Cohen believes that a man may not touch his wife once her water breaks, unless there is an unusually pressing need. Rav Ovadia Yosef (*Taharat Habayit Hakatzar* 2:6) rules that a woman in labor is not a *nidah* until she sees blood.

Physical Contact During Delivery

Of course, a woman is unquestionably a *nidah* once she sees blood. A student once suggested to Rav Aharon Lichtenstein (in a lecture to Yeshiva University rabbinical students) that the husband may nevertheless touch his wife during the delivery. The student reasoned that this is not an affectionate type of contact (*negiah shelo bederech chibah*), and some authorities permit non-affectionate contact. Rav Lichtenstein replied that such contact **is** affectionate (*bederech chibah*) and is forbidden once the wife becomes a *nidah*. Although contact between husband and wife in the delivery room is not sexual in nature, it is nonetheless of a loving nature and is hence prohibited. There is also another flaw in the student's argument. Some authorities do permit non-affectionate contact between men and women who are not related, but all authorities prohibit such contact between a married couple when the wife is a *nidah*.[3]

---

2. This is Rav Cohen's example. He mentions that this leniency is also applicable for other, similar needs.
3. Rav Moshe Feinstein (*Teshuvot Igrot Moshe, Even Ha'ezer* 2:14) permits traveling on a crowded subway even if one may brush against members of the opposite sex. Rav Elyakim (Getsel) Ellinson (*Hatznei'a Lechet* 2:57-59 and note 76) cites other authorities who also permit such contact, and he argues that this leniency may be followed in practice. Of course, he warns that every case must be judged independently to ensure that there are absolutely no affectionate overtones. Rav Ellinson notes that the *Beit*

GRAY MATTER

Another suggestion to permit a husband to touch his wife during childbirth is that she is considered a *cholah* (sick person). The Rama (*Yoreh De'ah* 195:16) allows a man to help his sick wife in a case of great need, if no one else can help her. Nevertheless, virtually all authorities reject applying the Rama's ruling to childbirth and prohibit the husband from touching his wife.[4] They understand that other people can help the wife during childbirth. Doctors and nurses are readily available to assist the wife during the delivery, so physical contact between the couple is not necessary in the vast majority of cases. In the rare case that the husband must touch his wife during delivery, such as if she suddenly gives birth in the car, physical contact is certainly permissible according to the Rama.

The Husband's Presence in the Delivery Room

Most contemporary authorities permit a husband to be present in the delivery room, although they do so with varying degrees of enthusiasm (see *Nishmat Avraham, Yoreh De'ah* 195:3). Rav Moshe Feinstein (*Teshuvot Igrot Moshe, Yoreh De'ah* 2:75) states no objection the husband's presence in the delivery room per se. Nonetheless, Rav Feinstein rules that the husband must avoid physical contact with his wife and may not watch the baby emerge from the birth canal. Watching the delivery is prohibited because even a husband may not look at that part of his wife's body.

While most authorities agree that the husband may attend delivery when needed, many of them express some reservations.

Shmuel (20:1) prohibits even non-affectionate contact, although Rav Ellinson challenges the *Beit Shmuel*'s proof. Rav Ellinson emphasizes, however, that all of the lenient authorities nonetheless prohibit all contact between a *nidah* and her husband.

4. These authorities include Rav Moshe Feinstein (*Teshuvot Igrot Moshe, Yoreh De'ah* 2:65), Dayan Y.Y. Weisz (*Teshuvot Minchat Yitzchak* 5:27), Rav Chaim David Halevi (*Aseih Lecha Rav* 4:58), Rav Yosef Dov Soloveitchik (reported by Rav Yosef Adler), Rav Aharon Lichtenstein (in a lecture at Yeshiva University), and Rav Yehuda Henkin (*Teshuvot Bnei Banim* 1:33).

A Husband's Participation in Childbirth

Rav Shlomo Zalman Auerbach (cited by *Nishmat Avraham*, Y.D. 195:3) and Rav Chaim David Halevi (*Aseih Lecha Rav* 4:58) discourage the husband's attendance, although they add that it is permitted when the wife is truly scared. Rav Yehuda Henkin (*Bnei Banim* 1:33) objects to granting blanket permission for every husband to attend delivery, enumerating the prohibitions that he may come to violate. Rav Henkin adds, however, that a husband must accompany his wife into the delivery room if she specifically requests his presence out of fear. Rav Henkin also suggests that the husband should not accompany his wife if there are other women in the same delivery room without their husbands. Rav Henkin explains that this husband's presence, while helping his wife, hurts the emotional state of the other women.

The *Minchat Yitzchak* (5:27) strongly objects to the husband's presence in the delivery room. He argues that a wife can manage without him, so her insistence on his presence is mere lightheartedness (*kalut hada'at*). Dr. Avraham Steinberg (*The Journal of Halacha and Contemporary Society*, 1:2:121, Fall 1981) challenges this assertion as being "in dispute with the scientifically proven evidence." Elsewhere (p. 108), Dr. Steinberg notes that scientific articles (such as *The New England Journal of Medicine*, 303:597-600) describe how companionship during delivery has many health benefits (although it does not necessarily have to be the husband's companionship).

The situation of a woman giving birth fundamentally differs from that of many ill people. As Rav Yehuda Henkin (*Teshuvot Bnei Banim* 1:33) notes, sick individuals often not need to be active in order to overcome their illness, whereas a woman in labor must remain calm while working intensely to deliver the baby. Therefore, meeting the mother's psychological needs is of great importance. If the couple has studied Lamaze breathing or the Bradley method together, the husband coaches his wife, so his presence is crucial. Furthermore, the husband can serve as an advocate for his wife's needs, if the medical staff does not pay proper attention to her. Anecdotal evidence indicates that this role can often be quite important.

In light of these considerations, many contemporary authorities permit a husband to attend childbirth, at least when his wife requests his presence. The sensitivity to the psychological needs of a woman giving birth is deeply rooted in *Chazal*. The Gemara (*Shabbat* 128b) presents the following rule:

> We assist a woman to give birth on *Shabbat*, and for her sake we desecrate *Shabbat*... as our Rabbis taught: If she requires a light, her friend must kindle a light for her.... Regarding a blind woman in labor, we might think that since she cannot see, it would be forbidden to light a candle at her request [on *Shabbat*]. This passage comes to inform us **that we set her mind at ease** [and light the candle for her].

Based on this passage, both Rav Moshe (*Teshuvot Igrot Moshe*, *Orach Chaim* 1:131) and the *Chazon Ish* (*Igrot Hachazon Ish* 1:141) permit husbands to accompany their wives by car on *Shabbat* to the hospital. The paramedics and doctors take care of her medical needs, while the husband helps keep her mind at ease, contributing towards a safer delivery. The Talmud Yerushalmi (*Shabbat* 14:3, cited in *Nishmat Avraham*, *Yoreh De'ah* 195:3) also indicates that there is a connection between one's emotional state and one's physical health. In fact, nearly all contemporary authorities recognize that mental illness can be just as life-threatening as physical illness (see *Contemporary Halakhic Problems* 2:299).

Conclusion

Many authorities discourage the husband's presence in the delivery room. Nevertheless, if the need is great enough, nearly all authorities permit the husband to attend childbirth. In such a situation, he should avoid physical contact with his wife after she becomes a *nidah* and may not watch the actual birth. May God bless His nation with many healthy children.

Women and Leadership Positions

Halachic literature contains much discussion about the permissibility of a woman serving in a communal leadership position.

The Rambam's Ruling

Those who claim that women may not serve in leadership positions cite the Rambam's famous ruling (*Hilchot Melachim* 1:5):

> We do not appoint a woman as king, as the Torah states (*Devarim* 17:15), "Appoint a king" - but not a queen. Similarly, a woman may not be appointed to any leadership position among the Jewish people.

The *Kesef Mishnah* and Radbaz, both commenting on the Rambam, cite the *Sifrei*'s comment on the aforementioned verse as the source for this ruling. However, the *Sifrei* merely states that a woman may not be appointed to the position of **queen**. The Rambam has no explicit source for his extension of the *Sifrei*'s ruling to **all** leadership roles.

Rav Moshe Feinstein (*Teshuvot Igrot Moshe, Yoreh De'ah* 2:44-45) suggests a basis for the Rambam's ruling. The Gemara (*Yevamot* 45a) states that not only does the Torah forbid appointing a convert as king, but it also forbids appointing him to any position of authority. Rav Moshe posits that the Rambam derives from this passage that the position of king is the paradigm for every leadership position. Whoever may not be appointed king

GRAY MATTER

may not hold any leadership role. The Rambam thus concludes that, just as we may not appoint a queen, we may not appoint a woman to any position of leadership.

What Is Considered Authority?

Rav Moshe Feinstein defines the term "position of authority" based on the Gemara (*Kiddushin* 76b), which teaches that a convert should not be appointed as an inspector of weights and measures. Rav Moshe explains that even if a position is not prestigious, it can still be viewed as authoritative. The difference between a person with authority and a regular worker is that a regular worker is hired to do the bidding of his employer, whereas someone in a position of authority is hired to, at times, act against the will of his employer. The inspector of weights and measures is in a position of authority because he does not permit his employer to act dishonestly, regardless of the employer's wishes. The inspector, unlike other workers, is hired to enforce an outside set of rules on his employer.

Elsewhere (*Teshuvot Igrot Moshe, Yoreh De'ah* 4:26), in a somewhat cryptic responsum, Rav Moshe adds that a job's purpose must be to enforce rules upon the employer in order for it to constitute authority.[1] If, however, a position contains a certain measure of power over others (such as subordinates), this is insufficient to exclude converts from that position. For example, Rav Moshe discusses the possibility of appointing a convert as a *rosh yeshivah* (dean) or *mashgiach ruchani* (spiritual guidance counselor of a Yeshivah). Although these jobs include certain administrative powers, such as the ability to reject and expel students, Rav Moshe nonetheless permits a convert to hold them. He explains that these powers are "merely like the authority of a boss over his workers," as opposed to an "appointment to act against the will of the employer, empowered by the Torah law."[2]

---

1. It is our hope that Rav Moshe's responsum is presented here accurately, as the responsum is extremely cryptic.
2. It is unclear if Rav Moshe would equate a woman with a convert.

Women and Leadership Positions

According to his criteria, Rav Moshe concludes (*Teshuvot Igrot Moshe*, Y.D. 2:45) that a professional *kashrut* supervisor is in a position of authority. He is hired by a food company to enforce the laws of *kashrut* even when the company would like to disregard them. Rav Moshe adds, though, that there is a very easy way to permit a woman to supervise *kashrut*. The food company can hire a rabbi to supervise it, and the rabbi, in turn, may hire the woman to oversee the *kashrut*. The rabbi bears ultimate accountability for the food's *kashrut*, while the female supervisor is merely obeying the directions of her employer, the rabbi.

Not everyone agrees with Rav Moshe's definition of authority. For greater discussion of how to define authority, see Rav J. David Bleich's *Contemporary Halakhic Problems* (2:254-267).

Other Rishonim

Although the Rambam rules that a woman may not be appointed to a position of authority, Rav Moshe and Rav Chaim David Halevi (*Techumin* 10:118-123) note that many *Rishonim* appear to disagree with the him.

One opinion cited in *Tosafot* (*Nidah* 50a s.v. *Kol*) permits a woman to serve as a *dayan* (rabbinical judge). This view clearly believes that a woman can be appointed to a position of authority.

The *Sefer Hachinuch* (*Mitzvah* 497) cites the *Sifrei*, which states that a woman may not be appointed as king. However, the *Sefer Hachinuch* does not explicitly exclude a woman from any

---

According to the Rambam's position (which Rav Moshe is following), it is the same prohibition for both women and converts to hold positions of authority. However, Rav Moshe writes that he is inclined to rule leniently with a convert because the Torah requires us to act kindly toward converts, leaving open the possibility that, in a questionable case, he would rule more strictly with a woman.

other position of authority. In the next *mitzvah* (the prohibition of appointing a convert to be king), the *Sefer Hachinuch* emphasizes that a convert may not hold any position of authority. Apparently, when the prohibition applies to all forms of leadership, the *Sefer Hachinuch* writes so explicitly. Rav Moshe thus deduces that the *Sefer Hachinuch* does not explicitly exclude women from leadership roles (besides being a queen) because he does not agree with the Rambam.

Rav Moshe also suggests that both Rashi (*Kiddushin* 76b s.v. *Kol*) and the Ran (*Kiddushin* 31b in pages of the Rif, s.v. *Garsinan*) disagree with the Rambam's opinion. They explain that the source for the rule that a convert may not be appointed to any position of authority is the redundancy of words from the root *s.y.m.* (verbs of appointing) in *Devarim* 17:15, the verse that requires the king to be a natural born Jew ("*mikerev achecha*"). The Torah is teaching that **all** leadership appointments must be *mikerev achecha*. Regarding women, however, the prohibition is derived from the word "*melech*" ("king" - and not queen) and bears no connection to the word "*tasim*" ("You shall appoint"). Rav Moshe explains that Rashi and the Ran view the prohibition against women as precluding the position of queen but permitting other leadership appointments.

Finally, Rav Moshe claims that the Ramban (*Shevuot* 30a s.v. *Vechein*) and the Rashba (*Shevuot* 30a s.v. *Velo*) may also disagree with the Rambam, based upon their analysis of the status of Devorah. Devorah both judged individual people and led the nation like a queen (see *Shofetim* 4:4-5). The Ramban and Rashba do not appear to view the prohibition against a queen as applicable to Devorah's judiciary role (although the prohibition raises a problem for Devorah's role as a national leader). They do assert that women are disqualified from serving as judges,[3] but they do not connect this with women's disqualification from serving as queen.

---

3. It is accepted as the Halachah in *Shulchan Aruch*, *Choshen Mishpat* 7:4, that a woman may not serve as a *dayan*. While the *Pitchei Teshuvah* (C.M. 7:5) cites a dissenting opinion, he personally accepts the *Shulchan Aruch's* view.

WOMEN AND LEADERSHIP POSITIONS

On the other hand, the Ritva (*Shevu'ot* 30a s.v. *Shevu'at*) does agree with the Rambam. He states unambiguously that the *Sifrei*'s prohibition against appointing a queen applies to all leadership positions.

Rav Moshe Feinstein

Rav Moshe writes (in his *teshuvot* quoted above) that although many *Rishonim* disagree with the Rambam, the Rambam's view should nonetheless be followed in practice. He explains that this issue is a dispute regarding a biblical prohibition, and the *Shulchan Aruch* did not resolve it, so we must observe the strict opinion. Thus, a woman should not be appointed to the board of a synagogue. Rav Moshe does permit relying on the other *Rishonim* in a case of great need. For example, he permitted a poor widow to become a *mashgichah* (*kashrut* supervisor), despite the fact that it is a position of authority (similar to the supervisor of weights mentioned in *Kiddushin* 76b), so that she could make a living.

Rav Chaim David Halevi

Rav Chaim David Halevi questions the Rambam's view by pointing to the historical fact that the righteous Queen Shlomtzion ruled over the Jewish people for nine years during the Second Temple period. He notes that the Talmud never criticizes the fact that she served as leader of the Jewish people, and *Chazal* even say very positive things about her (see *Vayikra Rabah* 35:10).[4]

Rav Halevi does not reject the Rambam's view, but he suggests that even the Rambam would permit a woman to lead the nation if she was willingly accepted by the people. Rav Halevi

---

It should be noted that the *Pitchei Teshuvah* also cites prominent authorities that permit a female expert in Halachah to rule on halachic questions.

4. It is not clear why Rav Halevi raises this question against the Rambam specifically, considering that everyone appears to agree that a woman cannot be appointed queen.

GRAY MATTER

claims that the prohibition is against a woman **taking power** over people, but it does not apply when the woman is **elected democratically**. Rav Halevi notes that this approach seems to correspond with the Ramban and Rashba's opinion (above) regarding Devorah - she could serve as a ruler because the nation accepted her rulings. Rav Halevi therefore rules that a woman may hold an elected position of authority.

Other Authorities

The position of Rav Halevi parallels the view of his mentor, Rav Ben-Zion Uzziel (*Teshuvot Mishpetei Uzziel*, *Choshen Mishpat* 6). Interestingly, Rav Yehuda Amital adopted this ruling in practice. This author asked Rav Amital how, in 1988, he allowed a woman to run on the parliamentary list of the political party Meimad, in light of the Rambam's ruling. He replied that the Rambam's ruling does not apply to a democratically elected position. On the other hand, Rav Avraham Yitzchak Kook (*Ma'amarei Hare'iyah* pp. 189-194) opposes any participation by women in elections.

Monetary Issues

Hasagat Gevul: Economic Competition in Jewish Law

Hasagat gevul (literally "infringement of boundary") is often used to refer to unfair business competition.[1] In the past few years, many accusations of *hasagat gevul* have been brought before *batei din*. These cases often arouse much controversy, especially since the Halachah is sometimes at odds with American society's tendency to favor unrestricted competition.

Aggadic Background

Before examining the halachic texts that address this issue, there are two relevant aggadic passages from the Gemara. While aggadic passages are usually not halachically binding,[2] they do set a tone that influences halachic decisions. In *Yevamot* (78b), the Gemara draws an equation between eliminating an individual's ability to earn a livelihood and murder. In *Makkot* (24a), the Gemara records that King David outlined eleven fundamental principles of halachic life, among them that one should not compete with another person's business. These passages give moral weight to those who generally favor restricting business competition.

The Gemara

The primary halachic discussion of business competition appears in *Bava Batra* (21b). The Gemara records that one may

---

1. For a discussion of how this term attained its modern usage, see Rav Simcha Krauss's essay in *The Journal of Halacha and Contemporary Society* (29:5-29).
2. See *Encyclopedia Talmudit* (1:62) for more details on this issue.

not set up a fishing net too close to another person's fishing net and thus catch all the fish that would have gone into the original net. Because the fish would have otherwise gravitated automatically to the original net, they are viewed as if they have already reached its owner's possession.[3] However, *Amoraim* dispute a less flagrant form of competition, in which one person is operating a mill in a *mavuy* (alley),[4] and another wishes to open a similar establishment there. Does the first person have the right to prevent his competitor from opening in the same *mavuy*?

Rav Huna asserts that the owner of the first mill may prevent the newcomer from setting up shop, as the newcomer will interfere with the first inhabitant's livelihood. Rav Huna the son of Rav Yehoshua, on the other hand, argues that this is permitted. Rashi (s.v. *Shani Dagim*) explains that the competitor may claim, "Whoever will come to me will come to me, and whoever will come to you will come to you." The Gemara indicates that the latter position fits with the majority opinion in a similar debate from the time of the *Tannaim* (see *Tosafot, Bava Batra* 21b s.v. *Peshita*). The Gemara thus seems to permit starting a competitive business, if its owner does not aim to inflict direct damage on his opposition.

The Halachah normally follows the majority opinion,[5] and the Halachah generally follows the later *Amora*,[6] so virtually all *Rishonim*[7] follow Rav Huna the son of Rav Yehoshua's view, as do the *Shulchan Aruch* (*Choshen Mishpat* 156:5) and most of its

---

3. See Rashi, s.v. *Shani Dagim*, and *Nimukei Yosef, Bava Batra* 11a in pages of Rif s.v. *Bar Mevo'ah*; see *Teshuvot Chatam Sofer, Choshen Mishpat* 79, for a summary of alternative explanations of this passage.
4. An Israeli rabbinical court ruled that a "neighborhood" is the contemporary halachic equivalent of a Talmudic *mavuy* (*Piskei Din Rabbaniyim* 6:3).
5. *Yachid verabim Halachah kerabim*; see *Mo'eid Katan* 20a and *Tosafot* s.v. *Kol*.
6. *Halachah kevatrai*; see *Encyclopedia Talmudit* 9:341-345. In this case, Rav Huna the son of Rav Yehoshua lived later.
7. These Rishonim include the Rif (*Bava Batra* 11a in pages of Rif), *Tosafot* (*Bava Batra* 21b s.v. *Peshita*), the Rambam (*Hilchot Shecheinim* 6:8), and the Rosh (*Bava Batra* 2:12).

HASAGAT GEVUL: ECONOMIC COMPETITION IN JEWISH LAW

commentaries (see *Aruch Hashulchan, Choshen Mishpat* 156:6-7). The Rif, Rambam, and *Shulchan Aruch* do not even mention the Gemara's restriction regarding the fishing nets, so perhaps they understood that the Gemara eventually rejected that law. In fact, the Meiri (*Bava Batra* 21b) explicitly rejects the restriction on setting new fishing nets near old ones. It would thus seem that the Halachah sanctions nearly unrestricted free enterprise.

Nonetheless, Rav Huna the son of Rav Yehoshua adds that such competition is only permitted when the new competitor comes from the same *mavuy*, for he is just as entitled as the first businessman to earn a livelihood in that area. The new competitor can claim, "You do work on your home turf, and [so too] I do work on my home turf." However, one who comes from a different city and challenges the established local business is unfairly encroaching. Rav Huna the son of Rav Yehoshua inquires whether one who comes from a different *mavuy* but resides in the same city is considered sufficiently local to be granted the right to compete. Due to the fact that the Gemara never reaches a conclusion regarding such a person (*teiku*), the *Rishonim* rule that there is insufficient basis for preventing a resident of another *mavuy* in the same city from opening a competing business.[8] The *Shulchan Aruch* (*Choshen Mishpat* 156:5) rules accordingly.

The Gemara adds that even an outsider is permitted to compete if he pays taxes to the local authority. The *Tur* (*ibid.*) writes that an outsider who pays taxes is permitted to compete "like the residents of the city," and the *Shulchan Aruch* (*ibid.*) accepts this presentation. However, *Tosafot* (*Bava Batra* 21b s.v. *Ve'i*) assert that, even if the outside resident pays taxes to the local authority, he may only open a business in a **different** *mavuy* in that city. The Rama rules like *Tosafot*.[9]

---

8. See Rif and *Nimukei Yosef* s.v. *Lo Chayat, Bava Batra* 11a in pages of Rif; Rosh, *Bava Batra* 2:12; and *Tur, Choshen Mishpat* 156.
9. The *Rishonim* also debate precisely what constitutes the necessary type of tax for this purpose. See the commentary attributed to Rabbeinu Gershom (*Bava Batra* 21b s.v. *Bar Mata*), *Hag'hot Ashri* (*Bava Batra* 2:12), *Bach* (C.M.

GRAY MATTER

The Aviasaf's Interpretation

As mentioned above, Rav Huna the son of Rav Yehoshua appears to permit most competition, and, according to the Meiri (and possibly Rambam, Rif, and *Shulchan Aruch*), he does not even prohibit placing one's fishing net right in front of someone else's net. Even if one assumes that Rav Huna the son of Rav Yehoshua does prohibit placing the fishing net in such a manner, it is still not clear what level of competition he means to prohibit. The case of the fishing nets might be a uniquely extreme case, as the fish were sure to go into the original net. Alternatively, that case might come to prohibit any new store that will undoubtedly cripple the original store's income, even if the new entrepreneur does not directly block the incumbent's merchandise. Consequently, there has been a dispute since the time of the *Rishonim* regarding where to draw the line between legitimate economic competition and unfair damage to someone else's livelihood.

The *Aviasaf* (cited by the Mordechai, *Bava Batra* 516, and Hag'hot Maimoniot, *Hil. Shecheinim* 6:8) defines unfair competition in a most broad manner. He forbids opening a store at the entrance to a *mavuy satum* (a dead-end alley) if a similar establishment is already located farther within the *mavuy satum*. Such competition is unfair, for it will definitely ruin the original shopkeeper's business. Potential customers will see the new store upon entering the *mavuy satum* without ever noticing the other establishment farther in. Rav Yosef Karo (*Beit Yosef, Choshen Mishpat* 156 s.v. *Vekatav Hamordechai*) claims that the *Aviasaf* is following Rav Huna's opinion in the Gemara (prohibiting opening a new mill where one already exists). As mentioned above, most *Rishonim* rule against Rav Huna (in favor of Rav Huna the son of Rav Yehoshua). Rav Karo thus ignores the *Aviasaf*'s view in his *Shulchan Aruch* (C.M. 156:5) and rules that all local competitors are unrestricted in their ability to open rival businesses.

---

156 s.v. *Umah Shekatav Im*), *Beit Yosef* (C.M. 156 s.v *Hacheilek Hasheini*), and *Biur Hagra* (C.M. 156:23).

HASAGAT GEVUL: ECONOMIC COMPETITION IN JEWISH LAW

The Rama (*Darchei Moshe* 156:4), however, explains that, according to the *Aviasaf*, even the lenient[10] Rav Huna the son of Rav Yehoshua prohibits opening a new business at the start of a *mavuy satum*. The reason for this is that the new business will surely cripple the business inside the *mavuy*. Not surprisingly, therefore, the Rama takes a stricter stance than the *Shulchan Aruch*, for he understands that the *Aviasaf*'s ruling fits into the accepted position in the Gemara. In a responsum (10), the Rama adjudicates a famous sixteenth-century dispute between two Italian publishers who both printed editions of the Rambam's *Mishneh Torah*. The one who published it first objected to the existence of a rival edition of the *Mishneh Torah*. The Rama rules against the second publisher, reasoning (based on the *Aviasaf*'s ruling) that all *Amoraim* forbid opening a store if it will clearly ruin the original entrepreneur's business. The Rama thus concludes that the second publisher should not be patronized, as he was unfairly ruining the original publisher's livelihood.

Other Limitations on Competition

Even if one does not accept the *Aviasaf*'s ruling, it is still possible to apply some limits to free enterprise. For example, the *Mas'at Binyamin* (27, quoted by *Pitchei Teshuvah*, *Choshen Mishpat* 156:3) addresses a town that was permitted to have only one store of a particular type. One such store already existed, and someone wanted to start an identical one. The *Mas'at Binyamin* writes that even the lenient Rav Huna the son of Rav Yehoshua forbids the new competitor from opening. Since there was not even a theoretical chance of both stores surviving, the new storeowner was assuredly damaging the incumbent (*bari hezeika*). The *Pitchei Teshuvah* points out that nowhere in his responsum does the *Mas'at Binyamin* cite the *Aviasaf*'s ruling as a precedent. Perhaps the *Mas'at Binyamin* would permit opening a

---

10. For purposes of clarity, we will refer to opinions that permit competition as lenient and ones that limit it as strict or stringent. Obviously, from the point of view of the original proprietor, the more "lenient" opinions cause greater hardship, while the more "stringent" ones benefit him.

GRAY MATTER

store at the entrance to a *mavuy satum*. Regarding a *mavuy satum*, at least some chance exists that people will decide to walk into the *mavuy* and buy from the original merchant, even if this is unlikely. In this town, by contrast, the law made it completely impossible for two stores of the same type to coexist.

The Rashba (*Teshuvot* 3:83) also limits free enterprise. He extrapolates from the Gemara's case of the fishing nets that, while one may open a rival business, he may not actively pursue people who are known to be regular customers of the first proprietor. Just as one who places his net in front of the first net swipes fish that were heading straight toward it, this type of advertising steals customers who would have undoubtedly bought from the original proprietor.

Responsa of Acharonim

The *Chatam Sofer* (*Choshen Mishpat* 61 and 118, cited by *Pitchei Teshuvah* 156:3) understands that even Rav Huna the son of Rav Yehoshua permits competition when the new store will only **decrease** the profits of the original proprietor. However, competition that will **eliminate** the original proprietor's ability to earn a livelihood is forbidden. The *Chatam Sofer* quotes the *Aviasaf* as a precedent and asserts that Rashi agrees with the *Aviasaf*. Rashi (mentioned above) explains that the lenient view in the Gemara permits competition because "whoever will come to me will come to me, and whoever will come to you will come to you." Surely, argues the *Chatam Sofer*, Rashi would agree that if the new competitor's presence made it nearly impossible for consumers to go to his rival's store, this claim is untenable. Everyone would forbid opening the new store in such a case. The *Chatam Sofer* thus concludes that none of the *Amoraim* ever sanctioned destroying someone else's livelihood completely.

The *Chatam Sofer* (*Choshen Mishpat* 79) adds that a community may administer lashes to one who competes unfairly. He bases this on the aforementioned responsa of the Rama (who appears to forbid non-Jews, too, from competing unfairly) and

HASAGAT GEVUL: ECONOMIC COMPETITION IN JEWISH LAW

Mas'at Binyamin, both of which view unfair competition as a heinous offense. It is worth noting that the *Chatam Sofer* explicitly prohibits unfair competition even when the original merchant knows another trade or can support himself with other money.

Not all *Acharonim* subscribe to the *Chatam Sofer*'s limitations on competition. For example, the *Chatam Sofer* notes that the *Chavot Ya'ir* (*Teshuvot* 42) actually derives the reverse from the aggadic passage (cited above from *Makkot* 24a) in which King David praises one who does not enter his fellow's trade. The *Chavot Ya'ir* reasons that David considers this trait a sign of **piety** precisely because it is **technically permitted** (as long as one is a local resident). David commends one who refrains from competing with his friend for going **beyond** the letter of the law.[11] The *Pitchei Teshuvah* also cites the *Beit Efrayim* (*Choshen Mishpat* 26-27), who writes that common practice in his community was apparently not to follow the *Aviasaf*'s view. His community permitted entrepreneurs to open new hotels at the city gate, despite the fact that all who entered the city saw the new hotels before seeing the older hotels inside the city.[12]

Contemporary Authorities

Rav Moshe Feinstein (*Teshuvot Igrot Moshe, Choshen Mishpat* 1:38) rules in accordance with the *Chatam Sofer* that one may not open a business if it will destroy someone else's livelihood. Rav Moshe rules that a loss of livelihood is not defined by a loss of one's home or his ability to put food on the table. Instead, he claims, taking away one's ability to afford as much as the average person in his socioeconomic class constitutes

---

11. Of course, the *Chatam Sofer* himself sharply attacks this claim and tries to prove that King David's eleven principles are all technically binding, just as the 613 *mitzvot*, which they symbolize, are all obligatory.
12. The *Pitchei Teshuvah* cites many authorities on each side of the debate regarding limiting competition.

destroying his livelihood.[13] It should be noted that the case addressed by Rav Moshe also included other reasons to prohibit the new competition.[14]

Rav Ezra Basri (*Teshuvot Sha'arei Ezra* 2:131) does not quote the *Aviasaf*, although he does rule in accordance with the opinion of the Rashba (quoted above) that one may not lure away the original proprietor's regular customers.[15] Rav Basri permits selling *chametz* before *Pesach*[16] in a neighborhood where another rabbi has already been selling *chametz*, but he prohibits publicizing or advertising the rival business, so as not to take away regular customers from the first rabbi. Rav Basri adds that if any community establishes an official policy in these matters, the policy is halachically binding. For example, if the local Religious Affairs Councils in Israel were to appoint specific rabbis to sell *chametz*, this designation would preclude all other rabbis from running a competing sale.

---

13. The *Chatam Sofer* himself distinguishes between weakening someone's business ("*chulshat chiyuteih*") and totally ruining it ("*pisuk chiyuteih*"), and he only prohibits the latter. *Pisuk chiyuteih* could have been interpreted as driving the person into poverty, but Rav Moshe adduces a proof from the laws of *ribbit* (the prohibition to charge interest) that it should be understood more broadly.
14. The new competitors in this case were providing the same service as the incumbent, but they were not doing it for personal profit. Rav Moshe felt that their lack of interest in making money from the service made it less legitimate for them to ruin someone else's opportunity to earn a livelihood. They could not claim, "You do work on your home turf, and [so too] I do work on my home turf," because they did not need the work for their livelihood in the same way that their competitor did.
15. It should be noted that Rav Basri is a Sephardic authority, which might explain why he bases his ruling on the Rashba, a Sephardic *Rishon*, rather than the various Ashkenazic *Rishonim* and *Acharonim* quoted earlier in our chapter.
16. It is common for people to give some money to the rabbi who sells their *chametz* to a non-Jew.

HASAGAT GEVUL: ECONOMIC COMPETITION IN JEWISH LAW

Some authorities are even more lenient about competition. The *Beit Efraim* (C.M. 26) rules against the *Aviasaf*'s view, and the Tel Aviv Beit Din (*Piskei Din Rabbaniyim* 4:9-32) also leans this way. Rav Yosef Adler reports that Rav Yosef Dov Soloveitchik adopted a similar approach when an established kosher pizza store sought to block another pizza store from opening in the same area (Bergen County, New Jersey). The local rabbis (Rav Adler and Rav Macy Gordon) consulted with Rav Soloveitchik, who ruled in favor of the new entrepreneurs. The Rav insisted that in America there are no restrictions on competition, although he did not explain his reasoning.

There is also another possible reason to permit competition in America today. Murray Laulicht (a prominent Orthodox attorney) informed this author that almost all restrictions of economic activity violate civil antitrust statutes. This point may be significant, and the issue of whether *dina demalchuta dina* (the principle that the law of the land is halachically binding) applies in a given situation must be carefully examined.[17]

No clear consensus has emerged regarding rules for when to permit competition, so the ruling in each case depends upon the understanding of the particular *dayanim* involved.

Five Cases of Consensus

Although most issues of competition are subject to debate, there are at least five cases where nearly all authorities appear to agree.

---

17. This issue might hinge on the dispute between the *Rama* (C.M. 73:14) and the *Shach* (73:39). See Professor Steven Resnicoff's extensive review of the debate among halachic authorities as to whether Halachah should assimilate secular bankruptcy laws (*The Journal of Halacha and Contemporary Society* 24:5-54). Also see the fascinating debate between Rav Shlomo Dichovsky and Rav Avraham Sherman (*Techumin* 18:18-40 and 19:205-220) as to whether Halachah should assimilate secular equitable distribution laws.

GRAY MATTER

I. Better Prices or Merchandise

The Rama (C.M. 156:7, based on the Ri Migash, quoted by the *Tur*, C.M. 156) rules that a new competitor may not be restricted if his prices or the quality of his merchandise are preferable for the Jewish consumers.[18] According to the *Aruch Hashulchan* (C.M. 156:11), this ruling also applies to a merchant who is selling different merchandise, even if his prices and quality are no better. However, the *Aruch Hashulchan* warns that the leniency toward a competitor with cheaper prices only applies if the competitor is not engaging in predatory pricing. If the old merchant was charging a high price, he explains, the new competitor may charge a more reasonable one. However, if the old merchant was charging a reasonable price, such that further lowering his price would prevent him from turning a profit, the new competitor may not open.

II. Necessary Monopolies

The *Chatam Sofer* (*Choshen Mishpat* 79) rules that communities should ensure that industries which require monopoly protection (i.e., protection from competition) receive it.[19] Rav Dr. Aaron Levine (*Free Enterprises and Jewish Law*, pp. 19-20) suggests that power companies and urban transportation are contemporary examples of enterprises that need monopoly protection in order to survive.[20] Some may argue that basic

---

18. In the Rama's responsum (10) prohibiting a second edition of the Mishneh Torah, the second edition was of worse quality than the first edition.

19. See *Teshuvot Igrot Moshe* (C.M. 2:39) regarding the negative effect of having rival organizations supervise *kashrut* in the same community. Rav Moshe instructs the local rabbinical council in Pittsburgh, Pennsylvania to maintain sole control of *kashrut* supervision.

20. At the time that this is being written, the issue of protecting a monopoly over power is being debated in parts of America, and protecting a monopoly over public transportation is a matter of great debate in Israel.

Jewish service providers in small Jewish communities similarly need monopoly protection to survive.[21]

III. Teaching Torah

The Gemara (*Bava Batra* 21b-22a) states that even Rav Huna permits unrestricted competition in the area of Torah education, since competition fosters improved Torah knowledge (*kin'at sofrim tarbeh chochmah*). This idea applies only to Torah study, but not to other religious services.[22] For example, Rav Ezra Basri (*Shaarei Ezra* 2:131) rules that the laws of *hasagat gevul* apply to the sale of *chametz* before *Pesach*, because *kinat sofrim tarbeh chochmah* only applies to teaching Torah per se. Even when competition is technically permissible between Torah scholars, Rav Basri (based on the *Chatam Sofer's* conclusion) adds that rabbis must be extra strict about only competing fairly, to set a proper example for everyone else.

IV. Business Districts

Many contemporary authorities believe that a competing store occasionally enhances the business of the first storeowner. Under certain circumstances, the new store helps transform the area into a center for a certain type of businesses. Residents of Manhattan are familiar with garment districts, flower districts, furniture districts, and other similar commercial zones. Such areas attract large amounts of consumers, who spend more money than if they were patronizing a single store. Rav Moshe D. Tendler (in a

---

21. Ezra Frazer points out that such a situation may be analogous to a case addressed by the *Chatam Sofer* (C.M. 61). Two people were vying for the job of town butcher, one who had held the position for a long time and one who had substituted for this butcher and now wanted to be a butcher himself. The *Chatam Sofer* takes into consideration that the town was not capable of supporting two butchers as a reason to rule against the newer candidate. (In the end, he rules in favor of the newer candidate due to certain unique circumstances surrounding the specific people involved.)
22. See *Chatam Sofer*, *Choshen Mishpat* 19 and 79 s.v. *Mah*.

lecture at Yeshiva University) and Rav Basri (personal communication) permit competition in such circumstances, as the original storeowners benefit from the newcomers.

V. Contemporary Neighborhoods

It should be noted that changing patterns in the geography of business impact halachic discussions of competition. Many businesses today do not cater exclusively to their local neighborhoods. For example, the Tel Aviv Beit Din has written that competition between insurance agents should not be restricted according to the distinction between local residents and outsiders, as the insurance industry is not a neighborhood-based field (*Piskei Din Rabaniyim* 6:3). Following this reasoning, geographic location would not limit stores that conduct much of their business through the World Wide Web. Thus, each business must be individually evaluated, based on contemporary business conditions, to determine if the rules of *hasagat gevul* apply to it.

Conclusion

This area is particularly complex, as it depends on both many unresolved halachic disputes and changing business conditions. It is thus important to present all cases to *dayanim* who are Torah scholars and who understand the intricacies of business (see *Aruch Hashulchan*, C.M. 15:6). It should not surprise people to find that different *batei din* rule differently in these matters, considering the many unresolved disputes involved.

Halachah and Copyright Laws

According to many authorities, Halachah accepts the concept of copyright laws, which would make them binding according to both Jewish law and civil law. A ruling of the Jerusalem Beit Din (printed in *Techumin* 6:169-184) illustrates this assertion. Rav Ezra Basri (a member of the Beit Din) notes that virtually all halachic authorities accept the concept of copyright laws, so the Beit Din ruled that the defendant (who violated copyright law) could not be acquitted by claiming to follow the minority opinion, which maintains that Halachah does not recognize the concept of copyright.[1]

Although many authorities recognize copyright laws,[2] there are differing opinions as to why this is so. This article outlines five approaches from some of the greatest halachic authorities of the past three-hundred years.

Rav Yosef Shaul Nathanson - Equity

Rav Yosef Shaul Nathanson (*Teshuvot Sho'eil Umeishiv* 1:1:44) explicitly asserts that Halachah recognizes the concept of

---

1. For further information on this topic, see Rav Israel Schneider's essay "Jewish Law and Copyright", (*The Journal of Halacha and Contemporary Society* 21:84-96), the eighth chapter of Rav Aaron Levine's *Economic Public Policy and Jewish Law*, and the essays of Rav Zalman Nechemia Goldberg and Rav Ezra Basri in *Techumin* (6:169-207).
2. See, however, Rav J. David Bleich (*Contemporary Halakhic Problems* 2:121), who writes, "Jewish laws with regard to an author's proprietary interest in his published or unpublished work is far from unequivocal."

intellectual property and copyright law. He does not offer a prooftext for this assertion, but he writes that it would be counterintuitive to claim that Halachah would fail to recognize the internationally accepted rules of copyright. It would appear that Rav Nathanson is arguing that we must accept these laws based on considerations of equity. Indeed, the Ramban, commenting on the Torah's exhortation (*Devarim* 6:18), "*Ve'asitah hayashar vehatov be'einei Hashem*" ("You shall follow what is proper and good in the eyes of God"), emphasizes the need to conduct oneself in an ethical manner. He explains that the Torah commands us to follow what is considered proper and ethical behavior even in situations that are not directly addressed in the Torah. Following copyright laws is a fulfillment of this exhortation.[3]

Rav Yitzchak Shmelkes - Dina Demalchuta Dina

Rav Yitzchak Shmelkes (*Beit Yitzchak, Yoreh De'ah* 2:75) writes, "I am not aware of any Torah source that prohibits copying a Torah work[4] without the authority and permission of the author." However, he states that one must obey copyright laws that the civil government enacts due to the Talmudic rule of "*dina demalchuta dina*." This rule, literally, "the law of the government is the law," obligates Jews to follow many laws of the land in which they dwell.[5]

In Jewish communities today, there is an added reason that Jews must obey the civil government's laws. Unlike previous generations, Jews today do not live in autonomous communities with their own business practices. The "local business customs" of any Jewish community are thus its local civil laws. Explaining

---

3. For further analysis of Rav Nathanson's approach, see *Techumin* (7:366).
4. The *Beit Yitzchak's* logic presumably applies to copying anything illegally. He speaks of copying a Torah work merely because this is the case that was presented to him for adjudication.
5. For a summary of this topic, see Rav Hershel Schachter's essay in *The Journal of Halacha and Contemporary Society* (1:103-132).

why Halachah should recognize American rent control laws, Rav Yosef Eliyahu Henkin (*Kitvei Haga'on Rav Y. E. Henkin* 2:96) writes:

> Since we are residents of the United States, whose laws are enacted by elected officials, chosen by citizens, to uphold justice, and we Jews do not maintain organized communities with communal heads (*tovei ha'ir*), the government's laws are halachically binding because of *dina demalchuta dina*. Although these [laws] do not always conform to the *Shulchan Aruch*, if they relate to issues which depend on custom, [the civil laws] are the nation's custom. When a case comes before Jewish *dayanim* (rabbinical judges), they must rule according to the civil laws, except for the laws of inheritance,[6] which do not depend on custom.

Rav Henkin does note that not all authorities apply *dina demalchuta dina* to laws that are designed to maintain order, when these laws contradict Halachah (as opposed to taxes, which all authorities consider binding).[7] Nonetheless, he claims that all would agree that when there are no Jewish courts to legislate rules for an effective society,[8] the civil government's laws to maintain order must be followed.[9] This reasoning appears especially true in the area of copyright law, as virtually all countries in the world maintain them, and contemporary business cannot function without them.

---

6. Rav Henkin explains the unique status of inheritance earlier in the same chapter (paragraph 3).
7. See *Shach, Choshen Mishpat* 73:39.
8. See *Contemporary Halakhic Problems* (4:3-16), where Rav J. David Bleich laments the lack of a central, universally recognized *beit din* and suggests how to remedy the situation.
9. Nonetheless, Judah Dick (an Orthodox attorney from Brooklyn) stated (in a public lecture) that *batei din* in the Williamsburg section of Brooklyn, New York rule that rent control laws are not halachically binding.

GRAY MATTER

Chazal teach us that when government discipline is lacking, pandemonium ensues (*Avot* 3:2). Similarly, if copyright laws were not enacted (and obeyed), economic pandemonium would result.

Noda Biy'hudah - Making a Profit at Someone Else's Loss

Rav Zalman Nechemia Goldberg (*Techumin* 6:195-197) applies a responsum of Rav Yechezkel Landau as a source for recognition of intellectual property rights. Rav Landau (*Noda Biy'hudah, Choshen Mishpat* 2:24) adjudicates a dispute in which a Torah scholar wrote a commentary on parts of the Mishnah. He paid a publisher to print the Mishnah and his commentary together in one book. After the work was printed, the publisher discarded the characters used in printing the commentary but saved the typeset of the Mishnah's text. The publisher then printed another edition of the Mishnah without the scholar's commentary. The scholar sued the publisher for compensation, arguing that the new edition of the Mishnah would hurt sales of the edition containing his commentary. The scholar claimed that the publisher acted unfairly, as he was paid to print the Mishnah on the scholar's behalf. It would not be proper to use the fruits of this printing against him.

The publisher defended his actions by claiming that the typeset characters belonged to him, so he could use them as he pleased. Rav Landau rejected the publisher's claim, stating that he caused unfair monetary damage to the scholar. Publishing another edition of the Mishnah caused a reduction in demand for the edition with the scholar's commentary. Rav Landau ordered the publisher to compensate the scholar, as using the typeset characters constituted benefitting at the scholar's expense.

Rav Zalman Nechemia Goldberg discusses the possibility of applying this ruling to the situation of copyright law. If someone copies a computer program, for example, the copier benefits from the program and causes a loss to the producer of the program, as the copied version hurts the sales of the computer program.

Copying it therefore constitutes benefitting at another's expense (*zeh neheneh vezeh chaseir*), so the copier must compensate the producer of the program.

Chatam Sofer - Hasagat Gevul (Illegal Encroachment)

The *Chatam Sofer* (*Choshen Mishpat* 49, 69, 79) provides another source for the concept of ownership over intangible property. In discussing why one may not republish a prayer book set that was edited and arranged by a particular publisher, the *Chatam Sofer* cites a passage from the Gemara (*Bava Batra* 21a-b) as a source for the prohibition. The Gemara records, "Fishing nets must be kept away from fish [which has been targeted by another fisherman] the full length of their ability to swim."

The targeted fish are ownerless until they are actually trapped. Nevertheless, *Chazal* require the other fishermen to distance themselves from the targeted fish. *Tosafot* (*Kiddushin* 59a s.v. *Ani*) cite Rabbeinu Meir (Rashi's son-in law), who explains that this Halachah applies when the first fisherman baited the particular area with dead fish, leading other fish to gather in that area. Competitors may not capitalize on the investment made by the first fisherman.

The *Chatam Sofer* formulates a general principle based on this case from the Gemara. He asserts that one who invested effort in attaining a certain goal (even if it is intangible) possesses an exclusive right to the resulting profits of that investment. Hence, the creator of intellectual property, such as a computer program or a music tape, may retain the exclusive rights to the profits resulting from his creation. A violation of this right encroaches on someone else's business rights.

Rav Zalman Nechemia Goldberg - Shiyur

Rav Zalman Nechemia Goldberg (*Techumin* 6:185-207) suggests that the concept of *shiyur*, that one who sells an object can retain certain rights to it, may apply to copyright laws. For example, the Gemara (*Bava Metzia* 34a) discusses a case in which one sells his sheep but retains the rights to the sheep's future production of wool and offspring. The original owner still owns the sheep as far as their wool and offspring are concerned.[10]

Rav Goldberg argues that a store that sells a copyrighted computer program or music cassette only sells the purchaser the right to derive personal enjoyment from it. He does not sell, however, the right to copy the merchandise. The buyer cannot claim that, as the new owner, he may copy the product at will, because he does not own the right to copy the product. Copying the merchandise in such a case constitutes outright theft.[11]

Conclusion

Halachic authorities offer at least five reasons to abide by civil copyright laws. Indeed, Rav Moshe Feinstein (*Teshuvot Igrot Moshe*, *Orach Chaim* 4:40:19) and Rav Eliezer Waldenberg (*Tzitz Eliezer* 18:80) both rule that one must follow these laws. Failure to abide by these laws can unfortunately lead to *chilul Hashem* (desecration of God's name), as well. Therefore, before copying cassettes, compact discs, or computer programs, one must ascertain that it is permissible to do so. Nevertheless, many authorities, most notably Rav Shlomo Zalman Auerbach, permit copying small portions of a tape or book if one would not have otherwise bought the item.[12] For a discussion of other situations in which it may be permitted to copy something, see *Pitchei Choshen* 4:9:11 (and note 27). This author has found that consulting with attorneys who are well-versed in copyright laws can be useful when rendering halachic decisions about these matters.

---

10. For other examples of *shiyur*, see *Gittin* 82 and *Bava Kama* 78b.
11. If someone went ahead and copied something illegally under these circumstances, Rav Goldberg forbids buying the item from him. See *Techumin* (7:360-380) for criticism of Rav Goldberg and Rav Goldberg's response.
12. See *Nishmat Avraham* (4:204-206) and *Techumin* (7:367). Rav Shlomo Zalman permits copying small portions of a book even if the author explicitly writes that he explicitly forbids copying any amount. See, however, *Pitchei Choshen* (4:9, note 27), who prohibits disobeying the author's explicit demand.

The Torah's View of Gambling

This author once asked Rav Yosef Dov Soloveitchik if it is permissible to go to a casino for a single visit. The Rav replied succinctly: "It's a bad habit, don't do it!" Rav Mordechai Willig encouraged this author to publicize the Rav's statement. Similar sentiments are expressed by the *Mishnah Berurah* (670, *Biur Halachah* s.v. *Venohagim*), the *Aruch Hashulchan* (*Orach Chaim* 670:9), Rav Moshe Feinstein (*Teshuvot Igrot Moshe, Orach Chaim* 4:35), Rav Yehudah Amital (in a discussion with this author), Rav Aharon Lichtenstein (in a discussion with this author), Rav Hershel Schachter (in a lecture delivered at Yeshiva University), and Rav Mordechai Willig (in a speech delivered at a National Conference of Synagogue Youth convention). We will explore the basis for this attitude in the Gemara, *Rishonim*, and *Shulchan Aruch*.

Talmudic Background

The main Talmudic discussion of gambling appears in *Sanhedrin* (24b-25a). The Mishnah there lists different types of men who are disqualified from serving as witnesses, including a dice player (*mesacheik bekubiya*). The Gemara cites two explanations for disqualifying a dice player. Rami Bar Chama believes that one's winnings in dice playing constitute theft, as the losing party does not willingly give his money to the winner. Rather, it is a situation of *asmachta*, where someone accepts a disproportionately large financial responsibility under the assumption that he will never have to pay it. Rashi (s.v. *Asmachta*) explains that Rami Bar Chama considers gambling to be *asmachta* because each gambler agrees to pay, should he lose, only due to the mistaken belief that he will win. Hence, when he hands the money to the winner, he does so unwillingly.

GRAY MATTER

On the other hand, the Gemara records that Rav Sheishet does not view the losing gambler's payment as an *asmachta*. According to Rav Sheishet, the Mishnah only disqualifies a gambler who has no other profession, because he fails to engage in any constructive activity (*eino oseik beyishuvo shel olam*). The Rambam (*Hilchot Gezeilah Va'aveidah* 6:11) explains that a person should involve himself in learning and other activities that contribute positively to society, whereas even permissible forms of gambling (such as gambling with a non-Jew) contain no socially redeeming value.

Rishonim

The Rambam (*Hil. Gezeilah Va'aveidah* 6:10-11) rules that gambling with a Jew constitutes theft on a rabbinical level. Regarding gambling with a non-Jew, while there is no theft involved, he prohibits it because it is a total waste of time, whereas man should spend his time acquiring wisdom and developing the world.[1] The Rambam's opinion is somewhat difficult, because he appears to contradict himself in *Hil. Eidut* (10:4), where he implies that even gambling with a Jew involves no technical prohibition. It is also unclear how his opinion fits into the Gemara quoted above.[2]

Rashi, Rabbeinu Tam, and the Ri debate why Rav Sheishet maintains that gambling does not constitute *asmachta*. Rashi (*Sanhedrin* 24b s.v. *Kol Ki Hai Gavna*) explains that when one plays dice, he does not have any control over whether he will win or lose, for rolling dice successfully does not depend on skill. Hence, if one agrees to pay in the event that he loses, he does so wholeheartedly, knowing that he might lose. On the other hand, situations of *asmachta* arise when a person is certain that he will

---

1. Regarding the validity as a witness of one whose only occupation is gambling with non-Jews, see Raavad's comment there, *Kesef Mishneh* on *Hil. Eidut* 10:4, and *Shulchan Aruch, Choshen Mishpat* 370:3.
2. See *Magid Mishnah, Hil. Gezeilah Va'aveidah* 6:10; *Lechem Mishneh, Hil. Eidut* 10:4; *Kesef Mishneh* on both these sources; and *Aruch Hashulchan*, C.M. 207:23.

fulfill his promise and thus avoid paying the penalty. For example, the Mishnah (*Bava Batra* 168a) discusses a person who promises his creditor that, as a penalty, he will pay more money than he owes if he does not repay his loan by a certain date. He agrees to pay the extra money only because he is certain that he will be able to pay the creditor by the due date. Therefore, if the borrower defaults, the penalty is an *asmachta*, as he did not expect to actually pay the penalty. The gambler, on the other hand, understands that he might lose his money, so he consents to his loss, making the gambling payment a permissible transaction according to Rav Sheishet.

The Ri fundamentally agrees with Rashi's explanation of Rav Sheishet, but he adds a number of points to provide a full account of the parameters of *asmachta*. He outlines three basic categories of conditional agreements. The first category is when one makes an agreement whose terms are reasonable (*lo gazim*), and one is fully in control of the situation (*beyado*). This conditional agreement is valid and does not constitute *asmachta*. The classic example of this category is a sharecropper who agrees to compensate the owner of a field if he fails to work the field according to their agreement (*Bava Metzia* 104a). The payment is not a penalty; rather, it constitutes appropriate compensation to the owner of the field for the lost profits. In addition, the sharecropper himself chooses whether he will work the field.

The second category described by the Ri is accepting a debt without seriously believing that one will ever have to pay it, such as when one agrees to pay an exaggerated penalty should he fail to do something. For example, if a sharecropper agrees to pay the owner of the field an exorbitant sum as a penalty for failing to work the field, the agreement is an *asmachta*, because the sharecropper undoubtedly never expected to pay such a great sum (*Bava Metzia* 104b). He agreed to the financial penalty only inasmuch as he believed that he would work the field properly and never need to pay it. Accordingly, the penalty constitutes an *asmachta* and is not legally binding.

GRAY MATTER

The Ri considers playing dice to be a third category. Winning and losing are totally random, so the players recognize that they might lose and consciously agree to pay the required sum. No one is under the false impression that his superior skills give him a better chance of winning. Since each competitor knows in advance that he may reasonably need to pay this sum, playing dice is not an *asmachta* according to Rav Sheishet.

Rabbeinu Tam offers a different explanation. He suggests that playing dice would be *asmachta* if it were a unilateral agreement. However, playing dice involves a bilateral agreement, whereby one agrees to pay when he loses games because he wants the ability to collect when he wins. Rabbeinu Tam believes that *asmachta* invalidates an agreement only if the person commits himself to pay without receiving any potential profit in return, such as in the aforementioned case concerning defaulting on a loan.

The Shulchan Aruch and Its Commentaries

The Rama (*Choshen Mishpat* 207:13) cites the theories of both the Ri and Rabbeinu Tam to explain why playing dice is not an *asmachta*. Elsewhere, the Rama (C.M. 370:3) does not forbid occasional gambling, as the Halachah accepts the opinion of Rav Sheishet. Rav Yosef Karo (same source), however, rules in accordance with the view of the Rambam,[3] that dice playing constitutes theft on a rabbinical level, asserting that the agreement between the two parties involved is an *asmachta*.

Accordingly, Sephardic Jews may not even gamble occasionally, since for them the rulings of Rav Yosef Karo constitute the halachic norm. Indeed, Rav Ovadia Yosef (*Yabia Omer*, vol. 7, C.M. 6) rules that a Sephardic Jew may not buy lottery tickets. Even the Rama limits the permissibility of gambling

---

3. Rav Yosef Karo believes the Rambam's view to match the opinion of Rami bar Chama; see his aforementioned comments in the *Kesef Mishneh*.

occasionally to those games in which the winner is determined entirely at random.⁴ In order to engage in such an activity, one must ascertain that the game does not constitute an *asmachta* in any way. This task is far from simple, since crucial distinctions between valid and invalid agreements are very subtle. Rav Aharon Lichtenstein (cited in *Daf Kesher* 1:83-85) notes that sports betting pools, for example, appear to be prohibited even for Ashkenazic Jews. In that form of gambling, each participant believes that his superior understanding of sports will help him bet on the right teams, so he does not expect to pay for losing.

Moreover, the Rama (*Choshen Mishpat* 207:13) cites the opinion of Rabbeinu Tam, that gambling is permitted only when the prize money is placed on a table owned by both parties (see *Bi'ur Hagra*, C.M. 207:37). Most cases of gambling do not fulfill this requirement, as they usually take place in the home of a single player or in a casino.

Raffles and Lotteries

A possible exception to the halachic problems with gambling is a lottery conducted to raise funds for a charity. Rav Yosef Adler reports that Rav Yosef Dov Soloveitchik permitted purchasing a lottery ticket if the purpose of the lottery is to raise money for a charity, because the rule of *asmachta* does not apply to charitable contributions (*Shulchan Aruch*, *Yoreh De'ah* 258:10). *Asmachta* occurs only when someone does not intend to truly obligate himself, but the losers of a charity fundraiser feel comfortable relinquishing their money, knowing that it will be used for a positive purpose.⁵

Rav Aharon Lichtenstein (cited in *Daf Kesher* 1:83-85) offers a different reason to permit lotteries and raffles, explaining

---

4. This is because the Rama accepts the three categories of the Ri.
5. It is unclear whether this leniency applies to lotteries that donate only a small percentage of their profits to charity.

GRAY MATTER

that one who purchases a ticket buys a right to compete in the lottery. At the time of this purchase, the buyer consents fully to the sale. Should the buyer regret the sale after he loses the lottery, it is too late to undo the sale. Undoing such a sale would be the equivalent of one who purchases a stock demanding to abrogate the sale after a subsequent stock market crash. For Sephardic Jews, it has already been noted that Rav Ovadia Yosef prohibits purchasing lottery and soccer pool tickets.[6] Nonetheless, Rav Ovadia cites Rav Yosef Chaim of Baghdad (*Rav Pe'alim*) as permitting raffles in which the prize is an object, as the winner does not directly take the money of the other participants. Common practice in the observant community is to conduct raffles as fundraisers.

Moral Considerations

The Rivash (432) describes gambling as "disgusting, abominable, and repulsive," noting its terrible effect on society even according to those who do not technically define it as theft. Rav Ovadia Yosef (*Yabia Omer*, vol. 7, C.M. 6) adds to the Rivash's comments:

> Also, regarding the lottery, there are many people who buy a lot of tickets, [spending] almost their entire salary, thinking that one number may win, and in the end... they lose all their money and property.

Due to moral objections, the authorities cited at the beginning of this chapter similarly condemn engaging even in

---

6. Rav Ovadia adds that even Ashkenazic Jews should not buy tickets in Israeli soccer pools ("Toto"), as these tickets support soccer games played on *Shabbat*. We have already noted that, according to Rav Aharon Lichtenstein, these pools may constitute an *asmachta*, as their participants believe that their superior understanding of soccer enables them to bet correctly.

THE TORAH'S VIEW OF GAMBLING

"recreational gambling," in addition to the potential problems of theft. In 1996, Rav Mordechai Willig instructed a convention of the National Conference of Synagogue Youth to refrain from all forms of gambling (including horse racing, football pools, and rotisserie leagues), due to the aforementioned rulings of the Rambam (*Hilchot Gezeilah Va'aveidah* 6:10-11). Rav Willig admitted that many Ashkenazic authorities disagree with the Rambam's claim that all gambling with a Jew is actual theft. However, no one would question the truth of the Rambam's statement that gambling, even when there is no theft involved, is a total waste of time, is the antithesis of wisdom, and contributes nothing positive to the world. Rav Willig cited many of the catastrophic results of habitual gambling, repeatedly decrying gambling and its results as "*churbano shel olam*" - destroying society.[7]

Rav Hershel Schachter (in a lecture at Yeshiva University) even objected to lotteries commonly conducted at weddings to determine which guest will keep the table centerpiece, based on a similar law in the *Shulchan Aruch* (*Orach Chaim* 322:6). He explained that the activity prohibited by the *Shulchan Aruch*, casting lots to determine which child in a family will receive the biggest portion of food, reflects a general prohibition against activities that teach people the thrill of gambling.

The *Mishnah Berurah* and *Aruch Hashulchan* (cited at the beginning of the article) strongly discourage playing cards on *Chanukah*. Rav Moshe Feinstein refers to card playing and bingo as despicable activities ("*devarim mecho'arim*"). Rav Aharon Lichtenstein commented (to this author) that casinos and gambling halls are "symbols of decadence in society." Rav Yehuda Amital said, "People are seeking forms of excitement in life [which are unhealthy]." Rav Soloveitchik put it succinctly, as mentioned earlier - "It is a bad habit; don't do it!"

---

7. See *The Jerusalem Report* (August 16, 1999, pp. 26-32) regarding the disproportionately high incidence of gambling problems in Israel and Jewish communities worldwide.

GRAY MATTER

The Torah (*Vayikra* 19:2) exhorts us: "*Kedoshim tih'yu*" ("Be holy"). Many great rabbis have declared that gambling is incompatible with the Jewish people's goal of being a holy people. While it is highly unusual for the *Aruch Hashulchan* to strongly condemn a practice of the observant community, he does so regarding the practice of many Jews to gamble on *Chanukah*. Perhaps he reacted so harshly because he served as the rabbi of a city (Novaradok, in pre-World War I Lithuania), where he may have seen the devastating effects that gambling often has on individuals, their families, and society as a whole. In short, let us remember the words of the *Mishnah Berurah* regarding gambling, "*Hashomer nafsho yirchak mizeh*" ("He who values his soul will stay away from it").

The State of Israel

Exchanging Land for Peace
Part I: Hashkafic Considerations

Peace negotiations and agreements between Israel and her neighbors have aroused much controversy in recent years. In the next two chapters, we discuss the permissibility of ceding Israeli land in the attempt to achieve peace with other nations. In this section, we will address the hashkafic issues (claims based on religious perspective as opposed to religious law).

The Importance of the Land of Israel

Before discussing the technical permissibility of ceding land, it should be emphasized that everyone recognizes the great importance of *Eretz Yisrael* (the Land of Israel). The great love that the Jewish nation has for *Eretz Yisrael* fuels the passionate debate regarding this issue. The following anecdote from the Gemara (*Ketubot* 112a) illustrates the love we have for *Eretz Yisrael*:

> Rabi Abba kissed the rocks of Acco. Rabi Chanina repaired the roads of *Eretz Yisrael* (Rashi: "Because of his love of *Eretz Yisrael* he made this effort, so that no one would cast aspersions on the quality of roads in *Eretz Yisrael*"). Rabi Ami and Rabi Assi moved the students [during the summer] from the sun to the shade and [during the winter] from the shade to the sun (Rashi: so they would not complain about Israel's weather). Rabi Chiya bar Gamda used to roll in the dirt of *Eretz Yisrael*, as the Scripture (*Tehillim* 102:15) states, "For your servants desire her stones and find charm in her dirt."

GRAY MATTER

We even love the rocks and dirt of *Eretz Yisrael*, despite their lack of economic worth. While everyone agrees that *Eretz Yisrael* is very important to the Jewish people, some believe that *Eretz Yisrael*'s central role in Judaism, and especially its role in the redemption process, precludes any discussion of ceding land, even if the result would be peace. Others feel that circumstances might arise where exchanging portions of *Eretz Yisrael* for peace is permissible.

Hashkafic Opposition to Any Cession

Rav Yaakov Moshe Charlap believed that *Eretz Yisrael* is so vital to the Jewish people that it may never be yielded. He wrote a fiery reaction to the division of Palestine suggested by the Peel Commission in 1937 (published in *Techumin* 9:271-273 [see p. 280 for a map outlining the proposed boundaries]). When there was not yet a Jewish state, Rav Charlap opposed accepting anything short of the entire *Eretz Yisrael:*

> There is no doubt that if it should come to, God forbid, being forced to sign an international agreement which would include concessions on our rights to *Eretz Yisrael*, it is better for the signers to cut their thumbs off [!] than to cut away any portion of... beautiful Zion, upon which God's beauty appears. Just as one who claims that the entire Torah is of Divine origin, save for one letter, is deemed a heretic, similarly one who says that all of *Eretz Yisrael* belongs to the Jews, save for one inch, detracts from the holiness of the Land.[1]

---

1. It should be noted that two outstanding authorities, Rav Chaim Ozer Grodinski (*Techumin* 9:293-295) and Rav Tzvi Pesach Frank (*Techumin* 9:276-277), permitted accepting the proposal of the Peel Commission. Their rulings do not necessarily indicate how they would feel about ceding land today, because the land that the Peel Commission gave to the Arabs had not yet been under Jewish control.

EXCHANGING LAND FOR PEACE PART I

Opponents of "land for peace" also cite certain aggadic statements to support their position. They often quote Rabi Shimon Bar Yochai's statement (*Berachot* 5a) that God presented the Jewish people with three precious gifts, which are acquired only through great difficulty: Torah, *Eretz Yisrael*, and the World to Come. They also point to the Rashbam's explanation of why God subjected Avraham to the ordeal of binding Yitzchak (*Bereishit* 22:1). He suggests that God meted out a punishment to Avraham for making a peace treaty with Avimelech, King of the Philistines.

The passionate love for *Eretz Yisrael* is further fueled by what some believe regarding the resettling of the Land of Israel in the past century. Rav Tzvi Yehudah Kook is said to have often cited the Gemara (*Sanhedrin* 98a) to show that the State of Israel represents the *atchalta dig'ulah*, the beginning of the Final Redemption:

> Rabi Abba states that there is no greater indication that the Redemption has arrived than what is described by the *Navi* (Yechezkel 36:9), "Hear ye, O mountains of Israel, your branches should bear fruit for My nation, Israel."

The Maharsha (commenting on this passage) presents two alternative interpretations whether the fruits spoken of are natural fruits or "supernatural fruits." Rav Tzvi Yehudah's belief that the Gemara's promise was already fulfilled presumably adopts the first interpretation.

The deep commitment to *Eretz Yisrael* is further reinforced by the belief of some that the current return to Israel is irreversible. This attitude may stem from the promises of many prophets that God will not reverse the Final Redemption. Amos, for example, concludes his book with these sentiments (9:13-15):

> I shall return my nation, Israel, to the land, and they will rebuild abandoned cities, and they shall

settle [them], and they shall plant vineyards and drink their wine, and they shall create gardens and eat their produce. And I shall plant them on their land, and they will no longer be removed from their land that I have given them, says Hashem your God.

Indeed, there is a story told of Rav Yitzchak Herzog's return trip to Israel in 1943, while the Battle of El Alamein was raging, which conveys this firm belief. Upon being warned of the danger inherent in the return trip to Israel at that time, Rav Herzog's replied that the *Beit Hamikdash* was destroyed twice and will not be destroyed again. Rav Herzog uttered these words when the Nazis (may their evil names be blotted out) were only ninety miles from *Eretz Yisrael* and were expected to defeat the allies at El Alamein.

The Ramban, in his commentary to *Vayikra* (26:16), states that the destruction describes there refers to destruction of the First Temple, and the similar destruction described in *Devarim* (Chapter 28) alludes to the destruction of the Second Temple. Rav Hershel Schachter (*Be'ikvei Hatzon* 32:15-16) understands that according to the Ramban, no destruction will occur in Israel subsequent to the destruction of the Second Temple. Rav Schachter notes that the Ramban, in his description of the Second Temple's destruction, focuses on the destruction of the **Jewish government**, and not on the destruction of the Temple itself. Since what happened then is never supposed to repeat itself, Rav Schachter suggests that the redemption becomes irreversible once a sovereign Jewish state has been established in *Eretz Yisrael*.

Hashkafah Behind Exchanging Land for Peace

Rav Yehuda Amital (*Alon Shevut* 100:34-62) argues that we must prioritize our national values. From the core values of the physical Jewish people, the Torah, and the Land, Rav Amital seeks to prove that a clear hierarchy exists (following the order that we have listed them), so saving people takes precedence over the Land of Israel. Thus, if it is in the interest of saving lives to relinquish sections of *Eretz Yisrael*, we must do so.[2]

In a similar vein, Rav Ovadia Yosef (*Techumin* 10:8) cites the a story from World War I to emphasize that the desire for redemption should not override the value of human life:

> People said to Rav Chaim Soloveitchik, during a conversation, that if this war (the First World War) would bring the redemption, perhaps it was worthwhile. Rav Chaim rebuked them and said, "It is better that many redemptions should be delayed from the Jewish people than that one Jewish life should be lost. And so, if the question were to come before us, that by sacrificing one Jew the Messiah would come, of course we would rule that it is better for the Messiah not to come, and a Jew should not die. Does not *pikuach nefesh* override every *mitzvah* in the Torah, including the Messiah and the redemption?"

As we have already noted, the *hashkafah* of those who permit returning land in no way intends to belittle the value of *Eretz Yisrael*. Rav Aharon Lichtenstein, who also permits exchanging land for peace, once cited a story involving Rav Tzvi Yehudah Kook to illustrate this point. Rav Tzvi Yehudah cried the day the State of Israel was established out of disappointment that much of *Eretz Yisrael* would wind up under non-Jewish control. Rav Lichtenstein firmly stated that even if one does not agree with Rav Tzvi Yehudah's view regarding the exchange of land for peace, his view regarding the sanctity of *Eretz Yisrael* must be accepted. For the Jewish people, *Eretz Yisrael* is not merely a national homeland, but the Holy Land given by God to His nation. Surrendering land for peace must involve great pain for a Jew, analogous to amputating a limb to save the life of an individual.

---

2. This author has heard Rav Yaakov Meidan respectfully counter Rav Amital's claim. Rav Meidan argues that the needs of the Land and people of Israel are identical. It can thus never be in the interest of the people to relinquish control of sections of *Eretz Yisrael*.

Exchanging Land for Peace
Part II: Halachic Arguments

Aside from their hashkafic considerations, each side in the debate about ceding land in return for peace presents halachic claims. We will begin by citing a number of sources around which the debate focuses, after which we will explain how each side interprets these sources.

The Opinion of the Ramban

The Torah (*Bemidbar* 33:53) commands, "And you shall conquer the land [of Canaan] and settle in it, because it is for you I have given the land to inherit it." The Ramban comments:

> In my opinion, this is a positive commandment with which we are commanded to settle and conquer the land,[1] as it is given to us and we must not reject our inheritance from God.

The Ramban explains his position at greater length in his critique of the Rambam's *Sefer Hamitzvot* (additional positive commandment #4). He concludes his comments by stating:

> Accordingly, [conquering and living in *Eretz Yisrael*] is a positive commandment that applies in all generations and obligates each individual, even

---

1. For a discussion of whether to translate the Ramban's term as "sovereign control" or "military conquest," see the debate between Rav Nachum Rabinowitz and Rav Yaakov Ariel in *Techumin* (4:302-306 and 5:174-186).

EXCHANGING LAND FOR PEACE PART II

during the time of exile, as is evident from many places in the Talmud. The *Sifrei* says that "it happened that Rabi Yehudah Ben Beteira, Rabi Matya Ben Charash, Rabi Chananya Ben Achi, Rabi Yehoshua, and Rabi Natan were departing *Eretz Yisra*el. They came to Platia and recalled *Eretz Yisrael*. Their eyes swelled with tears, and they tore their garments and mentioned the following verse: 'And you shall conquer and settle in it, and be certain to do this.' They proclaimed that settling and conquering the land of Israel is equivalent to all of the *mitzvot*."

From these comments of the Ramban, we see that he considers it a *mitzvah* to conquer the land of Israel. The Ramban does not address surrendering this land for peace, but we shall soon see how those who oppose ceding land support themselves with his comments.

The Argument of the Minchat Chinuch

The *Sefer Hachinuch* (425) writes that if someone has the opportunity to kill a member of the seven Canaanite nations **without endangering himself**, failing to do so violates the *mitzvah* to destroy them (*Devarim* 7:10). The *Minchat Chinuch* (a commentary on the *Sefer Hachinuch*) finds the *Sefer Hachinuch*'s ruling puzzling. Why should this *mitzvah* only apply when there is no danger involved? Although most *mitzvot* do not require that we sacrifice our lives to fulfill them, here the Torah requires us to do **battle** with the seven nations. It is understood, the *Minchat Chinuch* points out, that the Torah's laws do not assume that a miracle will occur (as explained by the Ramban's comments to *Bemidbar* 5:20 and 13:2). Since the normal course of the world is that people die in battle, we see that the Torah commands us to fight with the seven nations even at risk to ourselves.[2]

---

2. Although the *Minchat Chinuch* concludes with an expression of some doubt, a number of *Acharonim* do embrace his argument, including Rav

141

GRAY MATTER

The argument for prohibiting exchange of land for peace combines the comments of the Ramban and *Minchat Chinuch*. It claims that the Torah obligates us to conquer *Eretz Yisrael* with force, so this *mitzvah*, by its very nature, entails risking our lives. We thus cannot surrender portions of *Eretz Yisrael* even if we are certain that it will save lives, for this would violate our obligation to conquer. Among those who make this argument is Dayan Yehoshua Menachem Aaronberg (*Teshuvot Devar Yehoshua* 2:48 and *Techumin* 10:26-33). Of course, Dayan Aaronberg notes, if there is concern that military defeat (Heaven forbid) will remove more territory from Jewish control, the obligation to wage war does not apply.

Response to the "Ramban - Minchat Chinuch Argument"

The above argument against relinquishing land for the sake of peace is based on the Ramban's belief that it is a *mitzvah* to conquer *Eretz Yisrael* even if it involves loss of life. Rav Yehuda Amital (*Alon Shevut* 100:34-62) counters that the Rambam (Maimonides) believes that the *mitzvah* to conquer *Eretz Yisrael* does not apply today. He questions the ability of a rabbi to rule that we must risk life in accordance with the Ramban (Nachmanides), if the Rambam does not agree with his assertion. Moreover, some *Acharonim* interpret the Ramban as ruling that only the *mitzvah* of **settling** the land, but not conquering the land, applies today. The *Pe'at Hashulchan* (*Hilchot Eretz Yisrael* 1:3) rules in accordance with this view.[3]

According to this approach we are no longer commanded to conquer *Eretz Yisrael*. Thus, if surrendering land will lead to peace, it would be permissible to do so. The *mitzvah* of settling the land of Israel can still be fulfilled in those areas that remain

---

Naftali Tzvi Yehudah Berlin (*Meromei Sadeh*, *Eruvin* 45a and *Kiddushin* 43a) and Rav Yitzchak Zev Soloveitchik (*Parshat Beshalach*, p. 32; cited by Rav J. David Bleich, *Contemporary Halakhic Problems* 3:296-297).
3. The *Pe'at Hashulchan* is considered authoritative regarding *mitzvot* of the Land of Israel.

Exchanging Land for Peace Part II

under Israeli control. Rav Aharon Lichtenstein, in a speech at Yeshivat Har Etzion in which he defended the Camp David accords with Egypt, cited Rav Yosef Dov Soloveitchik, Rav Moshe Feinstein, and Rav Yitzchak Hutner as believing that Israel is permitted to exchange land for peace.

The Prohibition of Lo Techaneim

The Mishnah (*Avodah Zarah* 19b) prohibits the sale of Israeli real estate to non-Jews, providing another possible reason to prohibit ceding land. This is based on the Torah's words, "*Lo techaneim*" (*Devarim* 7:2). The Gemara (*Avodah Zarah* 20a) interprets these words as "*lo titein lahem chanayah bakarka*" ("Do not give them permanent dwelling in the Land"). Some prohibit giving land to non-Jews even to save lives (see *Teshuvot Dvar Yehoshua* 2:48), while others argue that this prohibition may be ignored if lives would thereby be saved (see Rav Ovadia Yosef, *Techumin* 10:34-47). Rav Ovadia also points to the minority of authorities, such as the *Bach* (*Choshen Mishpat* 249:2), who claim that *lo techaneim* does not apply to non-Jews who do not worship idols, such as Muslims.

A Questionable Peace

Until now, we have discussed the question of surrendering land to secure peace. The issue that Israel faces now is whether to surrender land in exchange for an uncertain peace. The country is divided as to whether the current peace process will bring peace or further danger to Israel. Even Israel's top generals disagree as to whether ceding land in this case will actually bring peace. The question that arises now is whether land may be exchanged when we are uncertain of the results of this action. In this situation, Rav Hershel Schachter (*Journal of Halacha and Contemporary Society*, 16:79-80) offers one suggestion for determining how to proceed:

> The question at hand seems comparable to that of a sick individual who must decide the course of action his doctors should undertake. The Poskim

discuss the case of a patient who is fatally ill but who could receive treatment that would prolong his life although cause painful side effects. In such a situation, since there is no consensus whether going ahead with such treatment is desirable, the decision is left to the sick individual [see *Nishmat Avraham, Yoreh Deah* 155:2 and 349:3, and *B'ikvei Hatzon* 34 -H.J.]. Likewise, in the case of a nation in mortal danger, faced with a solution of dubious value, the decision on the course of action to be taken should be in the hands of the majority of those affected.[4]

Professor Eliav Schochetman (*Techumin* 17:107-120) disagrees with this approach. He cites numerous sources to demonstrate that the nation cannot decide matters of Halachah. Moreover, he cites the ruling of Rav Mordechai Eliyahu that in a case where doctors disagree regarding the plan of action for a sick patient, the doctors should adopt a policy of maintaining the status quo (*sheiv v'al ta'aseh*). Similarly, reasons Professor Schochetman, since there is disagreement among military experts if exchanging land for peace is prudent or reckless, the status quo should be maintained.

Conclusion

It is important to recognize the complexity of this issue. Many great rabbis permit exchanging land for peace, while many others forbid it. May God help the State of Israel attain everlasting security and peace.

---

4. See *B'ikvei Hatzon* (32:9), where Rav Schachter discusses precisely who should be permitted to vote in such a referendum.

The Halachic Status of the Falash Mura

During the past few decades, thousands of Ethiopian Jews whose ancestors converted to Christianity, known by their Ethiopian name, the Falash Mura, have returned to observance of Halachah. This chapter presents a halachic perspective on their status as Jews, based on an article by Rav Menachem Waldman in *Techumin* (16:243-272).

Is One Who Abandons Judaism Still Jewish?

The Gemara (*Yevamot* 47b) states that once a convert has completed the conversion process (as soon as he emerges from the *mikvah*), he is considered a Jew even if he later reverts to his non-Jewish lifestyle or religion. In a similar vein, the Gemara (*Sanhedrin* 44a) cites a verse from the book of *Yehoshua* (7:11) in which God proclaims, "An **Israelite** has sinned." The Talmud infers from this formulation that despite committing a sinful deed, the person remains a Jew ("*Yisrael af al pi shechata Yisrael hu*").

On the other hand, the Gemara (*Yevamot* 17a) states that *Chazal* proclaimed the ten lost tribes to be Gentiles ("*goyim gemurim*").[1] Assyria exiled these tribes from Israel in the First Temple period, and they completely assimilated into their surrounding cultures. Treating them as non-Jews seemingly contradicts the Gemara's statement that Jews, no matter how much they sin, always remain Jewish. The *Rishonim* present two

---

1. See *Chulin* 6a for a similar proclamation regarding the Samaritans. For a fascinating explanation of this proclamation, see the commentary of the *Chatam Sofer* to *Shulchan Aruch Orach Chaim* 39.

approaches to resolve the apparent contradiction. The Me'iri (*Avodah Zarah* 26b s.v. *Na'aseh*), representing the minority among the *Rishonim*, states:

> If a Jew practices another religion, he is no longer considered a Jew, except in matters concerning personal status, such as marriage and divorce. His child [presumably he means "her child," as he is referring to a case where a woman converts to another religion -H.J.], however, is even considered non-Jewish regarding those matters.

The *Ba'al Ha'itur* (cited by the *Beit Yosef, Even Ha'ezer* 44 s.v. *Yisrael Mumar*) cites and rejects an opinion that resembles the Me'iri's. Indeed, most *Rishonim* reject the approach of the Me'iri and state that a Jew who converts to another religion remains Jewish.[2] They regard even the children of an apostate as Jews, provided that their mother is Jewish. These *Rishonim* believe that the rabbinical proclamation regarding the ten tribes is unique, due to their total assimilation over many generations. Hence, it does not apply to Jews who have converted to other religions, unless they assimilate socially into non-Jewish society to the point where their Jewish roots are not identifiable.[3]

The *Shulchan Aruch* (*Even Ha'ezer* 44:9) codifies the majority opinion as normative, and most of the commentaries to the *Shulchan Aruch* do not challenge his ruling. The *Be'er Heitev* (44:7), however, cites Mahari Mintz (*Teshuvot* 12) and Maharshdam as writing that a marriage between a Jew who has converted to another religion and another Jew is valid only on a **rabbinical** level, implying that they believe he is no longer a full-fledged Jew. Furthermore, the *Be'er Heitiv* (44:8) quotes Mahari

---

2. See Rambam, *Hilchot Issurei Bi'ah* 13:17; Rosh, *Yevamot* 4:36, and *Korban Netaneil ad. loc.*; and *Tur, Even Ha'ezer* 44.
3. See the responsum of Rav David Darshan, the Rama's student (printed erroneously in *Teshuvot Harama* 62), and Rav Aharon Lichtenstein's essay in *Judaism* (12:260-280) for further discussion of this issue.

ben Chaviv as distinguishing between a Jew who was forcibly converted to another religion (who remains Jewish) and a Jew who converted willingly (who loses his status as a Jew). Nevertheless, the *Pitchei Teshuvah* (44:9) cites the *Noda Biy'hudah* (2:162), who states unequivocally that the minority view is rejected by halachic authorities.[4] The *Be'er Heitev* (44:8) also cites the Re'eim, who asserts that even "after many generations" of following a different religion, the descendants of those who converted to a different religion remain Jewish. Of course, Jewishness is passed down from mother to child only, so the child of a Jewish man and non-Jewish woman is not Jewish (see Rashi on *Devarim* 7:4).

Rav Waldman reports in the aforementioned essay that, despite their conversion to Christianity a century ago, the Falash Mura remain a socially distinct (though not religiously distinct) group within the general Ethiopian community. Non-Jews refer to them as "Israel" and know that they have Jewish roots. Furthermore, non-Jewish society views them as strange and of a lower stature, and refuses to marry them. Rav Waldman writes that the intermarriage rate of the Falash Mura was extremely low (approximately 0.3 percent), and the few intermarriages occurred mostly among those who moved to cities far from their ancestral villages. Accordingly, the fact that the Falash Mura lived as Christians for quite some time seems not to detract from their status as Jews.

Are Ethiopian Jews Truly Jewish?

A prerequisite to determining the halachic of the status of the Falash Mura is determining the halachic status of Ethiopian Jewry in general. This thorny and complicated question has been hotly debated, and Rav Waldman summarizes the debate (*Techumin* 4:314-326). Rav Ovadia Yosef (*Yabia Omer* 8:11) claims that Ethiopian Jewry is undoubtedly Jewish in origin, and

---

4. Rav Moshe Feinstein (*Teshuvot Igrot Moshe*, E.H. 4:83) affirms the *Noda Biy'hudah*'s assertion.

its members need not undergo conversions. Most authorities, however, doubt the status of all Ethiopian Jews and require them to conversion upon arrival in Israel, out of concern that they are not Jewish.[5] The authorities who subscribe to this view include former Israeli Chief Rabbis Yitzchak Herzog, Yitzchak Nissim, and Shlomo Goren (all cited in *Techumin* 4:324-326) and Rav Moshe Feinstein (*Techumin* 12:98 and *Teshuvot Igrot Moshe, Yoreh De'ah* 4:41).

Must One Who Left Judaism "Reconvert"?

Upon establishing that a Jew who "converted" to a different religion remains a Jew, it follows that he need not "reconvert" when he returns to Judaism. Indeed, the Talmud never requires such an individual to immerse in a *mikvah*. However, a number of *Rishonim* mention that the practice emerged for someone returning to Judaism, after practicing another religion, to immerse in a *mikvah*, and the Rama (*Yoreh De'ah* 268:12) codifies this practice. Although this immersion is not required, strictly speaking, it is an act of great significance, expressing the depth of one's commitment to leave his past sins and return to God and the Jewish people.

The following ruling of Rav Aharon Lichtenstein, related by Dr. David Berger, demonstrates the importance of this immersion. An older woman, who had "converted" to Catholicism in her youth, but returned to Judaism in her later years, asked Dr. Berger if she must immerse in a *mikvah*. She told him that she found it somewhat difficult to immerse, due to her age. Dr. Berger posed the question to Rav Lichtenstein, who ruled that the woman should make a great effort to immerse, despite the difficulty. He explained that "it is the least that she could do" in light of her earlier abandonment of Judaism.

---

5. See *Techumin* (7:295-313), where Rav Shaul Yisraeli argues that Ethiopian men who were circumcised in Ethiopia need not undergo a second circumcision when participating in such a conversion.

THE HALACHIC STATUS OF THE FALASH MURA

Are Falash Mura Permitted to Marry Other Jews?

Authorities have also raised concern for *mamzeirut* regarding the Falash Mura (and all Ethiopian Jews), assuming that they were Jewish prior to their conversion in Israel. This concern arises because they did not practice the laws of Jewish divorce.[6] Regarding the Karaites, who similarly did not observe Jewish divorce laws, the Rama (*Even Ha'ezer* 4:37) forbids marrying a Karaite even if the Karaite repents and accepts the authority of the Oral Law. He explains that Karaites are considered possible *mamzeirim* (*mamzeirim misafek*)[7] due to the invalid divorces that they performed throughout the centuries. At first glance, it would appear that this ruling of the Rama should apply to Ethiopian Jews.[8]

However, two different approaches exist to free all Ethiopian Jews from the stigma of *mamzeirut*.[9] The more straightforward approach, endorsed by Rav Ovadia Yosef (*Yabia*

---

6. A *mamzeir* (described in the *Sifrei's* comments to *Devarim* 23:3) is any child born to a Jewish woman from an adulterous or incestuous relationship with another Jew. This creates profound problems for communities which do not perform proper *gittin* (divorce documents), because a woman who marries according to Halachah remains halachically married to her first husband until receiving a *get*. If a woman "remarries" without a *get*, this constitutes adultery, and any children born from this marriage are *mamzeirim*. A *mamzeir* is prohibited to marry anyone, Jew or non-Jew, other than a convert to Judaism or a fellow *mamzeir*.

7. It should be noted that a *mamzeir misafek* is treated like a *mamzeir* only on a rabbinical level (*Kiddushin* 73a), so once any other doubt exists, there is greater room to be lenient.

8. Not all authorities accept the Rama's ruling against marrying Karaites. See Radbaz (*Teshuvot* 1:73), *Pitchei Teshuvah* (E.H. 4:45), *Yabia Omer* (8:12), and Rav Eliyahu Bakshi Doron's essay in *Techumin* (18:77-83). Also see *Tzitz Eliezer* (12:66), citing Rav Tzvi Pesach Frank, and Rav Avraham Sherman's essay in *Techumin* (19:192-200), who prohibit Karaites from marrying Jews.

9. See *Teshuvot Moznei Tzedek* (vol. 1, *Even Ha'ezer* 2) who nonetheless questions the permissibility of marrying Ethiopian Jews. The overwhelming majority of authorities do not appear to accept his view.

Omer 8:11), argues that their divorces did not conform to Halachah, but their marriages (*kiddushin*) were also conducted in a halachically invalid manner. The invalidity of their divorces does not produce *mamzeirim*, because the improperly divorced couples were never married. Rav Waldman (*Techumin* 11:214-240) demonstrates in detail that Ethiopian Jews' marriages were not valid.[10]

Rav Yitzchak Herzog (*Techumin* 4:324-325), Rav Shaul Yisraeli (*Techumin* 7:312), and Rav Hershel Schachter (*The Journal of Halacha and Contemporary Society* 9:143-160) espouse a different approach, saving Ethiopian Jews from *mamzeirut* by virtue of a *safeik s'feika* (a double doubt). First, they argue, there was so much intermarriage, coupled with the improper performance of conversion ceremonies, that many of today's Ethiopian Jews are descendants of non-Jews. As non-Jews, the problem of *mamzeirut* does not apply to them (see *Kiddushin* 66b). Rav Herzog adds that perhaps they were all originally non-Jews who improperly converted to Judaism and thus remained non-Jews. Dr. Karen Bacon (*The Torah U-Madda Journal* 3:1-7) uses genetic tests to prove that Ethiopian Jewry contains a large number of people who were originally non-Jewish.[11]

Even if they are Jews, each Ethiopian Jew is only a *safeik mamzeir* (a possible *mamzeir*), as it is not known which individuals descend from women who remarried without halachic divorces. In light of this double doubt, Rav Herzog, Rav Yisraeli, and Rav Schachter argue that, after the completion of the conversion process in Israel, Ethiopian Jews may marry within the ranks of the Jewish people.

---

10. We discuss the halachic status of marriages without valid ceremonies in section II of this book.

11. See *Nefesh Harav* (p. 53 note 26), where Rav Hershel Schachter cites sources to demonstrate that historical evidence may be used to establish the necessary facts for a halacihc ruling. Two letters criticizing Dr. Bacon's study appear in the subsequent volume of *The Torah U-Madda Journal*, and she ably responds to both of them (pp. 243-245).

Conclusion

Most authorities require the Falash Mura, as well as other Ethiopian Jews, to undergo a conversion. While some doubt surrounds the Falash Mura's status, Rav Waldman advocates saving them, along with rest of Ethiopian Jewry. It should be noted that Rav Waldman published his essay in 1996, but since then thousands more of the Falash Mura have requested to immigrate to Israel. At present, many in Israel have questioned the sincerity of these potential immigrants' commitment to Judaism, as well as challenging Rav Waldman's claims about the observance of the Falash Mura already living in Israel. This author lacks access to reliable sources of information for accurately evaluating the present religious dedication of the Falash Mura in Ethiopia or Israel.

Should Yeshivah Students Serve in the Israeli Army?

Throughout the State of Israel's short existence, it has granted military exemptions to full-time Yeshivah students. These exemptions and the decision by some Yeshivah students to serve in the army nonetheless have both generated much debate and discussion.

Should a Spiritual Person Serve in an Army?

People often ask, how can someone thoroughly engrossed in spiritual matters serve in the army, a rugged and physically intense experience? Our own male role models answer this question. Avraham, Moshe, Yehoshua, and David all scaled the heights of spirituality, yet they excelled at waging war. The Gemara (*Mo'ed Katan* 16b) describes this phenomenon, "[David] would soften himself as a worm when he studied Torah, but he hardened himself like wood when he fought in war."

Rav Yehuda Amital (*Hama'alot Mima'amakim*, pp. 62-63) cites David's model as a paradigm for *hesder* students. They grapple with the subtlety of a great Talmudic commentary, such as "*Ketzot*," "*Netivot*," or "Reb Chaim," while on the other hand serving with great distinction in the Israeli army. Indeed, it is widely reported that religiously observant soldiers comprise a significant percentage of the junior officers in certain Israeli army units (although these officers do not necessarily participate in the *hesder* program).

Other sources similarly describe holy people as potent warriors. The Rambam (*Hilchot Melachim*, Chapter 11) presents a profile of the Messiah. He studies Torah and is devoted to the

SHOULD YESHIVAH STUDENTS SERVE IN THE ISRAELI ARMY?

Written and Oral Torah. He will compel the entire Jewish people to follow the Torah, and he will lead the nation in battle. The Ramban (*Bereishit* 26:29) explains what motivated Philistine kings to make covenants with our forefathers, who led a small nomadic tribe, seemingly posing little threat to the Philistine emperor:

> Avraham was very great and mighty, as he had in his house three hundred sword-bearing men and many allies. He himself was a lion-hearted soldier who pursued and vanquished four very powerful kings. When his success became evident as being divinely ordained, the Philistine king feared him, lest he conquer his kingdom... And the son emulated the father, as Yitzchak was great like [Avraham], and the king was afraid to fight him, lest [the king] be driven from his land.

Aside from these individuals, the Bible contains other examples of wars where the spiritual elite fought. Rashi (*Bemidbar* 31:3) asserts that the soldiers in the wars against *Amaleik* (*Shemot* 17:8-16) and *Midyan* (*Bemidbar* 31) were specifically chosen based on their religious piety. The Radak and Malbim (*Shofetim* 5:14) explain that, after defeating the army of Canaan, the prophetess Devorah gave special praise to the people of Machir and Zevulun precisely because their religious leaders fought in the battle. All of these sources clearly teach that no fundamental problem exists with spiritual leaders serving in an army. The advisability of their service in the Israeli army today, however, remains to be determined.

The Model of the Tribe of Levi

Some point to the tribe of Levi as a model for those who study and teach Torah full- time, while never serving in the army. Indeed, the Rambam's concluding remarks in *Hilchot Shemitah Veyoveil* (13:12-13) depict the tribe of Levi in this manner, "**They do not wage war** like the rest of Israel, nor do they inherit land in Israel." Moreover, the Rambam writes:

GRAY MATTER

[Being a part of the spiritual elite] applies not to the tribe of Levi alone, but to each and every person throughout the world whose spirit has uplifted him and whose intelligence has given him the understanding to stand before God, to serve Him, to worship Him, to know God; and he walks upright, since he has cast off from his neck the many considerations which people seek. Such a person has been sanctified as the Holy of Holies, and the Lord shall be his portion... forever and ever, and shall grant him adequacy in this world, as he has granted to the *Kohanim* and the Levites. As David... says, "Oh Lord, the Portion of my inheritance and of my cup, You maintain my lot."

This passage is often cited to excuse contemporary Yeshivah students from serving in the Israeli army. This application, however, contains several possible problems. The Rambam often ends sections of the *Mishneh Torah* with aggadic (non-legal) statements. Thus, perhaps he does not intend his comments at the end of *Hilchot Shemitah Veyoveil*, which conclude *Sefer Zera'im*, as a technical legal assertion. Furthermore, the Rambam points to King David, one of our greatest military leaders, as an example of such a spiritual person, so the Rambam might not intend to apply the parallel with Levi to military exemptions. Even if one does accept such an application, it remains unclear to what percentage of the population such a grand description applies.[1]

---

1. Rav Aharon Lichtenstein (*Tradition*, 19:199-217) writes the following pragmatic point regarding the application of the Rambam's words:
> [The Rambam] presents and idealizes the portrait of a selfless, temporal, almost ethereal person - one whose spirit and intelligence have led him to divest himself of all worldly concerns and who has devoted himself "to stand before God, to serve Him, to worship, to know [Him]"... To how large a segment of the Torah community - or *a fortiori*, of any community - does this lofty typology apply? To two percent? Five percent? Can anyone... confront a mirror and tell himself that he ought not to go to the army because he is "*Kodesh Kodashim*," *sanctum sanctorum*, in the Rambam's terms?

SHOULD YESHIVAH STUDENTS SERVE IN THE ISRAELI ARMY?

Did Levites Actually Serve in the Army?

The Talmud never states explicitly that the Levites did not serve in the army. The *Sifrei* (commenting on *Bemidbar* 31:4) addresses this issue regarding the war between the Jews and *Midyan*, but textual variants lead to opposing conclusions. Rashi's text of the *Sifrei* (in his commentary on that verse), understands that the Torah **includes** ("*lerabot*") Levi in the army that fought against *Midyan*. However, the Gra's text of the *Sifrei* reads "to **exclude** (*lehotzi*) the tribe of Levi" from that war. This passage in the *Sifrei* thus proves nothing about Levi's role in the army.

While the Rambam does mention Levi's military exemption at the end of *Hilchot Shemitah Veyoveil*, it is uncertain how much weight this carries, because he does not present this rule in *Hilchot Melachim*, where he discusses military exemptions at length. In fact, the Radak (*II Shmuel* 23:20) claims that in wars against the enemies of Israel, even the *Kohanim* (the most sanctified part of the tribe of Levi), who ordinarily avoid contact with dead bodies, must take an active part in killing the enemy.[2] David's great warrior, Benayahu ben Yehoyada, exemplified this practice. Despite being a *Kohein*, he served as a high-ranking officer in King David's army and eventually became the head of King Shlomo's army. Moreover, the Gemara (*Kiddushin* 21b) and the Rambam (*Hilchot Melachim* 8:4) discuss the laws of a *Kohein* who fights in wars, indicating that this was done in practice.[3]

On the other hand, whenever the Torah takes a census of those who are fit to wage war ("*kol yotzei tzava*"), it excludes the tribe of Levi, implying that this tribe does not fight in the army. The Rashbam (*Bemidbar* 1:47) even refers explicitly to their

---

2. From the Radak's comment in *I Melachim* (2:25), it sounds as if he only believes that *Kohanim* are **permitted** (but not obligated) to take part in fighting enemies. However, he writes there that he is merely restating what he wrote in *II Shmuel* 23:20.
3. The Talmud discusses whether a *Kohein* is permitted to take an *eishet yefat to'ar* (see *Devarim* 21:10-14).

exclusion for the army. Hence, using the Levites as a paradigm for excusing Torah scholars from serving in the army remains debatable, for the status of Levi is itself uncertain.[4]

Milchamot Mitzvah

In Halachah, there are two types of wars (see *Sotah* 44b). One type, *milchamot reshut* ("discretionary wars"), consists of wars fought to enlarge the borders of Israel and wars fought to bring glory to its king.[5] The other type, *milchamot mitzvah*, includes wars against *Amaleik* and the seven Canaanite tribes. The Rambam (*Hilchot Melachim* 5:1) also categorizes "saving the Jewish people from enemies who have attacked them" as a *milchemet mitzvah*. It follows from the Rambam that all the wars that the State of Israel has fought should be classified as *milchamot mitzvah*, for almost everyone regards them as saving Jewish people from enemies who have attacked them.[6]

While the Mishnah (*Sotah* 43a) lists those people who need not fight in battle,[7] it later (44b) limits these exemptions. The Mishnah rules that they only apply to a *milchemet reshut*, "but in a *milchemet mitzvah* everyone must go fight, even a groom from his

---

4. For a complete discussion of the status of Levi in the army, see Rav Yehoshua Hagar-Lau's *Ha'oz Veha'anavah* (pp.127-141).
5. For further discussion of *milchamot reshut*, see Rav Yehuda Amital's article in *Techumin* (8:454-461).
6. See *Contemporary Halakhic Problems* (1:13-18) and Rav Shlomo Yosef Zevin's *Le'or Hahalachah* (p. 65).
7. These people include one who has bought, inherited, or built a new house or storehouse, but did not yet use it; one who is in his first year of using a house or storehouse; one who plants, buys, inherits, or grafts (within one species) either a new vineyard or five fruit trees, but has not yet reaped their fruits; one who is in his first year of reaping fruits from either a vineyard or five trees; one who is halachically engaged (*me'oras*) or has to perform a levirate marriage (*yibum*); one who is in his first year of marriage; and one who is afraid to go to battle. Interestingly, this list includes neither Levites nor Torah scholars.

chamber and a bride from her canopy." In fact, the *Keren Orah* (*Sotah* 44b) writes explicitly, "Everyone must participate in a *milchemet mitzvah*. **Even Torah scholars** must interrupt their studies."[8]

Preemptive Strikes

As we have already noted, the Rambam considers defensive wars to be *milchamot mitzvah*. It is unclear from his language if this includes preemptive strikes to deter a threatening enemy.[9] Determining the status of such wars is critical for establishing whether those who are exempt from *milchamot reshut* must take part in such attacks.

In order to understand the status of preemptive attacks, we must first solve a more basic problem. The Rambam's categorization of a war to defend the Jewish people as a *milchemet mitzvah* appears to contradict the Gemara (*Sotah* 44b). The Gemara considers attacking a nation to prevent it from eventually attacking Israel a *milchemet reshut*. Explaining the Rambam's ruling in light of this passage in the Gemara determines the status of preemptive attacks.

The *Lechem Mishneh* (*Hilchot Melachim* 5:1) claims that a battle fought purely to intimidate an enemy (so that it will not dare to attack Israel) is in fact a *milchemet reshut* (as indicated by the Gemara). When the Rambam describes a *milchemet mitzvah*, the *Lechem Mishneh* implies, he only includes military activities that respond to an actual enemy attack. It seems that according to the *Lechem Mishneh*, preemptive strikes might not be *milchamot mitzvah*, although it is not entirely clear where he draws the line between offensive and defensive battles.

---

8. See Maharsha (*Sotah* 10a s.v. *Mipnei*). He asserts that a *chatan* (bridegroom) must fight in a *milchemet mitzvah*, and it is unclear from his language if he also applies this obligation to a Torah scholar. Also see *Chatam Sofer* (*Bava Batra* 7b).

9. See Rav Avraham Sherman's essay in *Techumin* (7:336-350).

GRAY MATTER

The *Aruch Hashulchan He'atid* (*Hilchot Melachim* 74:3-4) strongly disagrees with the *Lechem Mishneh* and writes that "it's obvious beyond any doubt" that a king must preemptively attack anyone who poses a threat to the Jewish people. The *Aruch Hashulchan* asserts that the Rambam describes even offensive strikes to save Jews as *milchamot mitzvah*. However, the *Aruch Hashulchan* suggests, all defensive wars differ from wars against *Amaleik* and the tribes of Canaan. A nation can usually launch strikes to enhance its security without the entire nation's participation, so the standard exemptions from the army apply to such a war. In this sense, defending Jews is like a *milchemet reshut*, as the Gemara indicated.[10]

Ha'osek Bemitzvah Patur Min Hamitzvah

The Talmud (*Berachot* 11a and *Sukkah* 25a) posits the rule of *ha'osek bemitzvah patur min hamitzvah* - while one is involved in the performance of one *mitzvah*, he is excused from performing another one. The Ra'ah and Ritva (*Sukkah* 25a) assert that not only is the one involved in performing a *mitzvah* **excused** from other *mitzvot*, but he is **forbidden** to perform them. Accordingly, some argue that Yeshivah students engage in constant Torah study, so they may not abandon their learning to serve in the Israeli army. This suggestion is somewhat problematic, because we generally assumed that *ha'osek bemitzvah patur min hamitzvah* does not apply to Torah study.[11] The Gemara (*Mo'eid Katan* 9a-9b) explains that if others are not able to perform a specific *mitzvah*, the student must interrupt his studies to perform that *mitzvah*. This being the case, Torah scholars should be obligated to serve in the Israeli army as long as the army needs them.

---

10. For further discussion of this issue, see *Contemporary Halakhic Problems* (3:251-292). Rav Avraham Sherman dedicates a significant portion of his aforementioned essay to determining the halachic status of the Lebanon War of the early 1980s.

11. See, however, Rav Aharon Lichtenstein's article in *Sefer Kavod Harav*, pp. 187-201, where he suggests that *oseik bemitzvah patur min hamitzvah* fundamentally applies to Torah study.

SHOULD YESHIVAH STUDENTS SERVE IN THE ISRAELI ARMY?

Rav Zalman Melamed (*Techumin* 7:330-334) argues, however, that the Israeli army (in 1986) can function without the service of every man in the country. If he is correct, Torah study could exempt Torah scholars based on *haoseik bemitzvah patur min hamitzvah*, as others perform the *mitzvah* to defend Israel. Furthermore, the democratically elected government of Israel releases those who study in Yeshivah from the army (albeit due to political considerations). Rav Moshe Feinstein (*Teshuvot Igrot Moshe, Yoreh De'ah* 4:33) writes that this governmental exemption constitutes recognition that those who sincerely study Torah deserve a draft exemption. He consequently rules that one who has a strong desire to learn Torah and strives to become great in Torah scholarship should study in Yeshivah and avoid the draft. This idea may be especially true if the army itself does not desire to draft Yeshivah student. Writing in 1986, Rav Avraham Sherman (*Techumin* 7:343) notes that many in the army's top brass do not believe that it will benefit the army to draft those Yeshivah students who want exemptions.

Rabanan Lo Tzrichei Netiruta

Rav Yechiel Michel Tukachinsky (*Hatorah Vehamedinah*, reprinted in *Betzomet Hatorah Veham'dinah* 3:212-213) exempts Yeshivah students from the Israeli army based on the Gemara's statement that rabbis need not contribute towards the construction of a protective wall around their town (*Bava Batra* 8a). The Gemara explains that this exemption exists since "rabbis do not require protection" ("*rabanan lo tzrichei netiruta*"). Similarly, argues Rav Tukachinsky, rabbis need not serve in the army, as they do not require protection.

Rav Yehudah Shaviv (*Techumin* 1:37) cites the *Chatam Sofer*'s opinion that the Gemara only excuses rabbis from paying communal taxes, but they still must fight in defensive wars. Rav Aharon Lichtenstein (*Techumin* 7:314-329 and *Tradition* 19:199-217) also asserts that one would have to reach a very high spiritual level to fall into the category of those who do not require protection.

GRAY MATTER

The aforementioned Gemara also exempts rabbis from actively participating in communal construction projects. Rav Tukachinsky bases the exemption of Yeshivah students on this Halachah as well. Rav Shaviv, however, claims that the Rambam cites this Halachah (*Hilchot Talmud Torah* 6:10), yet he never compares communal construction projects to military service. Hence, Rav Shaviv argues, Torah scholars are not exempt from military service.

Regarding the Israeli army today, one might suggest that Rav Tukachinsky and Rav Shaviv's debate depends upon the type of unit in which one would serve. Combat units involve directly defending the people of Israel, so their soldiers do more than just routine community service. However, those soldiers who have profiles[12] numbering lower than 72 generally may not serve in combat units. These soldiers (colloquially known as "*jobnikim*") perform all kinds of activities, ranging from gathering intelligence information (which may directly save lives) to mowing the lawn at army bases. Those "*jobnikim*" who would do the latter type of jobs might have a stronger claim that their work is a communal contribution which has little to do with fighting *milchamot mitzvah*. As such, studying Torah should exempt them from service.[13]

Aggadic Statements

A number of aggadic (non-legal) statements appear in the Talmud that are commonly cited to support exempting Torah scholars from army service.[14]

---

12. "Profiles" are numbers, no higher than ninety nine, that the army assigns to each soldier based on his physical and mental fitness.
13. The status of one's obligation to participate in communal projects from wh.ich he does not benefit is complex. See Rav Lichtenstein's aforementioned article in *Techumin* for further discussion.
14. In general, aggadic segments of the Talmud are not legally binding. For example, Rav Yechezkel Landau (*Teshuvot Noda Biy'hudah, Yoreh De'ah* 2:61) writes, "Midrashic and aggadic statements are intended solely to teach theology and ethics; they are not written with the intention of deciding

SHOULD YESHIVAH STUDENTS SERVE IN THE ISRAELI ARMY?

Rav Eliezer Waldenberg (*Hilchot Medinah* 3:3:4) cites an aggadic statement from the Gemara (*Makkot* 10a) to prove that Yeshivah students do not have to serve in the army. The Gemara states:

> What is the meaning of the [Psalmist's] words "Our feet stood within thy gates, oh Jerusalem"? [It is this:] What enabled us to "stand" in war? The gates of Jerusalem - the place where students engaged in the study of Torah.

Rav Waldenberg and many others explain this text to mean that Yeshivah students do not have to serve in the army, because their study enables the soldiers to succeed. One could argue, however, that if this were truly the case, there would be an unambiguous halachic source exempting Yeshivah students from military service. Rather, perhaps the Talmud is referring to the studies of those people who cannot serve in the army due to illness or age.

Another frequently cited source supporting military exemption appears in *Masechet Nedarim* (32a):

> Rabi Avahu said in the name of Rabi Elazar, "Why was our father Avraham punished by having his descendants pressed into Egyptian servitude for two hundred and ten years? Because he coerced Torah scholars into serving in his army."

A similar idea appears in *Sotah* (10a), explaining why King Asa was stricken with illness at the end of his life. The Gemara suggests that he was punished for using Torah scholars in his army. It is important to note that Rabi Elazar's opinion is only one of several possible causes that the Gemara cites for the

---

halachot. Therefore, one may not base a halachic ruling on them." Nonetheless, the precise legal status of aggadic statements is somewhat complicated; see *Encyclopedia Talmudit* 1:132.

enslavement in Egypt, and the other opinions might disagree with his idea. Furthermore, Rav Lichtenstein asserts that, at most, these texts contend that the Israeli Government should not coerce Yeshivah students into army service. They do not necessarily serve as a basis for the Yeshivah students' lack of initiative to serve.

Other Considerations

Rav Lichtenstein writes that serving in the Israeli army constitutes an act of great kindness. It also fulfills the Torah's command, "Do not to stand idly by your brother's blood" ("*Lo ta'amod al dam rei'echa*" - Vayikra 19:16). In addition, these students are performing the great *mitzvah* of *yishuv Eretz Yisrael* - settling and developing the Land of Israel. On the other hand, those who opt to learn in Yeshivah and avoid military service believe that they contribute toward the spiritual development of the Land of Israel. They also feel that their Torah study helps ensure that God protects the people of Israel physically. Furthermore, Rav Avraham Sherman (*Techumin* 7:336-350) reports that, during his tenure as an army chaplain, he witnessed many observant Jews who abandoned Torah and *mitzvot* after their experiences in the IDF influenced them negatively.[15]

Conclusion

There does seem to be a strong halachic basis for claiming that there is a *mitzvah* to serve in the IDF, as it defends the Jewish people. Nonetheless, many rabbis argue that service in the Israel Defense Forces is a *mitzvah* that others, who do not study full-time, are able to perform. However, there are prominent rabbis, such as Rav Aharon Lichtenstein, who view army service for Yeshivah students as a moral imperative.

---

15. Rav Sherman's printed his article in 1986. It should be noted that much progress has been made since that time to improve the situation of religious soldiers. Nonetheless, units still exist where it is difficult to remain religious.

LAWS OF SHABBAT

The Laws of Creating an Eruv
Part I: Defining the Four Domains

The construction of *eruvin* has generated much controversy in many Jewish communities. Our extended discussion seeks to shed light on the various opinions and practices regarding *eruvin* and thereby encourage mutual respect for the different practices regarding the use of *eruvin* today.

Disagreements about creating an *eruv* center around three primary issues: whether an area is suitable for creating an *eruv*, how to create the *eruv*, and how to rent the enclosed area in a democratic society. We will begin by discussing which areas are appropriate for creating *eruvin*.

The Four Domains

The Gemara (*Shabbat* 6a) delineates four domains (*reshuyot*) for the laws of *Shabbat*. A **reshut hayachid** (private domain) is surrounded by walls of a minimum height of 10 *tefachim* (about 40 inches),[1] and has a minimum area of four *tefachim* by four *tefachim*. Common examples of a *reshut hayachid* include buildings and fenced-in yards. One is permitted to carry within a *reshut hayachid* on *Shabbat*.[2]

---

1. A *tefach* is a handbreadth, which is between three and four inches. See *Encyclopedia Talmudit* 20:659.
2. However, in certain situations, it is necessary to perform *sechirat reshut* and *eruv chatzeirot*, as is explained in part four of our discussion of the laws of *eruvin*.

GRAY MATTER

A **reshut harabim** (public domain) is an area where carrying on *Shabbat* is forbidden, such as a city square or a street that passes directly from one end of town to the other. It must be at least 16 *amot* (about 28 feet)[3] wide, unroofed, and with less than three walls (see *Shabbat* 99a).[4] Rav Hershel Schachter points out that a *reshut harabim* must not be private property (*The Journal of Halacha and Contemporary Society*, 5:12, based on *Eruvin* 59a). Some opinions maintain that 600,000 people must pass through it daily, and we will discuss this debate later. Additionally, some authorities consider any inter-city highway a *reshut harabim*, even if it does not meet all of the other requirements (Ramban, *Eruvin* 59a).[5] Carrying four *amot* (about six to seven feet) within a *reshut harabim* on *Shabbat* is biblically prohibited, as is carrying from a *reshut hayachid* into a *reshut harabim* and vice versa.

A **mekom petur** (literally an "exempt site") is a place within a *reshut harabim* whose area is less than four *tefachim* by four *tefachim* (see *Mishnah Berurah* 345:30). It must also be **either** at least three *tefachim* high **or** enclosed by walls that are three *tefachim* high. One may carry into or out of a *reshut harabim* or a

---

3. For summaries of the various opinions regarding the size of an *amah*, see *Encyclopedia Talmudit* (2:28-29).
4. There is some debate regarding the question of whether such a street also makes all public areas in its town into a *reshut harabim*. This will be discussed when we address the various cities in which this issue arose.
5. See Rav Hershel Schachter's essay in *The Journal of Halacha and Contemporary Society* (5:13). Rav Schachter has told this author that only a limited-access highway falls into this category. For example, Rav Schachter believes that New Jersey Route 34 (in the Matawan *eruv*) and Route 46 (in the Parsippany *eruv*) are **not** highways for this purpose. These roads may thus be included inside *tzurot hapetach*. Also see *Teshuvot Bnei Banim* (1:19, pp. 66-67) and *Aruch Hashulchan* (O.C. 345:26), both of whom rule more leniently than Rav Schachter. It should be noted that the Jerusalem *eruv* includes Israel's Route 1 (Jerusalem-Tel Aviv highway). See *The Contemporary Eruv* (p. 54 note 119), where Rav Eliezer Waldenberg is cited in defense of including Route 1 in the *eruv*.

THE LAWS OF CREATING AN ERUV PART I

reshut hayachid from a *mekom petur*. Common examples include narrow garbage cans and fire hydrants. It is widely accepted that a *mekom petur* exists only in a *reshut harabim*.[6]

The fourth and final domain is a ***karmelit***. In this domain, it is rabbinically forbidden to carry. A *karmelit* is essentially any place that does not fit the descriptions of the other domains. This includes the sea and all public places that do not meet the requirements of a *reshut harabim*.[7]

Converting into a Reshut Hayachid

In order to facilitate carrying in *karmeliyot* and *reshuyot harabim*, these areas must be transformed into private domains. Since the prohibition against carrying in a *karmelit* is only rabbinical in nature, the rabbis made it relatively easy to change a *karmelit* into a *reshut hayachid*. Surrounding it with *tzurot hapetach* (doorframes) renders the *karmelit* an enclosed area. A *tzurat hapetach* consists of a horizontal wire (or pole) that passes over the tops of two vertical poles, forming the shape of a doorway.

Rav Yehudah Halevi (*Kuzari* 3:51) explains why the rabbis provided a relatively simple way to remove the prohibition of carrying in a *karmelit*, by ruling that *tzurot hapetach* are sufficient to convert a *karmelit* into a *reshut hayachid*. He suggests that they made this enactment to prevent treating rabbinical restrictions with the same severity as the Torah's restrictions and to provide the Jewish people with some freedom of movement on *Shabbat*.

---

6. The Rama (O.C. 345:19) cites two opinions regarding whether or not a *makom petur* can also exist in a *karmelit*. The *Mishnah Berurah* (345:87) notes that most *Acharonim* incline to recognize the status of *mekom petur* only in a *reshut harabim*, and the *Aruch Hashulchan* (O.C. 345:45) rules accordingly. Also see *Biur Halachah* s.v. *V'yeish Cholkim*.

7. For a brief summary of the laws concerning these four domains, see Rav Shimon Eider's *Halachos of the Eruv* (pp. 1-4).

GRAY MATTER

The conversion of a *reshut harabim* into a *reshut hayachid* is much more difficult, because the prohibition of carrying in a *reshut harabim* is biblical. A wall or fence must surround the *reshut harabim* in order to change its status.[8] If a *reshut harabim* is enclosed on all sides by doors at night, it ceases to be a *reshut harabim*.[9] The classic example of this phenomenon appears in *Eruvin* (22a), where the Gemara states that "had Jerusalem's doors not been locked in the evenings, the city would have been considered a *reshut harabim*." In a few locations in the United Sates, "doors" have been "installed" to encompass an area that might otherwise constitute a *reshut harabim*.[10]

Does a Reshut Harabim Require 600,000 People?

In light of the halachic differences between them, it is quite important to determine if an area is a true *reshut harabim* or merely a *karmelit*. The precise definitions of these categories have been debated since the time of the earliest *Rishonim*. The main point of contention is whether an area requires 600,000 people to attain the status of a *reshut harabim*.

Rishonim

The Rambam (*Hilchot Shabbat* 14:1) does not mention that 600,000 people must be present for an area to be considered a

---

8. A fence whose vertical and horizontal links are less than three *tefachim* apart is the halachic equivalent of a solid wall, based on the concept of *lavud*. This principle considers a gap of less than three *tefachim* to be closed off.
9. While walls undoubtedly turn a *reshut harabim* into a *reshut hayachid*, it is unclear whether doors achieve the same result. The *Avnei Neizer* (O.C. 280) believes they do make the *reshut harabim* into a *reshut hayachid*. On the other hand, the *Chazon Ish* (*Orach Chaim* 78:1) argues that doors transform a *reshut harabim* into a *karmelit*, but all breaches still require *tzurot hapetach* in order to permit carrying within the enclosed area on *Shabbat*.
10. See *Netivot Shabbat* (Chapter 23) for a general review of the literature regarding doors that eliminate the status of *reshut harabim*.

THE LAWS OF CREATING AN ERUV PART I

reshut harabim. Rashi (*Eruvin* 6a s.v. *Reshut Harabim* and *Eruvin* 59a s.v. *Ir*), however, writes that a city that does not regularly have 600,000 people is not a *reshut harabim*, because it has less population than the Jews' encampment in the desert. · The practices and the activities of the Jewish encampment in the desert as recorded in the Torah serve as the paradigm for forbidden activities on *Shabbat* (see *Shabbat* 73b-74a). *Tosafot* (*Eruvin* 6a s.v. *Keitzad*) record that the *Behag* agrees with Rashi, whereas Rabbeinu Tam finds Rashi's opinion problematic.

A major problem with the opinion requiring 600,000 people for a *reshut harabim* is that the Gemara (*Shabbat* 6a) describes at length what constitutes a *reshut harabim*, without any explicit mention of requiring 600,000 people. Surely, the Gemara would not omit such a critical part of defining a *reshut harabim*. Rav Aharon Lichtenstein has told this author that he believes the opinion of Rashi and the *Behag* is among the most singularly difficult opinions of *Rishonim* in all of Halachah!

The Shulchan Aruch and its Commentaries

The *Shulchan Aruch* (*Orach Chaim* 345:7) cites (and presumably accepts) the view that an area is a *reshut harabim* even without 600,000 people, although he does cite the other view as a secondary opinion.[11] The Rama (O.C. 346:3) indicates that he accepts the requirement of 600,000.[12] Both the *Magen*

---

11. The *Shulchan Aruch*'s view is somewhat unclear, as he appears to contradict himself in *Orach Chaim* (303:18). There he writes that no places today qualify as *reshuyot harabim*. Presumably, his reason is that he requires 600,000 people for a *reshut harabim*. Regarding the practice of Sephardic Jews today, see *Yabia Omer* (vol. 4, *Orach Chaim* 47:4) and page 7 of Rav Mordechai Eliyahu's comments to Rav Zechariah Ben-Shlomo's *Hilchot Tzava*.
12. This is inferred from the Rama's statement that in our day there are no *reshuyot harabim*. While logic would dictate that the Rama is writing this because he believes that only a place with 600,000 people constitutes a *reshut harabim*, this inference presents a certain difficulty. The *Shulchan Aruch* (*Orach Chaim* 303:18) also writes that there are no true *reshuyot*

169

GRAY MATTER

Avraham (345:7) and the *Taz* (345:6) cite the view of the *Ma'sat Binyamin* (92) and the Maharshal (*Yam Shel Shlomo, Beitzah* 3:8), who rule that the presence of 600,000 people is not required. However, the *Magen Avraham* and *Taz* themselves disagree with these authorities and write that the majority view is that of Rashi, requiring 600,000 people. The *Aruch Hashulchan* (345:17) writes that the *eruvin* in the Jewish towns of Eastern Europe relied on this accepted leniency; otherwise, they could not have used *tzurot hapetach*.

The Mishkenot Yaakov's Criticism

In the early nineteenth century, the *Mishkenot Yaakov* (*Orach Chaim* 119-122) strongly criticized the construction of the Eastern European *eruvin*. His criticisms included the fact that their wires sagged,[13] and there were no places for hinges on the *tzurot hapetach* (as there are on true doorways).[14] Most of all, *tzurot hapetach* were used to create the *eruvin*, since the towns and villages were seen as *karmeliyot*. He asserted that the opinions of many more *Rishonim* had been published since the time of the *Shulchan Aruch*.[15] The discovery that many of these *Rishonim* rejected Rashi's opinion rendered his opinion that requires 600,000 people a **minority** opinion, whereas it had previously been considered the majority view. He argued that even the small towns and villages of Central and Eastern Europe should now be considered *reshuyot harabim*.

---

harabim, yet he appears to rule that 600,000 people are **not** required for a *reshut harabim* (O.C. 345:7). The *Magen Avraham* (345:7) points out this problem.

13. Sagging wires are problematic, because a *tzurat hapetach* must be constructed in the same manner as people makes ordinary doorframes (*ked'avdei inshei*; see *Eruvin* 94b). We will address this at greater length in our third chapter about *eruvin*.

14. See *Eruvin* 11b. Our practice is not to require a place for hinges; see *Aruch Hashulchan* 362:31.

15. See Rav Moshe Bleich's article, "The Role of Manuscripts in Halachic Decision Making" (*Tradition* 27:2:22-55), regarding the halachic weight of newly discovered manuscripts of *Rishonim*.

THE LAWS OF CREATING AN ERUV PART I

Reaction to the Mishkenot Yaakov's Criticism

Halachic authorities expressed mixed reactions to the *Mishkenot Yaakov*'s criticism. The *Beit Efraim* (26) defended the practice to rely on *eruvin* consisting of *tzurot hapetach*. The *Aruch Hashulchan* (362:18) wrote in the late nineteenth century that it was as if a heavenly voice proclaimed that the opinion requiring 600,000 people for a *reshut harabim* was [still] correct.

The *Mishnah Berurah*[16] strongly urges pious individuals (*ba'alei nefesh*) to be strict and refrain from carrying within an *eruv* that is based on the lenient opinion. However, he writes that one should not rebuke those who do rely on such *eruvin*. For a summary of this issue, see Rav Elimelech Lange's *Hilchot Eruvin* (21-28).

It is interesting to note that even those who are strict and do not rely on an *eruv* might be permitted to ask a Jew who does use the *eruv* to carry for them (see *Teshuvot Igrot Moshe*, O.C. 1:186).[17]

---

16. 345:23 and *Biur Halachah* s.v. *She'ein Shishim*.

17. Rav Shlomo Zalman Auerbach (*Teshuvot Minchat Shlomo* 1:44) rules that one who embraces the strict opinion in a disputed area of Halachah need not refrain from causing others to follow their practice of relying upon the lenient view. However, he addresses a rabbinical prohibition, and he notes that this matter is subject to debate regarding biblical prohibitions. Regarding *eruvin*, authorities debate whether carrying in a *reshut harabim* enclosed by *tzurot hapetach* is a biblical or rabbinical prohibition; see *Biur Halachah* (364:2 s.v. *Vehu* and s.v. *Ve'achar*). Elsewhere (*Minchat Shlomo* 2:35:17), Rav Shlomo Zalman suggests that one who adopts a *chumra* (stringency beyond the letter of the law) can ask someone who follows the letter of the law to violate this *chumra*. However, if one is strict because he believes a more lenient view to be mistaken, perhaps he should refrain from asking others to violate what he considers an absolute prohibition. (Even in the latter case, Rav Shlomo Zalman does not issue a definitive ruling.) When Ashkenazic and Sephardic communities follow different opinions, Rav Shlomo Zalman implicitly compares such a situation to a *chumrah*, because the one who causes others to act agrees that Jews from the other community need not be stringent.

The Laws of Creating an Eruv
Part II: List of Major Cities

As we explained in the previous chapter, some *Rishonim* requirement 600,000 residents for a city to attain the status of a *reshut harabim*. While this position prevents most towns and cities from having to cope with the issues regarding a *reshut harabim*, larger cities might nonetheless face them. In this chapter, we survey the opinions of contemporary authorities regarding certain specific cities.

Paris: *Rav Chaim Ozer Grodzinski and the Chazon Ish*

In the late 1930s, the rabbis of Paris asked Rav Chaim Ozer Grodzinski (the leading halachic authority at that time) if they could construct an *eruv* consisting of *tzurot hapetach* (vertical poles with strings running atop them) around their city. This method would only suffice if Paris were considered a *karmelit*, as opposed to a *reshut harabim*.

Rav Chaim Ozer consulted with the *Chazon Ish* (one of the most respected authorities in the laws of *eruvin*)[1] as well as the rabbis who supervised the Vilna *eruv*. Rav Chaim Ozer (*Teshuvot Achiezer* 4:8) opens his responsum by noting that over 600,000 people reside in Paris, so seemingly all authorities would consider it a *reshut harabim*. Consequently, an *eruv* consisting of *tzurot hapetach* cannot render it a private domain.

---

1. Rav Hershel Schachter and Rav Chaim Zimbalist have told this author that halachic authorities generally treat the *Chazon Ish* more authoritatively than even the *Mishnah Berurah* in the area of *eruvin*.

THE LAWS OF CREATING AN ERUV PART II

However, he notes that walls surround Paris on three sides, rendering it a *reshut hayachid* on a biblical level. There are bridges that pass over the walls, constituting breaches (*pirtzot*) in them.[2] Nevertheless, Rav Chaim Ozer claims that Paris is a *reshut hayachid* on a purely biblical level, since the walls on these three sides cover most of the perimeter (*omeid merubeh al haparutz*). Rav Chaim Ozer argues that, while any breach over ten *amot* (roughly fifteen to eighteen feet) invalidates a wall on a rabbinical level, breaches are insignificant on a biblical level as long as the majority of each of three sides of the perimeter remains enclosed.[3] Since the breaches in Paris's wall are only problematic on a rabbinical level, the erection of *tzurot hapetach* suffices to permit carrying. Rav Chaim Ozer and the *Chazon Ish* thus conclude that *tzurot hapetach* suffice in Paris.[4]

Warsaw: Rav Shlomo David Kahane

Rav Shlomo David Kahane (the Rav of Warsaw during the 1930s) faced an interesting problem with Warsaw's *eruv*. During

---

2. See *Noda Biy'hudah* (1:42) and *Mishnah Berurah* (*Sha'ar Hatziyun* 363:95).
3. Rav Moshe Feinstein (*Teshuvot Igrot Moshe, Orach Chaim* 2:90) also rules that a breach of more than ten *amot* constitutes a problem only on a **rabbinical** level. See, however, *Mishkenot Yaakov* (120) and *Mishnat Rabbi Aharon* (1:6:12), who disagree and claim that such breaches invalidate the wall on a **biblical** level.
4. Also see *Chazon Ish, Orach Chaim* 107:5-7. He addresses a situation where buildings are close enough to one another that they occupy more space than the open gaps between them. After complex calculations, the *Chazon Ish* rules that, whenever at least one street ends or curves inside the city, it loses the status of *reshut harabim*. For an explanation of his reasoning, see Rav Hershel Schachter's essay in *The Journal of Halacha and Contemporary Society* (5:15-19) and Rav Yosef Gavriel Bechhofer's *The Contemporary Eruv* (pp. 56-66). See *Beit Yitzchak* 5753, pp. 61-69, for Rav Mordechai Willig's thorough analysis of this issue. Rav Willig notes that the Meiri (*Eruvin* 20a s.v. *V'yeish*) appears to agree with the *Chazon Ish*. For criticisms of the *Chazon Ish*, see *Mishnat Rabbi Aharon* (1:6:12) and *Teshuvot Igrot Moshe* (*Orach Chaim* 5:28:1:3). Rav Shlomo Zalman Auerbach (*Minchat Shlomo* 2:35:22) takes the *Chazon Ish*'s view into consideration in case of great need.

It is unclear if Rav Chaim Ozer based his ruling in Paris on this opinion of the *Chazon Ish*.

its construction in the nineteenth century, Warsaw's *eruv* consisted of *tzurot hapetach*. It was effective because fewer than 600,000 people resided within it. However, in the twentieth century, Warsaw's population exceeded 600,000, seemingly invalidating the *eruv*. Rav Kahane (cited by Rav Menachem Kasher in *Noam* 6:34) rules that the *eruv* is nonetheless valid, asserting that the larger a city grows, the less chance there is for any one street to run straight through it, without curving significantly. One requirement for a *reshut harabim* is that a street must go **straight** through the entire city.[5] Accordingly, Warsaw does not meet this requirement and is still not a *reshut harabim*. Rav Moshe Feinstein criticizes this approach (see *Teshuvot Igrot Moshe, Orach Chaim* 1:140), rejecting the argument that the street cannot curve. He claims that a street that runs from one end of town to the other turns it into a *reshut harabim*, curves notwithstanding, provided that it meets the other criteria for a *reshut harabim*. Thus, in a place that meets the other requirements for a *reshut harabim*, *tzurot hapetach* do not suffice.

Flatbush: Rav Yosef Eliyahu Henkin and Rav Moshe Feinstein

During the 1970's, the construction of the *eruv* in Flatbush (a neighborhood of Brooklyn, New York) aroused great controversy. To this day, its permissibility remains disputed. The Va'ad Harabanim of Flatbush permits carrying inside the Flatbush *eruv*, while many rabbis and *rashei yeshivah* there, such as Torah Vodaath's Rav Yisroel Belsky (personal communication), forbid its use.

Rav Yosef Eliyahu Henkin (*Kitvei Hagaon Rav Y.E. Henkin* 2:25) strongly encourages the construction of *eruvin* in New York's five boroughs, including Brooklyn (whose population easily exceeded 600,000 already in his day). Although Rav Henkin does not explain why these places are not *reshuyot harabim*, a number of arguments have been offered to support his contention that Flatbush is not in this category. First, Rav Shlomo David

---

5. See *Shulchan Aruch* (O.C. 345:7) and Rav Mordechai Willig (*Beit Yitzchak* 25:63-65).

THE LAWS OF CREATING AN ERUV PART II

Kahane's argument regarding the Warsaw *eruv* seemingly applies to Flatbush, too, because no street within the Flatbush *eruv* runs straight from one end of the city to the other.[6]

Second, the ruling of Rav Chaim Ozer Grodzinski and the *Chazon Ish* also seems to apply to Flatbush. The faces of the buildings and the fences along the Belt Parkway appear to constitute the majority of a wall on three sides.[7] (Ironically, this lenient consideration is most often applicable in densely populated urban areas rather than smaller suburbs, which frequently have much empty space between buildings.)

Third, the *Aruch Hashulchan*'s unique (but highly questionable) approach might be taken into account (*Orach Chaim* 345:19-24). In his opinion, a street must be the only inter-city thoroughfare or commercial center in that city to be a true *reshut harabim*, with all other streets being minor in comparison. Accordingly, only in the time of the Talmud did true *reshuyot harabim* exist, because it was common for a town to have only one main street.[8] Nowadays, most towns and cities have more than one inter-city thoroughfare and commercial center, so we do not have true *reshuyot harabim*. Brooklyn certainly has multiple commercial centers and inter-city roads, so the *Aruch Hashulchan* would not consider it a *reshut harabim*.

Rav Moshe Feinstein (*Teshuvot Igrot Moshe, Orach Chaim* 4:87) vigorously disputes the *Aruch Hashulchan*'s argument, citing

---

6. Even Flatbush Avenue and Bedford Avenue bend at various points; Ocean Parkway does not extend from one end of Brooklyn to the other.
7. The *Chazon Ish* (O.C. 107:5-7) requires that there be at least one street in the town that either bends or ends inside the town. Brooklyn meets this requirement, as we have explained in the previous footnote.
8. The *Aruch Hashulchan* refers to the *sratiya* and *platiya* described in *Shabbat* (6a). It is unclear if the *Aruch Hashulchan* requires that a *reshut harabim* be **both** the only commercial center **and** the only inter-city route, or if he suffices with **either** condition. See his comments in O.C. 345:26, where it appears that he suffices with **either** condition.

a proof to the contrary from the Gemara (*Shabbat* 96b).[9] The *Divrei Malkiel* (vol. 3, p. 267) also writes that one may not rely on the *Aruch Hashulchan*'s novel insight, since it does not appear in any earlier source. Rav Aharon Lichtenstein (personal communication) conveyed sentiments similar to those of the *Divrei Malkiel* and Rav Moshe. Moreover, a careful reading of the *Aruch Hashulchan* seems to reveal that he sought to use his novel suggestion only as an adjunct (*senif*) to the view that a true *reshut harabim* requires 600,000 people. He never suggests relying on his idea without other grounds for leniency. Accordingly, the *Aruch Hashulchan*'s view cannot be relied upon as the sole reason for permitting carrying within an area that contains more than 600,000 people.

A fourth defense of the Flatbush *eruv* is the opinion of Rav Efraim Zalman Margoliot (*Beit Efraim, Orach Chaim* 26) that only pedestrians count when determining that 600,000 people travel in a street. He argues that the requirement for 600,000 people is based on a comparison to the encampment in the desert. The comparison can thus be made only to pedestrians, as the 600,000 people who were in the quintessential *reshut harabim* were all pedestrians. The Maharsham (1:162) and Rav Eliezer Waldenberg (cited in *The Contemporary Eruv*, p. 54 note 119) add that trains and cars are private domains unto themselves, so their occupants are not counted among the 600,000 people of a *reshut harabim*. Both Rav Moshe (*Teshuvot Igrot Moshe, Orach Chaim* 1:139:6) and Rav Binyamin Silber (*Teshuvot Az Nidberu* 6:70) reject this argument, pointing out that wagons (*agalot*) were used in the desert encampment's thoroughfares.

---

9. The Gemara describes how carrying in a *reshut harabim* occurred during construction of the *mishkan*. This work was not done in the main thoroughfare of the desert encampment, yet the Gemara states that it was done in a *reshut harabim*. Rav Moshe thus concludes that a city, like the desert encampment, can have multiple public centers and still be a *reshut harabim*, thus disproving the *Aruch Hashulchan*'s opinion.

THE LAWS OF CREATING AN ERUV PART II

Despite all of the arguments in favor of being lenient, Rav Moshe did not endorse the construction of the Flatbush *eruv* (see *Teshuvot Igrot Moshe, Orach Chaim* 4:87-88). He explicitly rejects all of the arguments presented and rules that the 600,000 people who regularly travel the streets of Brooklyn render it a *reshut harabim*.[10]

Kew Gardens Hills

Although Rav Moshe did not approve of constructing an *eruv* in Flatbush, he did permit the *eruv* in the Kew Gardens Hills section of Queens, New York. Rav Moshe stipulated the following requirements for the *eruv* to be acceptable:

1) All highways (Grand Central Parkway, Long Island Expressway, Van Wyck Expressway) were excluded from the *eruv*, because many authorities maintain that highways always constitute *reshuyot harabim*.[11] Similarly, the *eruv* in Teaneck, New Jersey excludes Route 4 due to concern that it is a *reshut harabim*.[12]

2) It was constructed in a manner that greatly reduces the possibility of breakage during *Shabbat*. A communal *eruv* that

---

10. Rav Moshe's concern was not for 600,000 **residents** but for 600,000 people **traveling** the streets at any time (drivers and pedestrians) within an area that is twelve *mil* by twelve *mil* (approximately eight miles by eight miles). He thus requires that the population be so great that 600,000 people are regularly found in the streets. Rav Moshe estimates that this requires at least 2.4 million residents. Rav Moshe is the lone authority who requires such a large population, and even he (O.C. 4:87) expresses reservations about his view, noting that no other authorities mention it. Nevertheless, Brooklyn is so populous that even Rav Moshe considers it a *reshut harabim*.
11. See Ramban to *Eruvin* 59a (s.v. *Verash Atzmo*), *Mishnah Berurah* (345:17), and *Teshuvot Bnei Banim* (1:17-20).
12. Route 4 also has the problem that it passes over the *tzurot hapetach* and is thus not encompassed by them (see *Mishnah Berurah* 363:118).

GRAY MATTER

uses as many pre-existing components as possible, such as preexisting telephone poles and wires, fences, hills, and train overpasses (see, however, *Teshuvot Igrot Moshe, Orach Chaim* 1:138), has the greatest chance of remaining intact.

3) An individual was appointed to inspect the *eruv* every Friday; it must be rigorously inspected before every *Shabbat* (see *Teshuvot Doveiv Meisharim*, 2:28, who disapproves of inspecting an *eruv* before Friday).

4) The rabbis of the community were required to approve of the *eruv* and mutually agree that it was built properly, as an *eruv* should promote peace and not be a source of tension within a community (see *Gittin* 59a).

Regarding the issue of *reshut harabim*, Rav Moshe wrote that "Kew Gardens Hills is small regarding these issues and the reasons I wrote [for not allowing an *eruv* in other parts of New York City] do not apply here." Although the borough of Queens has more than 600,000 inhabitants, Rav Moshe apparently viewed Kew Gardens Hills as a separate entity. *Tzurot hapetach* thus sufficed, since fewer than 600,000 people resided in it.

Tel Aviv

Not all halachic authorities agree with Rav Moshe's ruling to view certain neighborhoods as distinct entities within a large city. Rav Shaul Yisraeli (*Techumin* 10:140) writes that a city constitutes one halachic entity for purposes of defining a *reshut harabim*. Moreover, the sole halachic criterion defining an area as a city is a contiguity of homes (see *Shulchan Aruch, Orach Chaim* 398), but not municipal boundaries. Accordingly, he rules that the entire Tel Aviv metropolitan area (known as Gush Dan) should be viewed as one entity regarding the *reshut harabim* issue. Since more than 600,000 people reside in Gush Dan, it constitutes a *reshut harabim*.

THE LAWS OF CREATING AN ERUV PART II

The Tel Aviv *eruv* today consists of *tzurot hapetach*, so Rav Yisraeli offers a suggestion for how Gush Dan may yet be a *karmelit*. He explains that the overwhelming majority of the observant community in Tel Aviv relies on the *eruv* because it follows the *Shulchan Aruch*'s presentation (*Orach Chaim* 345:7) of the view that requires 600,000 people for a *reshut harabim*. He implies that 600,000 people must pass through a **particular street** every day for it to be a public domain. Rav Yisraeli notes that the *Mishnah Berurah* (345:24 and *Sha'ar Hatziyun* 345:25) rules that 600,000 people need not pass through a particular street for the town to be defined as a *reshut harabim*. According to the *Mishnah Berurah*, anywhere with 600,000 residents is a *reshut harabim*.[13]

The residents of Tel Aviv thus rely on an extraordinarily lenient approach. They follow the lenient understanding (*Shulchan Aruch*, to require 600,000 on one street) of the lenient opinion (Rashi, that 600,000 people are required for a *reshut harabim*)! Rav Yisraeli explains that it is possible to be so lenient only because we follow the opinion of those *Rishonim* (cited in *Biur Halachah*, 364:2 s.v. *Ve'achar*) who rule that *tzurot hapetach* suffice on a biblical level for even a *reshut* **harabim**. Because *tzurot hapetach* are only invalid in a *reshut harabim* on a rabbinical level, it is possible to permit lenient practices that would otherwise be unacceptable.

Rav Naaman Wasserzug (*Techumin* 11:163-169) provides a different defense of the Tel Aviv *eruv*. He argues that, on a Torah level, Tel Aviv is a *reshut hayachid*, because it is enclosed by "halachic walls" on three sides.[14] It has the sea on the west, the Ayalon Valley on the east, and the Yarkon Valley on the

---

13. Rav Moshe Feinstein (*Teshuvot Igrot Moshe*, O.C. 4:88) requires that the 600,000 people be within an area which is twelve *mil* by twelve *mil* (approximately eight miles by eight miles).
14. This is similar to the ruling of Rav Chaim Ozer Grodzinski and the *Chazon Ish* concerning Paris.

south.[15] According to this approach, the residents of Tel Aviv are not relying on such a radically lenient ruling.

Conclusion

In addition to the issues discussed in this chapter, this author's experience indicates that virtually every community *eruv* encounters challenges and difficulties during construction and maintenance. Accordingly, before relying on any community *eruv*, one must consult a halachic authority familiar with both the laws of *eruvin* and the details of the *eruv* in question. Our discussion in this chapter only addresses certain issues of interest regarding each *eruv*, but we have not researched the *eruvin* sufficiently to ensure that they are fit for use on *Shabbat*. Furthermore, due to the difficulties in maintaining an *eruv*, no one can ensure that *eruvin* that are presently acceptable will remain this way in the fsuture.[16]

---

15. The Halachah recognizes these places as valid walls; see *Shulchan Aruch* (*Orach Chaim* 345:2 and 362:3).

16. See this author's article "Advice for Proper Eruv Maintenance" in Yeshiva University's *Chavrusa* (April 1993, pp. 5-6).

The Laws of Creating an Eruv
Part III: Constructing the Tzurot Hapetach

In this chapter, we will address several issues that arise during the physical construction of an *eruv*. Before beginning to build and *eruv*, it must be determined if the area is a *reshut harabim* or merely a *karmelit*. If the area is a *karmelit*, surrounding it with *tzurot hapetach* suffices, whereas a *reshut harabim* must be enclosed by a wall, or at least by doors (*Shulchan Aruch*, O.C. 364:2, and *Mishnah Berurah* 364:8).

Constructing Tzurot Hapetach

Constructing a *tzurat hapetach* seems to be a simple and straightforward process. The Talmud (*Eruvin* 11b) states that a *tzurat hapetach* consists of two vertical poles with a horizontal pole directly on top of them (*kaneh mikan vekaneh mikan vekaneh al gabeihen*). However, the laws of *tzurot hapetach* are actually quite complex, particularly when constructing a community *eruv*. Community *eruvin* often use preexisting structures, which can significantly reduce the costs of building and maintaining an *eruv*. These structures, such as telephone poles, were not built for use in *eruvin* and often introduce halachic complexities.[1]

---

1. For an explanation of how such structures may be used as *tzurot hapetach* despite the fact that they were not constructed for this purpose, see *Chazon Ish*, *Orach Chaim* 111:5. See *Mishnah Berurah* (362:64) for more sources on this issue.

GRAY MATTER

Must the Vertical Poles Extend All the Way to the Horizontal One?

The Talmud (*Eruvin* 11b) records a dispute between Rav Nachman and Rav Sheishet about whether the vertical poles of a *tzurat hapetach* must extend all the way to the horizontal pole. The Halachah follows the opinion of Rav Nachman, that if the vertical poles are ten *tefachim* (approximately forty inches) high and are positioned precisely beneath the horizontal pole, the *tzurat hapetach* is acceptable. The horizontal pole need not touch the vertical poles and may be well above them (*Shulchan Aruch*, O.C. 362:11). The *Mishnah Berurah* (362:62) explains that the basis for this ruling is the principle of *gud asik* (literally, "stretch up"), which states that the Halachah views the vertical poles as extending upward to the horizontal pole.

Gud Asik: Eyesight or Plumb Line?

Although vertical poles of a *tzurat hapetach* need not touch the horizontal pole (or wire), they must be positioned directly underneath it. The poles cannot even be off by the slightest amount (see *Mishnah Berurah* 362:63). Halachic authorities debate how to determine the proper positioning.[2] Rav Yosef Dov Soloveitchik (as reported by Rav Yosef Adler) and Rav Moshe

---

2. Measurements for some areas of Halachah are estimated based on what appears correct to people, while other areas require precise measurements. For example, *terumah* (the fiftieth of grain which is given to *kohanim*) must be an estimate and may not be measured to precisely equal one-fiftieth (*Terumot* 1:7). On the other hand, *techum Shabbat* (the area that one may not leave on *Shabbat*) must be measured precisely (*Eruvin* 57b, 58b). In many areas, it is unclear whether an estimate or precise measurement is required. For example, the *Chazon Ish* (*Hil. Tumat Tzaraat* 8:1) writes that measurements for the spreading of a spot of leprosy are done by estimation. He bases himself on a passage in the Ramban's commentary to the Torah (*Vayikra* 13:5). However, the *Chazon Ish* does not mention that the Rosh (*Tosafot Harosh*, *Mo'eid Katan* 7a, cited in the *Tur*'s long commentary to *Vayikra* 13:5) requires the use of measuring implements to determine the leprosy spot's growth.

THE LAWS OF CREATING AN ERUV PART III

Feinstein (reported by Rav Elazar Meyer Teitz, from his uncle, Rav Pesach Rayman) both felt that it is sufficient to estimate the poles' positioning with one's eyes. Rav Zalman Nechemia Goldberg (personal communication) also permits using eyesight, although he requires building very wide vertical beams to allow for a wide margin of error in their positioning.

However, Rav Yitzchak Liebes, Rav J. David Bleich, Rav Hershel Schachter, Rav Feivel Cohen,[3] and Rav Mordechai Willig (all through personal communication) rule that a plumb line (or other device for measuring verticality) is necessary to ensure that everything lines up appropriately. The Gemara (*Eruvin* 94b) requires constructing "halachic walls" (and presumably *tzurot hapetach* as well) in the same manner that people usually build walls (*kede'avdei inshei*).[4] Builders and carpenters have used plumb lines for thousands of years; they appear in Amos (7:7-8) and the Mishnah (for example, *Kil'ayim* 6:9 and *Keilim* 29:3). Accordingly, a plumb line must be used in constructing a *tzurat hapetach*. Rav Shlomo Zalman Auerbach told this author that, while it is best to use a plumb line, one may rely on eyesight alone if it is "impossible" to construct the *eruv* otherwise.[5]

---

3. Rav Cohen believes that two sets of vertical poles must be constructed, one set that appears to be under the horizontal pole and one set that has been measured to be precisely under the horizontal pole (if the position determined by sight differs from the position determined by the plumb line). It is not clear, however, that Rav Moshe and Rav Soloveitchik invalidate an *eruv* that was measured by plumb line. It may be that they also recognize such an *eruv* but add that measuring by eyesight is **also** acceptable. Rav Shlomo Miller (in his letter of approbation for *The Contemporary Eruv*) presents an argument for why constructing an *eruv* with plumb line measurements suffices according to all authorities.

4. The significance of *kede'avdei inshei* is particularly emphasized by Rav Shlomo Kluger (*Teshuvot Ha'elef Lecha Shlomo* 156, 157, 161, 170, 173, 174).

5. Of course, the definition of "impossible" is debatable. Rav Hershel Schachter (in response to what this author quoted from Rav Shlomo Zalman) insisted that it is never impossible to measure precisely, especially with the invention of devices such as laser pointers. Similar to Rav Shlomo

GRAY MATTER

Rav David Lifshitz (Rav of Suwalk immediately before World War II) told this author that a plumb line was used when constructing *tzurot hapetach* in Suwalk. Rav Ephraim Oshry (Rav of the Kovno Ghetto) told this author that in Kovno they relied on eyesight alone. Rav Yosef Singer (Rav of Pilzno prior to World War II) also reported that he believes the rabbis he knew in Europe relied on eyesight alone. Accordingly, this debate has raged for at least 60 years. Rav Meir Goldwicht informed this author that Israeli communities today also have divergent practices regarding this issue. In order to avoid this problem, many communities erect vertical poles that reach the horizontal wire or pole. This method avoids the need to estimate from afar if the pole is directly under the wire.

Tachuv - A Horizontal Wire that Passes Through the Vertical Pole

Another major area of debate in constructing *tzurot hapetach* is the status of "*tachuv*," when the horizontal pole (or wire) does not rest atop the vertical poles, but is drilled through them instead. Cases of *tachuv* frequently arise today, as many wires on utility poles, especially those used for cable television, are attached to bolts that pass into holes in the poles. The issue of *tachuv* arises dozens of times in an average community *eruv*.

The Gemara relates that, in a valid *tzurat hapetach*, the horizontal pole is placed atop the vertical poles. Furthermore, if the vertical poles are not under the horizontal one, but to its side (*tzurat hapetach min hatzad*), the *tzurat hapetach* is unacceptable (*Eruvin* 11b). The Talmud does not specifically address a situation in which the horizontal pole passes through the vertical poles.

Zalman's ruling, the Rama (O.C. 456:3) permits estimating the measurement for separating *challah* when measuring precisely is not feasible (although he addresses a halachic impediment, rather than practical difficulty).

THE LAWS OF CREATING AN ERUV PART III

The *Acharonim* debate the acceptability of such a *tzurat hapetach*. The *Mishnah Berurah* (362:64) notes that the *Pri Megadim* was uncertain regarding this issue and therefore was inclined to rule strictly. On the other hand, Rav Shlomo Kluger (*Ha'elef Lecha Shlomo, Orach Chaim* 164), the *Aruch Hashulchan* (O.C. 362:32), the *Chazon Ish* (O.C. 71:9), and Rav Tzvi Pesach Frank (*Teshuvot Har Tzvi*, O.C. 2:18:3) rule that such *tzurot hapetach* may be used. They argue that, as long as the horizontal pole passes through the vertical poles at a point higher than ten *tefachim* off the ground, the portion of the vertical pole that is above the horizontal pole is ignored.[6] The *Chazon Ish* notes that if a horizontal pole was placed on top of a vertical pole and then another vertical pole was placed on top of the first one, the original *tzurat hapetach* remains acceptable. Similarly, a horizontal wire that passes through a hole in a vertical pole should be acceptable.

This issue has not been resolved; some rabbis rely on the lenient opinion, while others follow the strict one. Rav Dovid Feinstein has told this author that the leniency of *tachuv* should not be employed in community *eruvin*. Rav Shlomo Zalman Auerbach (*Teshuvot Minchat Shlomo* 2:35:25) writes that *tachuv* is undoubtedly acceptable. Rav Yehuda Amital told this author that the practice in Israel is to be lenient on this issue.

Obstructions Between the Vertical Pole and the Horizontal Pole

The *Acharonim* debate whether an obstruction (and not simply an open space) between a vertical pole and a horizontal pole invalidates a *tzurat hapetach*. The *Mishnah Berurah* (363:112) cites the *Taz* as ruling that a *tzurat hapetach* is invalid if a roof interrupts between one of its vertical poles and the horizontal pole or wire. His reasoning seems to be that *gud asik* (the theoretical "stretching" of the vertical pole to reach the horizontal one) only applies when nothing obstructs between the

---

6. The principle of ignoring what is unnecessary is known as *dal meihacha*. See, for example, *Sukkah* 2a.

Gray Matter

poles. An authority cited by the *Melamed Leho'il* (1:66) and an authority cited by the *Aruch Hashulchan* (*Orach Chaim* 363:46) disagree with the *Taz* and see no problem with a tangible separation between the poles. The *Melamed Leho'il* himself argues that obstructions between the vertical and horizontal poles are only forbidden by the *Taz* when they have a length or width greater than four *amot* (six to eight feet).[7] The *Melamed Leho'il* argues that if there is a smaller obstruction, no one invalidates the *tzurat hapetach*.

This question is of major importance when constructing a communal *eruv*, as telephone wires often do not pass directly over the telephone poles. In some communal *eruvin*, small beams are positioned under the desired wires and are then attached to the telephone poles. These poles often contain objects between the vertical beams or strips and the utility wire, such as boxes, campaign posters, and advertising billboards. Communities that attach wire molding to the telephone pole all the way up to the wire avoid this problem entirely.

The Tapered Pole - The Chazon Ish

Telephone and utility poles frequently have wires attached to their sides, rather than on top. It is thus important to determine whether one may use such a wire and pole as a *tzurat hapetach* without affixing additional materials to the telephone pole. One could argue that this would be acceptable, because telephone poles are often thicker on the bottom than they are on top. Therefore, a wire attached to the side of the pole on top passes directly over the extra thickness of the lower part of the pole. Perhaps this thickness constitutes a "vertical pole" of the *tzurat hapetach*. One must check, of course, that the extra thickness at the bottom sticks out under this wire for ten *tefachim* of the pole's height, for every vertical pole in a *tzurat hapetach* must be ten *tefachim* high.

---

7. The *Taz*'s example of an unacceptable obstruction is a roof of a building, which is typically wider than four *amot*.

THE LAWS OF CREATING AN ERUV PART III

Despite the above argument, the *Chazon Ish* (*Orach Chaim* 71:12) invalidates a wire on the side of a tapered pole, without explaining his reasoning. He adds that if there is an indentation cut in the pole, perhaps this pole and wire may then be used for a *tzurat hapetach*. The indentation must be ten *tefachim* above the ground. The accepted practice is to follow the *Chazon Ish*'s stringency.

Placing a Tzurat Hapetach in a Reshut Hayachid

Another important issue in *eruv* construction is whether a component of a *tzurat hapetach* may be located within a *reshut hayachid* (private domain). The *Mishnah Berurah* (363:113) cites the *Mekor Chaim*, who invalidates such a *tzurat hapetach*, and the *Mishnah Berurah* accepts his ruling.

There are two possible reasons for this strict ruling. One might argue that the *tzurat hapetach* is not noticeable (*nikar*) if it is situated within a *reshut hayachid* (such as a private yard). Alternatively, one might claim that the walls or fences that encompass a *reshut hayachid* are viewed halachically as extending "all the way to the heavens" (see *Shabbat* 7a), so the airspace above a *reshut hayachid* is halachically impenetrable. For example, a horizontal wire passing through a backyard enclosed by a fence would be invalid according to this opinion, as it is halachically blocked by the "upward extension" of the fence. Rav Hershel Schachter generally instructs *eruv* designers to be strict on this matter.[8]

Other *Acharonim* disagree with the *Mekor Chaim*'s stringency.[9] The *Chavatzelet Hasharon* (1:20) writes that the custom is to be lenient in this issue. He adds that his father, who was exceedingly strict concerning most halachic matters, ruled

---

8. Rav Schachter discusses this issue in *Be'ikvei Hatzon* (Chapter 13).
9. The *Aruch Hashulchan* does not mention this stringency. *Teshuvot Chatam Sofer* O.C. 91 and 96 and *Teshuvot Maharsham* 1:207 rule leniently regarding this issue in certain circumstances.

GRAY MATTER

leniently concerning this issue. Rav Hershel Schachter (in a lecture at Yeshiva University) relates that Rav Mendel Zaks told him that the custom in Europe was indeed to be lenient. However, Rav Schachter strongly urges communities to be strict in this matter. This issue has not yet been resolved, and practices vary from community to community.[10]

Flimsy and Zigzagging Wires

The *Shulchan Aruch* (*Orach Chaim* 362:11) codifies the Talmud's (*Eruvin* 11b) requirement that the vertical poles be sufficiently strong that they could theoretically support a door made of straw.[11] The *Shulchan Aruch* adds that the horizontal wire connecting the vertical poles does not have to be as strong and can even be made from a very light material, such as reed-grass (*gemi*).

Nonetheless, some suggest that the string may not be so flimsy that it sways in the wind. The *Mishnah Berurah* (362:66) presents two opinions regarding this issue. One focus of the argument is whether the horizontal wire has to be sufficiently sturdy that it can withstand "conventional" winds (*omeid beruach metzuyah*). He quotes the well-known rule that for a halachic wall (*mechitzah*) to be valid, it must be sturdy enough to withstand ordinary winds. This rule undoubtedly applies to the vertical poles of a *tzurat hapetach*, but one opinion claims that it does not apply

---

10. Rav Mordechai Willig once commented to this author that, in reality, all communities are lenient on this issue, because cars are considered *reshuyot hayachid*. Virtually every community *eruv* today uses *tzurot hapetach* that pass over cars, and the cars' walls should halachically block them, according to the stringent view. This point is also mentioned in *The Contemporary Eruv* (p. 79).

11. The thin strips of wire molding used in many *eruvin* today meet this requirement according to most authorities by virtue of the fact that they are attached to the utility pole, which is sufficiently strong (see *Sha'ar Hatziyun* 363:22).

THE LAWS OF CREATING AN ERUV PART III

to the horizontal strings (or poles). Another objection to flimsy wires is that normal doorframes are not constructed in such a manner (see *Eruvin* 94b). The *Aruch Hashulchan* (362:37) rules leniently regarding this concern, while the *Chazon Ish* (*Orach Chaim* 71:10) rules strictly.[12] Common practice appears to accept the lenient approach.

In a true doorframe, the horizontal beam goes straight from one vertical beam to the other. When constructing a *tzurat hapetach*, it happens sometimes that the wire will wrap around things, such as trees or poles, which it does not pass over. Consequently, the wire, which should parallel the top beam of a doorway, will zigzag between the vertical poles rather than going straight from one of them to the other. Rav Yehuda Henkin (*Bnei Banim* 1:19) suggests that the status of such a wire depends upon the same dispute as the status of a wire which is blown from side to side in the wind, for both wires move horizontally from being directly between the vertical poles. In defense of the lenient position, Rav Henkin claims that a minor zigzag is permissible, because the Gemara (*Eruvin* 11a) describes *eruvin* made of grapevines, which are not completely straight. Nonetheless, Rav Henkin claims that a curve of greater than twenty-two degrees invalidates the *tzurat hapetach*. Rav Yosef Adler reports that Rav Yosef Dov Soloveitchik also espoused this position. Rav Meir Arik (*Teshuvot Imrei Yosher* 2:133) claims that the wire is only valid if it does not sway or veer more than three *tefachim* in any direction.[13] This author has heard that *eruvin* designed by Rav Shimon Eider (such as the *eruv* in West Orange, New Jersey) allow for almost no zigzagging. For a discussion of this issue, see Rav Mordechai Willig's article in *Beit Yitzchak* (25:99).

---

12. The *Chazon Ish* invalidates the wire as long as the wind can move part of it outside a straight line between the two vertical poles. Rav Nata Greenblatt told this author that he constructed the Memphis, Tennessee *eruv* with unusually wide vertical poles in order that the wires do not sway beyond the width of the vertical poles.

13. For a criticism of this position, see *The Contemporary Eruv* (pp. 74-75).

GRAY MATTER

Sagging Wires

A related issue is whether the horizontal wire may sag. The *Mishkenot Yaakov* (111, cited by *Sha'ar Hatziyun* 362:56) and the *Chazon Ish* (*Orach Chaim* 71:10) rule that a sagging wire disqualifies a *tzurat hapetach*. If the wire sags, it probably sways in the wind, which is problematic according to some authorities (mentioned above). Furthremore a *tzurat hapetach* must be constructed in a manner that replicates the way people construct doorframes, and people do not manufacture doorframes that sag on top. Interestingly, Rav Yosef Dov Soloveitchik (cited in *Nefesh Harav* p. 170) recalled from his childhood that he visited his grandfather, Rav Chaim Soloveitchik, in Brisk and went with the *dayan* (rabbinic judge) of Brisk to check the community *eruv*. During that trip, the *dayan* tightened all the horizontal wires so that they would not sag, apparently following the *Mishkenot Yaakov*'s opinion.

Despite these rulings, Rav Tzvi Pesach Frank (*Teshuvot Har Tzvi* 2:18:8) permits sagging, as long as a significant part of the wire (about ten inches) does not come within ten *tefachim* of the ground. In addition, the *Aruch Hashulchan* does not cite the strict ruling of the *Mishkenot Yaakov* at all. The practice of most communities in Europe reportedly was to follow the lenient opinion in this area.

Communal practices today still differ in this area. Some communities follow a compromise approach that the horizontal wire may sag up to three *tefachim* (approximately 9-12 inches),[14] based on the concept of *lavud*, that a gap of less than three *tefachim* is considered closed.[15]

---

14. See Rav Shimon Eider's *Halachos of the Eruv* (p. 24).

15. Another common example of *lavud* is a chain link fence, which serves as a solid wall if the gaps between the links are less than three *tefachim* wide.

THE LAWS OF CREATING AN ERUV PART III

Slanted Wires

Because a *tzurat hapetach* should be built like a true doorway, a potential problem arises when one pole is taller than the other, putting the horizontal wire on a slant (even though it is taut). One could claim that this should be invalid, as most doorways are built with the horizontal beam perpendicular to the vertical beams. Nonetheless, the *Mishnah Berurah* (362:60) rules that even if the horizontal wire is slanted, the *tzurat hapetach* is acceptable. He cites (*Sha'ar Hatziyun* 362:46) the opinion of Rav Akiva Eiger, however, that an exceedingly slanted wire might disqualify the *tzurat hapetach*. Rav Aharon Kotler (cited in Rav Shimon Eider's *Halachos of the Eruv*, p. 23) rules that a slant of less than forty-five degrees is acceptable even according to Rav Akiva Eiger. The *Netivot Shabbat* (19:27 note 60) claims that a slant of more than twenty-two degrees is problematic.

Conclusion

We have reviewed some of the major issues concerning how to build a *tzurat hapetach*. While the laws of *eruvin* are extremely complex, it is an area where laymen can make a major contribution. Vigilant laymen who know the locations of their community's *tzurot hapetach* can help ensure its validity by notifying their rabbi whenever they notice downed or sagging wires. Similarly, people can help by noticing when telephone and utility workers make changes in the structure of poles and wires.[16]

---

16. See this author's article, "Advice for Proper Eruv Maintenance," in Yeshiva University's *Chavrusa* (April 1993, pp.5-6).

The Laws of Creating an Eruv
Part IV: Issues Once the Eruv is Erected

After constructing an *eruv*, three major issues remain: *karpeif*, *eruv chatzeirot*, and *sechirat reshut*.

Karpeif

A potentially major obstacle in creating a viable community *eruv* is the existence of a *karpeif* within the enclosed area. A *karpeif* is an area at least 100 *amot* (between 150 and 200 feet) by 50 *amot* (between 75 and 100 feet) that is not used for human habitation or other human needs.[1] Accordingly, sports fields, playgrounds, and lakes used for boating do not constitute *karpeifiyot*. *Chazal* forbade carrying within a *karpeif* even if it is located within a *reshut hayachid* created by *mechitzot* or *tzurot hapetach*. This is because the *reshut hayachid* must be encompassed by *mechitzot* or *tzurot hapetach* that were built for the purpose of **human habitation** (*mukaf ledirah*). A wall or *tzurat hapetach* built to surround an uninhabited forest is not built for the sake of human habitation, so it does not permit people to carry on *Shabbat* within that forest.

Moreover, the presence of a *karpeif* forbids carrying in the entire enclosed area surrounding it, because an area's walls or *tzurot hapetach* must be erected purely for human habitation. If they also include a *karpeif*, however, they are erected for an area that is not entirely fit for human habitation.[2] This author's

---

1. See *Eruvin* 23a-b and *Shulchan Aruch, Orach Chaim* 358.
2. For an analysis of the *karpeif*'s impact on the walls, see *Biur Halachah* (358:9 s.v. *Hazra'im*).

experience indicates that this issue arises much more often in suburban and rural areas than in urban areas, as an urban setting contains fewer undeveloped areas. The *Chazon Ish* (O.C. 88:25) writes that the only way to prevent a *karpeif* from invalidating the rest of the *eruv*'s area is to encompass the *karpeif* with either *mechitzot* or *tzurot hapetach*, thereby excluding it from the *eruv*. The community is then *mukaf ledirah*, while the uninhabited *karpeif* is severed from it.[3]

The lenient positions of some authorities might also solve this problem. The *Biur Halachah* (358:9 s.v. *Aval*) cites one such approach from the *Devar Shmuel*. He rules that if a *karpeif* is situated within a city and is only a small part of the city, it does not prohibit carrying within that area.[4] The *Devar Shmuel* reasons that, in such a situation, the *karpeif* is negligible compared to the rest of the city and may be ignored.[5]

Halachic authorities have reacted to the *Devar Shmuel*'s leniency with mixed feelings. On one hand, the *Chazon Ish* (cited earlier) rejects this approach, as he sees no reason for a *karpeif* within a city to differ from one in a more rural area. The *Biur Halachah* expresses serious reservations concerning this leniency, but he seems to accept the conclusion of the *Chacham Tzvi*, that the *Devar Shmuel*'s opinion may be followed where it is impossible to construct an *eruv* otherwise.

---

3. Also see the *Biur Halachah* (358:9 s.v. *Aval*).
4. Of course, the *Devar Shmuel*'s leniency does not apply to *eruvin* that enclose very large forest areas, since his entire reason is that the *karpeif* is negligible compared to the inhabited area. When this author sought to construct an *eruv* in a certain summer community in Connecticut, Rav Hershel Schachter ruled that the *eruv* could not be built, because the *tzurot hapetach* would have had to encompass huge tracts of forest. Rav Schachter also did not permit relying on the extraordinarily lenient views of *Teshuvot Divrei Malkiel* (cited in *Melamed Leho'il* 1:65) and *Teshuvot Even Yekara* (O.C. 16), which would have facilitated constructing the *eruv*, as these views are not accepted by most halachic authorities.
5. Although the *Devar Shmuel* speaks of a city surrounded by walls, his ruling appears to apply equally to a city surrounded by *tzurot hapetach*; see *Melamed Leho'il* (1:65).

GRAY MATTER

This issue remains controversial, as some communities rely on the *Devar Shmuel* while others do not. A number of Israeli rabbis have told this author that the practice in Israel is to follow the lenient opinion of the *Devar Shmuel* (except in Bnei Brak, where the *Chazon Ish* resided). This is hardly surprising, since *eruvin* in Israel often encompass entire cities.[6] It is exceedingly difficult to exclude every *karpeif* within Israel's growing cities. Hence, in keeping with the approach of the *Biur Halachah*, they rely on the *Devar Shmuel*'s lenient ruling.

A number of authorities adopt a compromise approach that distinguishes between different types of *karpeifiyot* (plural of *karpeif*).[7] If a *karpeif* beautifies the city, it does not forbid carrying. If, however, humans in no way benefit from the area, it must be excluded from the *eruv*.

Eruv Chatzeirot

Even after a proper community *eruv* has been constructed and the area encompassed is thereby rendered a *reshut hayachid*, one may still not carry within it on *Shabbat*. Despite the fact that it is biblically permitted to carry from one *reshut hayachid* (one's house) to another (in our case, the outside area enclosed by the *eruv*), the Rabbis prohibited this in many cases. Similarly, this rabbinical prohibition often precludes carrying from one household to another even within the same building.[8] For

---

6. For example, according to information received from the Jerusalem Rabbinate in 1991, the circumference of Jerusalem's *eruv* is approximately 110 kilometers.
7. See *Orchot Chaim* (Chapter 358), *Teshuvot Melameid Leho'il* (1:65), and *Teshuvot Har Tzvi* (*Orach Chaim* vol. 2, *Harari Vasadeh* p. 249).
8. If there is only one Jewish resident in the building, this prohibition does not apply (*Shulchan Aruch*, *Orach Chaim* 382:1). It also does not apply if all of the residents eat together or if the landlord stores property in all of the residences (*Shulchan Aruch*, *Orach Chaim* 370:2,4). Rav Moshe Feinstein (*Teshuvot Igrot Moshe*, O.C. 1:141) rules that a landlord who rents out items (such as stoves or refrigerators) with every apartment is considering to be

THE LAWS OF CREATING AN ERUV PART IV

example, this prohibition applies to an apartment building with at least two observant[9] families. In such situations, it is required to make an *eruv chatzeirot* (referred to by *Chazal* as an *eruv*) in order to permit carrying.

An *eruv chatzeirot* (literally "mixing the courtyards") is consists of every household in the *reshut hayachid* contributing some bread to the collective group of households. The bread is stored in one of the houses within the encompassed area. The Halachah then views the participants as if they all live in that one house, removing even the rabbinical prohibition against carrying (see *Shulchan Aruch*, O.C. 366:1).

The Talmud (*Shabbat* 14b) records that King Shlomo instituted this requirement, and a heavenly voice acknowledged the profound wisdom in it. The reason for this rule, as explained

---

"storing" his property with the tenants, so no *eruv chatzeirot* is needed. On the other hand, the *Chazon Ish* (O.C. 92) and *Chelkat Yaakov* (1:207) require an *eruv chatzeirot* if the landlord's property in the apartments is rented to the tenants. The *Devar Avraham* (3:30) and Rav Yosef Dov Soloveitchik (cited in *Nefesh Harav* p. 170) also favor this opinion, although the *Devar Avraham* concludes that he is unsure of the Halachah in such a case. See *The Contemporary Eruv* (p. 110 note 231) for a defense of Rav Moshe's view. Rav Hershel Schachter (in a lecture at Yeshiva University) reported that Rav Moshe encouraged those who do make an *eruv chatzeirot* in such a situation to refrain from reciting a blessing, since he believed that this *eruv* is unnecessary. The *Chelkat Yaakov* also argues that the landlord's ability to unite all of the apartments by storing property in all of them only applies to observant Jewish landlords. Regarding non-observant and non-Jewish landlords, he claims that *sechirat reshut* must be performed even if the landlord stores his personal property in all of the apartments. Other authorities do not appear to accept this qualification.

9. If there are flagrantly non-observant Jews, *sechirat reshut* must be performed. We will discuss this procedure later in this chapter. The status of non-observant Jews today is somewhat unclear, as most of them desecrate *Shabbat* out of ignorance, not out of contemptuousness. See *Eruvin* (69a) and *Chazon Ish* (O.C. 87:14) for a discussion of this phenomenon.

GRAY MATTER

by the Rambam (*Hilchot Eruvin* 1:4), is that otherwise people would become confused about the laws of carrying. The process of the *eruv chatzeirot* is designed to familiarize the community with the laws of carrying. This goal seems to be a reason for the time-honored practice of storing the *eruv chatzeirot* in the synagogue (see Rama, O.C. 366:3). Rav Elazar Meyer Teitz told this author that his father, Rav Pinchas Teitz (of Elizabeth, New Jersey), prominently displayed the *eruv* in a place within the synagogue where it was easily seen, noting that this was commonly done in Europe. Another advantage of storing the *eruv* in the synagogue is that community members have full access to the *eruv*, which is an important requirement (see Rav Moshe Shternbach's *Teshuvot Vehanhagot* 1:250).

In practice, we do not require every household in a *reshut hayachid* to give some bread for the purpose of the *eruv*. Instead, everyone in the community is granted a portion of the *eruv* by the process known as *zachin le'adam shelo befanav*, acquiring something on behalf of another person (see *Shulchan Aruch, Orach Chaim* 366:9-10,15). This is accomplished by one person handing another the *eruv* food[10] and the second person lifting the *eruv* into the air.[11] It is lifted with the intention of acquiring the *eruv* on behalf of all present and future residents of the area encompassed by the *eruv*.

A blessing ("*al mitzvat eruv*") is recited prior to the procedure of acquiring the *eruv* on behalf of the community.[12] Then, the formula of "*behadein eruva*" is recited, explaining the *eruv*'s intended purpose (see *Shulchan Aruch, Orach Chaim* 366:15).

---

10. The practice is to use a box or two of kosher-for-*Pesach matzah*; see Rama, O.C. 368:5.

11. There is a dispute regarding whether it must be lifted one *tefach* (3-4 inches) or 3 *tefachim*; see *Shulchan Aruch, Choshen Mishpat* 198:2 and *Mishnah Berurah* 366:51.

12. For an explanation of why a blessing is recited on an *eruv chatzeirot*, see *Teshuvot Chatam Sofer* (O.C. 99).

THE LAWS OF CREATING AN ERUV PART IV

Sechirat Reshut

The procedure of *eruv chatzeirot* is effective solely for Jews who believe in the Oral Law and thus believe in the efficacy of an *eruv*. However, one must rent the apartments, homes, and common areas (such as streets and parks) from every non-Jewish and non-believing Jewish resident of the *reshut hayachid*. This procedure is known as *sechirat reshut*.

Renting every non-Jewish house within the *tzurot hapetach* is a virtually impossible task to accomplish in a community *eruv*. Fortunately, Halachah provides an alternative method of performing the *sechirat reshut* (see *Shulchan Aruch*, O.C. 391:1). The Jewish community may rent the entire enclosed area from the head of the city (*sar ha'ir*) or from one to whom this leader has delegated his authority.[13] The *Shulchan Aruch* rules that the head of the city has the halachic ability to rent out not just the public property within the *tzurot hapetach*, but also the homes of its residents. His ability to rent out private homes stems from his right to quarter soldiers and military equipment in those homes during a time of war without consulting the residents.[14] The United States Constitution (Amendment 3) forbids quartering soldiers under most circumstances. Nonetheless, the *Tikvat Zechariah* (pp. 39-40, cited in *The Contemporary Eruv* pp. 115-117), discussing the possibility of constructing an *eruv* in St. Louis in the 1890s, rules that a city government in America does have the right to lease private homes for *sechirat reshut*. He reasons that local governments may search and inspect private homes, in addition to maintaining the right to expropriate private land for public use (eminent domain).[15]

---

13. A representative may be used even if this representative knows he is acting against the will of the non-Jewish authority (*Shulchan Aruch*, O.C. 382:11). The *Shulchan Aruch* also discusses who qualifies as a representative.
14. The *Biur Halachah* (391 s.v. *Bameh Devarim Amurim*) adds that the leader must also be capable of deciding when to wage war. Otherwise, his power to quarter troops is irrelevant during times of peace.
15. Rav Hershel Schachter (in a lecture at Yeshiva University) stated that

GRAY MATTER

Others, including Rav Hershel Schachter (in a lecture at Yeshiva University), strongly question this reasoning. They point out that the right of eminent domain is rarely used and is quite difficult to apply. According to their opinion, it is forbidden to carry on *Shabbat* (even within an *eruv*) from one's home to the private property of a non-Jew or non-observant Jew.[16] Nonetheless, they acknowledge that the mayor and police do possess the authority to close the **public** areas of the city. One should consult his rabbi regarding which opinion to follow.

The *Netivot Shabbat* (Chapter 37, note 93) notes that all would agree that the mayor and police cannot rent out a foreign embassy located within a city, as international law recognizes it as sovereign territory of the nation it represents. Thus, it would be forbidden to carry into a foreign embassy even in an area encompassed by an *eruv*, such as Jerusalem or Washington, on *Shabbat*.

It is often unclear who is the appropriate authority to lease the area from (see *Mishnah Berurah* 391:18). In order to avoid this problem, rabbis usually perform *sechirat reshut* from a number of local authorities, such as the mayor and the police chief. A particularly interesting situation occurred when Rav Barry Freundel of Congregation Kesher Israel (Washington, D.C.)

Rav Moshe Feinstein also permitted performing *sechirat reshut* from a democratically elected mayor based on similar reasoning. See *Chazon Ish* (O.C. 82:9) for an alternative explanation of why *sechirat reshut* may be done from democratic governments. Also see *Teshuvot Minchat Shlomo* (2:35:24), who writes that the *sechirat reshut* performed today "merits investigation" (*"yeish ladun"*).

16. *Netivot Shabbat* (36:27). One could question why the presence of privately owned non-Jewish property inside the *eruv* does not affect the rest of the area. After all, we have already mentioned (regarding a *karpeif*) that a place where carrying is forbidden also prohibits carrying in the rest of the *eruv*, unless special *tzurot hapetach* are erected to separate the forbidden area. While walls enclose the houses themselves, their unenclosed front lawns should invalidate the *eruv*. See *The Contemporary Eruv* (p. 115).

established an *eruv* for his community. Due to the ambiguous nature of Washington's municipal authorities, Rav Freundel told this author that he performed *sechirat reshut* from United States President George Bush[17] and Washington Mayor Marion Berry, along with the heads of the police and city council.

When expanding a community *eruv*, care must be taken to ensure that the *sechirat reshut* includes the expanded areas. In addition, *sechirat reshut* should not be allowed to expire.[18] Many authorities require renewing *sechirat reshut* when the non-Jewish official from whom it was performed leaves his office. The *Netivot Shabbat* (37:28 and notes 96-99) cites these authorities, but he argues that *sechirat reshut* remains effective in democracies even when the government changes. He reasons that a newly elected government is bound by agreements made by its predecessors. In practice, Jewish communities today do not renew *sechirat reshut* every time the town government changes (also see *Har Tzvi, Orach Chaim* 17).

Conclusion

We hope that this discussion of the laws of *eruvin* has shown how this area of Halachah is particularly complex. It should be emphasized that we have reviewed only some of these complicated laws. For further discussion of them, see *Netivot Shabbat, The Contemporary Eruv*, Rav Shimon Eider's *Halachot of the Eruv*, Rav Elimelech Lange's *Hilchot Eruvin*, and Rav Hershel Schachter's essay in *The Journal of Halacha and Contemporary Society* (5:5-24). When dealing with practical questions in the laws of *eruvin*, it is important to consult rabbis who have extensive experience in this field.

---

17. Of course, had it been difficult to reach the President, *sechirat reshut* could have been done from a representative of his.
18. For a discussion of how long a *sechirat reshut* may last, see the *Mishnah Berurah* (382:48) and *Netivot Shabbat* (Chapter 37:28 and note 20).

Milking Cows on Shabbat
Part I: Using a Non-Jew and Milking to Waste

Observant dairy farmers face the challenge of how to milk animals on *Shabbat*. The next three chapters review the solutions to this problem through the most recent developments. Some of this section is based on the writings of Rav Shmuel David in his *Sh'eilot Ut'shuvot Meirosh Tzurim*.

Source of the Prohibition

The Gemara (*Shabbat* 95a) states, "*Choleiv chayav mishum mefareik*" ("Milking is a violation of the prohibition of *mefareik*, removal"). One who milks a cow removes a liquid from its natural place of origin,[1] which constitutes a *toladah* (derivative prohibition) of *dash* (threshing - i.e., removing the kernel of grain from the stalk).[2]

Most *Rishonim* understand that the Gemara's use of the term *chayav* clearly indicates that *mefareik* is a biblical prohibition. A minority view, held most notably by the Rashba (*Shabbat* 95a s.v. *Choleiv*), believes that milking is merely a rabbinical prohibition.[3]

---
1. See *Encyclopedia Talmudit* (7:738) for a lengthier definition of *mefareik*.
2. There are thirty-nine basic categories of prohibited work on *Shabbat* (*avot melachah*). Other acts are biblically prohibited because of the similarity between them and one of the thirty-nine categories. These are called *toladot*; see *Bava Kama* 2a.
3. This view is based on the Talmud Yerushalmi (*Shabbat* 7:2).

MILKING COWS ON SHABBAT PART I

The Gemara (*Shabbat* 75a) records a dispute about the scope of *mefareik*. The *Chachamim* (most sages) only apply *dash* (from which *mefareik* is derived) to *gidulei karka* (items that grow from the ground), while Rabi Yehudah applies it to other things, too. The Rashba argues that the majority opinion on *Shabbat* 75a believes that the prohibition of *dash* only applies to *gidulei karka*. Therefore, since animals do not grow from the ground, milking them cannot constitute a biblical prohibition.

Most *Rishonim* reject the Rashba's view for one of three reasons. Some argue that the Halachah follows the view of Rabbi Yehudah (*Shabbat* 75a) that *dash* applies even to items that do not grow from the ground (see *Tosafot, Shabbat* 95a s.v. *Hacholeiv*). Alternatively, some argue that animals such as cows **are** considered *gidulei karka*, since they are nourished by items that grow from the ground.[4] Some *Rishonim* accept neither of these claims, yet they forbid milking for other reasons. For example, Rabbeinu Tam[5] claims that milking on *Shabbat* constitutes *memacheik* (smoothing) of the udder.

Rav Ben-Zion Uzziel (*Teshuvot Mishptei Uzziel, Orach Chaim* 10) sought to rely on the minority view of *Rishonim* that milking is merely a rabbinic prohibition and thus permit milking cows in an unusual manner.[6] However, almost no modern-day authorities adopt this approach. Rav Avraham Yitzchak Kook (*Teshuvot Orach Mishpat* 64) represents the predominant view on this topic when he writes:

> It is extremely difficult to base a leniency in contradiction to the majority opinion of *Rishonim* who believe milking to be a biblical prohibition....

---

4. See the aforementioned passage in the Rashba, *Tosafot* (*Ketubot* 60a s.v. *Mefareik*), and *Maggid Mishnah* (*Hilchot Shabbat* 8:7).
5. *Tosafot, Shabbat* 73b s.v. *Mefareik*; also see the aforementioned passage in the Rashba.
6. See *Ketubot* 60a. Regarding the general concept of *shinui* (violating *Shabbat* in an unusual manner), see the introduction to the *Eglei Tal*, section 3.

GRAY MATTER

These authorities include the Rif, Rabbeinu Chananel, Rabbeinu Tam, the *Or Zarua*, and a simple reading of Rashi and *Tosafot*, and this is also explicit in the Rambam.... It is impossible to permit a Jew to violate what most *Rishonim* view as a biblical prohibition.

Maharam of Rothenburg - Milking by a Non-Jew

As Rav Kook intimates, it is permissible to ask a non-Jew to milk a cow on *Shabbat* to avoid causing the cow pain and suffering (*tza'ar ba'alei chaim*).[7] The source of this leniency is a ruling of the Maharam of Rothenburg (cited by the Rosh, *Shabbat* 18:3), based on a comment of the Gemara (*Shabbat* 128b). The Gemara permits supporting an animal with pillows and blankets if it falls into a water channel on *Shabbat*. Doing so entails violating a rabbinical prohibition,[8] yet it is permitted to alleviate an animal's suffering. The biblical imperative to alleviate an animal's pain supersedes the rabbinical prohibition. Similarly, reasons the Maharam of Rothenburg, one may set aside the rabbinical prohibition of *amirah lenochri* (asking a non-Jew to violate *Shabbat*) to alleviate the pain of a cow that needs to be milked. The *Shulchan Aruch* (O.C. 305:20) rules in accordance with the view of the Maharam of Rothenburg.[9]

---

7. Modern dairy farms use cows that produce large volumes of milk daily and suffer greatly unless they are milked two or three times a day.

8. Placing a pillow underneath an animal renders the pillow *muktzah*, as the pillow serves as a base for an animal, and animals are *muktzah* (*basis ledavar ha'asur*). Making a non-*muktzah* item *muktzah* (*mevateil keli meiheichano*) is rabbinically prohibited because it resembles *soteir*, destroying a utensil. In this case, the utensil is not physically destroyed, but it is rendered unusable for the remainder of *Shabbat*. See Rashi, *Shabbat* 128b s.v. *Veha*.

9. In practice, some possible restrictions are involved when employing a non-Jew to milk on *Shabbat*. The *Korban Netaneil* (*Shabbat* 18:70), commenting on the Maharam's leniency, lists these restrictions. First, the milk may not be used until the next day, as *Chazal* forbade using liquids squeezed on *Shabbat* until after *Shabbat* ends. (*Chazal* worried that using

MILKING COWS ON SHABBAT PART I

Twentieth-Century Israel

In modern times, Rav Kook endorses following the *Shulchan Aruch*'s ruling and hiring a non-Jew to milk cows on *Shabbat*. Rav Kook opposes seeking a way to enable Jews to milk the cows for fear that Jews present in the barn would inevitably come to violate *Shabbat*. Even if the milking could be done in a permissible manner, other ancillary problems to the milking frequently arise, such as fixing broken pipes and machinery. In a similar vein, Rav Shmuel David (*Techumin* 7:17) notes that one's very presence in a barn on *Shabbat* leads to very serious problems, such as helping an animal give birth and the status of farm animals as *muktzah*.[10]

However, non-Jewish labor was not a practical option in the earlier part of last century.[11] It seems that Arab farm workers brought diseases from their animals to the Jewish-owned animals. The reason for this was the primitive state of veterinary care at Arab farms. Thus, Jews needed an alternative solution for milking on *Shabbat*.

---

freshly squeezed liquids, or juice that leaked from a fruit, would cause people to violate *Shabbat* by squeezing more; see *Beitzah* 3a.) Additionally, milk squeezed on *Shabbat* by a non-Jew must be given to the non-Jew. If the Jewish owner would keep the milk, it would appear as if the non-Jew violated *Shabbat* for the Jew's **personal** benefit, whereas we only permit him to violate *Shabbat* for the **animal's** sake. If the Jewish owner wants the milk, he must buy it from the non-Jew (although he may pay a heavily discounted price; see *Biur Halachah* 305 s.v. *Bedavar.*) While the *Korban Netaneil* cites all of these restrictions, they are not all universally accepted. See *Shulchan Aruch* (O.C. 305:20) and the *Mishnah Berurah*'s comments thereupon.

10. Rav David addresses these issues at length in his book, *Sh'eilot U'tshuvot Meirosh Tzurim*, which discusses halachic life at Kibbutz Rosh Tzurim, Israel.

11. Interestingly, there was one early Jewish settlement, Nevei Yaakov, that employed Arabs to milk cows on *Shabbat*. For a description of how this was done, see *Birurim Behilchot Hare'iyah*, pp. 315-317.

GRAY MATTER

Milking to Waste - Chazon Ish and Rav Kook

A different way to permit milking on *Shabbat* is *chalivah le'ibud*, letting the milk go to waste by milking into a drain. This approach is based on Rashi's comment (*Shabbat* 145a s.v. *Legufo*) that milking a cow or squeezing a fruit *le'ibud* is not defined as an act of *mefareik* and is therefore permitted. Although many *Rishonim* agree with this assertion, some believe that milking to waste is rabbinically prohibited (see *Tosafot, Ketubot* 6a s.v. *Hai*), and the *Eglei Tal* (*dash*, subsection 27) accepts their strict view. Rav Kook (*ibid.*), while writing that one should not rebuke those who follow the lenient view, expresses serious reservations about relying on the authorities who permit milking to waste. He goes so far as to state that no respected Torah scholar could ever endorse milking to waste, as it contradicts the stringent view of many *Rishonim*. The *Chazon Ish* (*Hilchot Shabbat* 56:4), however, rules that if one is unable to hire a non-Jew to milk on *Shabbat*, he may rely on the opinion of Rashi that milking to waste does not constitute *mefareik*.

Milking Cows on Shabbat
Part II: Milking in Unusual Manners

Milking Onto Foods

The Gemara (*Shabbat* 144b) teaches that "one may milk a goat into a pot [filled with solid food] but not onto an [empty] plate." Rashi (s.v. *Letoch*) explains that the Gemara is speaking of squeezing the milk into a pot to improve the taste of food inside the pot. He permits this activity "since one does not need the milk as a liquid per se, rather as food (a component of a solid food). This is not the manner of *mefareik* and resembles separating food from food." In other words, *mefareik* does not apply when separating one solid food from another, and here the milk is considered solid food being removed from a cow (which is viewed as beef).[1]

It appears from Rashi that this leniency applies on both *Shabbat* and *Yom Tov*, for squeezing milk onto solid food is never defined as an act of *mefareik*. On the other hand, Rabbeinu Tam (*Tosafot* s.v. *Choleiv*) believes that permission to milk onto food applies only on *Yom Tov*. He notes that milking onto food is permitted because the milk is considered "food (based on its destination) being removed from food (the cow)." Only on *Yom Tov*, however, is the cow considered "food," because only on *Yom Tov* can an animal be slaughtered and eaten.[2] On *Shabbat*,

---

1. For an explanation of why the cow is considered food despite the fact that it may not be slaughtered on *Shabbat*, see Rashba, *Shabbat* 144b s.v. *Veha*.
2. Even on *Yom Tov*, there may be a distinction between different types of cows. Clearly, a cow that might be slaughtered and eaten on *Yom Tov* is considered food. Some cows, however, are designated for a purpose other

reasons Rabbeinu Tam, a cow is not food. Thus, even if one milks a cow onto food, he is separating "food" (milk) from something inedible, a violation of *mefareik*.

The *Shulchan Aruch* (O.C. 305:20 and 505) appears to rule in accordance with the strict opinion of Rabbeinu Tam. The *Shulchan Aruch* also emphasizes that the permission to milk onto food applies only when the food absorbs most of the milk. It certainly does not apply if one squeezes a large volume of milk onto a few crumbs of bread (see *Teshuvot Achiezer* 4:8 and *Techumin* 1:7-8). Consequently, milking into food is undoubtedly not a practical option for dairy farmers.

Milking to Waste with Milking Machines

The most viable option for religious dairy farms in the earlier part of the century was milking to waste, but downside of this procedure was that all of the milk was lost. With the advent of milking machines in Israel, however, milking to waste without actually losing the milk appeared possible. The machine could be set to send the milk down the drain, attached to the cow, and adjusted after the first drops of milk to send the subsequent milk into storage containers. The human act of milking (attaching the cow to the machine and squeezing the first drops)[3] sends the milk to waste, while no further squeezing of the udders (by humans) is necessary to redirect the milk.

Theoretically, it seems entirely permissible to use milking machines in this manner. Nonetheless, the *Chazon Ish* (O.C. 38:4) finds this procedure objectionable, drawing an analogy

---

than eating, such as cows that are designated specifically to produce milk. It is questionable whether such cows may be considered "food," as their owners surely do not intend to eat them. For a discussion of the permissibility of milking cows designated for such a purpose on *Yom Tov*, see *Mishnah Berurah* (505:1,4).

3. See *Shemirat Shabbat Kehilchatah* (27 note 159) regarding the need for the first drops of milk to flow before readjusting the machine.

MILKING COWS ON SHABBAT PART II

between it and a loophole discussed in the Gemara (*Shabbat* 8b). The Gemara states that one may carry on *Shabbat* from a *reshut harabim* (public domain) to a *mekom petur* (neutral domain) and from a *reshut hayachid* (private domain) to a *mekom petur*, whereas one may not carry from a *reshut hayachid* to a *reshut harabim* or vice versa. One could seemingly circumvent this prohibition by carrying from a *reshut harabim* to a *reshut hayachid* via a *mekom petur*. Nevertheless, the Gemara forbids this loophole. Although each step is permissible (i.e., carrying to and from a *mekom petur*), the net result of the actions is carrying from a *reshut harabim* to a *reshut hayachid*, so *Chazal* forbade it.

Similarly, the *Chazon Ish* reasons, one may not first set up the milking machine to milk to waste and subsequently adjust the machine to send the milk into storage containers.[4] Nonetheless, the *Shemirat Shabbat Kehilchatah* (27, note 159) records that even the most scrupulously observant farm settlements engaged in this practice. Moreover, prominent rabbis (cited there) report that none other than the *Chazon Ish* sanctioned this practice in case of great financial loss.[5]

How can we reconcile the contradiction between the written ruling of the *Chazon Ish* and the oral ruling he reportedly gave religious farmers? One might suggest that even the *Chazon Ish* fundamentally permits the action of switching from the drain to storage containers. Despite the cogency of his analogy to carrying via a *mekom petur*, it seems to contradict two axiomatic rules regarding post-Talmudic rulings. The first is that one cannot

---

4. Rav Shlomo Zalman Auerbach (cited in *Shemirat Shabbat Kehilchatah* 27 note 159) suggests having one person attach the cow to the milking machine and another person readjust the milking machine to store the milk. However, Rav Shlomo Zalman limits his proposal to situations where the person who attached the machine did not know that his colleague was going to redirect the milk flow. Accordingly, Rav Shlomo Zalman's suggestion cannot be used as a standard procedure for dairy farms.
5. Presumably, "great loss" means that the economic survival of the *kibbutz* depends upon not losing the milk. See *Techumin* (7:172 note 15).

GRAY MATTER

necessarily extrapolate from one rabbinical prohibition or leniency to another (see *Tosafot, Chullin* 104a s.v. *Umina,* and *Maggid Mishnah, Hilchot Shabbat* 6:9). Additionally, the Rosh (*Shabbat* 2:15) writes that we may not create new rabbinical prohibitions after the Amoraic period. Thus, the *Chazon Ish*'s ruling essentially was a *chumra* (stringency), which could be waived in case of great need.

Milking Through Grama

During the mid-1980s, the Zomet Institute developed machinery that solves the *Chazon Ish*'s objection to using milking machines for storing all but the first few drops. Zomet's invention switches the milk machine from the drain to storage receptacles **indirectly**. The Gemara (*Shabbat* 120b) teaches that doing a forbidden act **directly** is biblically prohibited, whereas doing it **indirectly** (*grama*) is biblically permitted.[6] For example, the Mishnah (*Shabbat* 120a) describes how one may indirectly extinguish a fire on *Shabbat*.[7] One may put barrels of water in the path of the fire, so that when the fire eventually reaches the barrels, it will cause them to explode, and the water will extinguish the fire. *Grama* is not totally permitted, though. The Rama (O.C. 334:22) rules that we may violate *Shabbat* through *grama* only in cases of great economic loss (see *Biur Halachah,* O.C. 334:22 s.v. *D'gram*)

The Gemara (*Sanhedrin* 77a) describes another classic *grama* situation. One person ties up another in the desert at night. The next day, the sun appears and the bound individual dies of sunstroke. Rashi (s.v. *Sof*) explains that one who kills in this fashion does not receive the death penalty, as he killed indirectly. The killing agent, the sun, was not present at the time of the killer's actions and only showed up later (*sof chama lavo*).

---

6. It should be noted that Rav Yosef Dov Soloveitchik (cited in *B'ikvei Hatzon* 7:4) defined *grama* in a somewhat stricter manner than many of his contemporaries. Accordingly, Rav Soloveitchik might prohibit some of the *grama* machinery developed for *Shabbat* in consultation with other authorities.
7. The Mishnah actually records a dispute regarding this issue. We have only cited the accepted view (Rambam, *Hilchot Shabbat* 12:4).

MILKING COWS ON SHABBAT PART II

Many of the *grama* products of the Zomet Institute (such as its famed *Shabbat* telephone) are based on the *sof chama lavo* model. The user turns on a switch with no immediate result. In a few seconds, an electronic eye detects a change in the switch's position and effects the desired result (see *Techumin* 1:515-524). The electronic eye parallels the sun in the aforementioned murder case. When one turns the switch, no action results immediately. The electronic eye that brings about the desired action is not present when the switch is turned on, and, like the sun, it only appears later. It consists of an electric impulse that checks at regular intervals (six to twelve seconds) to see if the switch has been moved. When it detects that the switch has moved, it reacts accordingly.

The Zomet Institute applies this principle to redirecting milk from the drain to storage containers through *grama*.[8] No person directly moves the machinery from waste to storage. Instead, a person moves a faucet, causing no immediate result. Several seconds later, an electronic eye discovers that the faucet has moved and causes the machinery to switch the milk flow from waste to storage.

While the Rama (O.C. 334:22) permits *grama* only in case of great financial need, here *grama* is being utilized routinely. Nonetheless, there are two reasons to permit its implementation on dairy farms. One can argue that this is a case of great financial need, as losing a day's worth of milk every week would deliver a major economic blow to any dairy farm. Furthermore, *grama* is employed merely to accommodate a concern which, even according to the *Chazon Ish*, may only be a stringency. Accordingly, there would be room to rule leniently even without pressing financial need.[9]

---

8. For a more detailed discussion of how this works from both halachic and engineering perspectives, see *Techumin* 7:144-173.

9. Regarding whether it is preferable to milk via *grama* or hiring a non-Jew, see *Teshuvot Minchat Shlomo* (2:24) and Rav Yaakov Ariel's essay in *Techumin* (19:343-348).

Milking Cows on Shabbat
Part III: Attaching a Milking Machine Turned Off

In addition to the milking methods that we have already discussed, an additional method of milking on *Shabbat* became feasible near the end of the twentieth century.

The Kibbutz Sdei Eliyahu Solution

In the eleventh volume of *Techumin* (pp.170-175), the Rav of Kibbutz Sdei Eliyahu, Rav Shlomo Rosenfeld, presents an innovative solution to the problem of milking cows on *Shabbat*. The proposal implements a solution suggested decades before by the *Chazon Ish* (*Orach Chaim* 38:4):

> It appears to me that one may connect the pipe [from the milking machine] to the udders when the electricity is not functioning and later the electricity will turn on automatically and milk the cows.

This approach is based on the *sof chamah lavo* case (*Sanhedrin* 77a), described in the previous chapter. This Talmudic passage establishes that one who ties up a victim at night is considered to have killed only **indirectly** if the burning sun kills the bound victim the following day. This act is *grama* (indirect) because the death agent was not present at the time that the villain tied up the victim. In the *Chazon Ish*'s ruling, the electricity parallels the sun. The electrical current is not active at the time that the milking machine pipes are attached to the cow's udders. The person who attaches the pipes is thus only indirectly violating *Shabbat*, as the milking procedure begins only after his action is over. Since *grama* is permitted in case of great monetary loss, the *Chazon Ish* permits milking cows in this fashion.

Problems with the Chazon Ish's Ruling and its Solution

As late as 1986, Rav Shmuel David (*Techumin* 7:158) wrote that the *Chazon Ish*'s ruling was impractical. He explained that the pipes of the milk machines did not remain attached to the cow's udders while the electricity was off. Before the milk machine was operating, no vacuum existed to hold the pipes to the udders.

However, five years later, Rav Shlomo Rosenfeld wrote that the members of Kibbutz Sdei Eliyahu discovered a way to create a vacuum effect, keeping the pipes attached to the cow's udders without electric power. Rav Rosenfeld's essay discusses this method in halachic and engineering detail and notes that leading authorities, such as Rav Shaul Yisraeli and Rav Yehoshua Neuwirth, approved of this method of milking cows on *Shabbat*. In fact Rav Uri Dasberg (*Techumin* 15:394-400) reported in 1995 that this approach had been adopted by many dairy farms. Moreover, dairy farmers related that this method had fewer technical difficulties in implementation than other solutions. In addition, the milk that goes to waste with other methods need not go to waste when milking by *grama*.

Rav Rosenfeld suggests that even the *Chazon Ish* would agree that Sdei Eliyahu's *grama* method is the preferred method for milking cows on *Shabbat*. Although the *Chazon Ish* also permitted milking to waste, that procedure is rabbinically prohibited according to some *Rishonim*. *Grama*, on the other hand, is explicitly permitted by the Rama (*Orach Chaim* 334:22) in case of financial loss, without any reservations.

GRAY MATTER

Problems with the Kibbutz Sdei Eliyahu Solution

In Rav Dasberg's article, he describes a problem with this method. It seems that a certain percentage of cows leak milk into the pipes even before the electric current starts to flow. The halachic question is whether this flow of milk is considered a *davar she'eino mitkavein*. A *davar she'eino mitkavein* is when a person intends to do a permissible act, but this action may also lead to an unintended prohibited result.[1] For example, a person drags a chair across a field with the intention of bringing it somewhere, he simply wants to transport the chair, which is allowed on *Shabbat*. Along the way, however, the chair might plow a furrow in the ground, although this is not the person's intention. A *davar she'eino mitkavein* is permitted on *Shabbat*, so if causing the milk to flow when the pipes are attached is defined as a *davar she'eino mitkavein*, the pipes may be attached on *Shabbat* (before the electricity is turned on).

Rav Shlomo Zalman Auerbach (*Teshuvot Minchat Shlomo* 2:35:7) forbids attaching the pipe to the udders, because it might cause some milk to be released. This action is not a *davar she'eino mitkaven*, he claims, since one essentially intends to milk the cow. Although the milk that flows immediately is not desired, since the person does not wish to violate *Shabbat*, one fundamentally wants the milking process to occur. Rav Shlomo Zalman thus claims that attaching a milking machine constitutes intentional milking whenever there is a reasonable possibility that this action will immediately dislodge drops of milk.

Lenient Rulings of Rav A.D. Auerbach and Rav Lichtenstein

Despite Rav Shlomo Zalman's opposition, two great halachic authorities, Rav Avraham Dov Auerbach (Rav Shlomo Zalman's son) and Rav Aharon Lichtenstein (both cited in

---

1. For greater elaboration on the parameters of a *davar she'eino mitkavein*, see the *Encyclopedia Talmudit* (6:631-655).

Techumin 15:394-410), rule leniently and consider the milk leakage a permitted *davar she'eino mitkaven*. Rav Avraham Auerbach reasons that there are three requirements for defining an action as a *davar she'eino mitkaven*. The forbidden result must occur unintentionally, the forbidden result must not occur inevitably (*pesik reisheih*), and it must be possible to identify the permitted act and forbidden result as two separate actions.

Rav Shlomo Zalman's opposition challenged the last point. He claimed that the permitted act, attaching the pipes, was the same act that commenced the prohibited milking process. In order to permit attaching the pipes, Rav A.D. Auerbach suggests that attaching the pipes to the udders is one (permissible) act, and the milk that flows later (after turning on the machine) is something entirely separate. Rav A.D. Auerbach claims that these two steps only become one unit when there is a 50% chance of milk starting to flow as soon as the pipes are attached. If, however, attachment of the pipes does not usually bring out milk, the later milk flow is a separate occurrence. Regarding the minority of cases, when attaching the pipes to the udders immediately squeezes milk, they are a *davar she'eino mitkavein*, as this flow is unintentional and does not happen inevitably. Rav Lichtenstein reportedly agrees in principle with this approach. In fact, he is even more lenient regarding the odds that milk will flow when the pipes are attached. According to Rav Lichtenstein, as long as the drops of milk do not emerge in a significant minority (approximately 20%) of the cases, the act is still regarded as a *davar she'eino mitkaven*.

Rav Zev Whitman (*Techumin* 15:409) suggests a way to make the Sdei Eliyahu milking machines acceptable for all opinions, including Rav Shlomo Zalman Auerbach. Rav Whitman proposes setting up the machinery so drops of milk that flow when the pipes are attached go to waste, because milking to waste is permitted according to many opinions. Rav Whitman presents a technical description of how to set up the milking machine so that these drops of milk should go to waste.

GRAY MATTER

Conclusion

We have reviewed several solutions to the problem of how to milk cows on *Shabbat*. It should be emphasized that this is not merely an issue of economic concern, but also the welfare of the animals is of concern, since many cows would not survive if they were not milked on *Shabbat*. We have seen how emerging technology can serve as an aid to Halachah and not a nuisance. We look forward to the day when all aspects of the State of Israel will operate in accordance with Halachah.

Postscript

Rav Zev Whitman (*Techumin* 18:313-327) discusses the complexities of how the Israeli dairy industry can cope with a three-day *Yom Tov*, which can occur on *Rosh Hashanah* even in Israel.

Laws of Holidays

The Second Day of Yom Tov for Visitors to Israel

Diaspora Jews who visit Israel on *Yom Tov* often wonder what they should do on *Yom Tov Sheini* (the second day of *Yom Tov*, only observed by Diaspora Jews). We will review the three basic opinions regarding this issue.

Introduction - Observance of Yom Tov Sheini

Until the fourth century C.E., Sanhedrin declared a new Jewish month only after accepting the testimony of two people who witnessed the new moon. Consequently, it often took weeks to notify all of world Jewry of the day on which a new month had started. Jews who lived a great distance from the Sanhedrin frequently did not know precisely when the new month had begun in time for the celebration of holidays in that month. The practice thus evolved to observe two days of *Yom Tov* in the Diaspora, due to a doubt regarding which day was the true date of the holiday. However, during the Amoraic period, the Sanhedrin ceased to establish the Jewish calendar by testimony and instituted a fixed calendar system. Once the calendar was set, there was no longer a reason to observe *Yom Tov Sheini*, as even a Jew on the other side of the world from Israel could calculate the proper day for each holiday. Nonetheless, the Gemara (*Beitzah* 4b) rules that *Yom Tov Sheini* must continue to be observed in the Diaspora:

> They sent from there [*Eretz Yisrael*]: Give heed to the custom of your fathers [to keep a second day of *Yom Tov* in the Diaspora]. It might happen that a non-Jewish government will issue a decree [preventing knowledge of the Jewish calendar], and it will cause confusion regarding the dates of *Yom Tov*.

GRAY MATTER

Rishonim debate whether observance of *Yom Tov Sheini* during "the period of the set calendar" is merely a custom or a full-fledged rabbinical enactment. For an analysis of this issue, see Rav Yitzchak Zev Soloveitchik's *Chidushei Hagriz* (*Hilchot Berachot* 11:16).

The Foreigner Traveling to Israel

The Mishnah (*Pesachim* 50a-b) teaches us a key rule regarding one who travels to a Jewish community with customs different from his own, "We impose upon him the restrictions of the location from which he departed and the restrictions of the location where he has arrived."

The Gemara (*Pesachim* 51a) comments that one remains bound by the restrictions of the place he left only when he intends to return there (*da'ato lachazor*). Assuming that *Yom Tov Sheini* has the same status as other customs, a Diaspora Jew visiting Israel must continue to observe two days of *Yom Tov*, provided that he intends to return to the Diaspora. The analogy between *Yom Tov Sheini* and other customs, however, is in dispute, so three major positions have developed regarding this issue.

Rav Yosef Karo

Rav Yosef Karo, in his *Teshuvot Avkat Rocheil* (26), rules that the Mishnah's principle does indeed apply to *Yom Tov Sheini*. He also notes that this was the common practice among the travelers to Israel, "who publicly gather to form *minyanim* to recite the *Yom Tov* prayers on *Yom Tov Sheini*." Later authorities confirm that this was the accepted practice in Israel (see *Teshuvot Halachot Ketanot* 4 and *Birkei Yosef* 496:7), and most authorities rule that a visitor from the Diaspora in Israel must keep two days of *Yom Tov* (*Mishnah Berurah* 496:13, *Pe'at Hashulchan* 2:15, and *Teshuvot Igrot Moshe, Orach Chaim* 3:74 and 4:108). The *Avkat Rocheil* and *Pe'at Hashulchan* both note the practice of publicly conducting *Yom Tov* services on *Yom Tov Sheini*.

THE SECOND DAY OF YOM TOV FOR VISITORS TO ISRAEL

The Chacham Tzvi

Rav Tzvi Ashkenazi (*Teshuvot Chacham Tzvi* 167) disputes Rav Karo's ruling. He argues that the Mishnah's rule of maintaining the restrictions of the place that one left does not apply to the observance of *Yom Tov Sheini* by visitors to Israel. He explains that *Yom Tov Sheini* differs from regular customs, which theoretically apply anywhere, because it is geographically linked to the Diaspora. While the **residents** of a particular community normally develop its customs, *Yom Tov Sheini* was instituted for the **physical area** of the Diaspora. However, when one is in Israel, he is in a place where *Yom Tov Sheini* has no meaning, regardless of where he normally resides. Only other customs, which could theoretically exist even where they are not practiced, is it reasonable for someone who always did them in his own community to observe them while visiting elsewhere.[1] According to the *Chacham Tzvi*, a visitor in Israel is prohibited from observing *Yom Tov Sheini*, lest he violate the prohibition of *bal tosif* (adding to the Torah's precepts). Although the *Chacham Tzvi* is definitely the minority view on this issue, his position has attracted some support from other authorities (*Shulchan Aruch Harav* 496:11 and *Teshuvot Sho'eil Umeishiv* 3:2:28). According to this view, it follows that an Israeli visitor to the Diaspora should fully observe *Yom Tov Sheini,* as one's permanent place of residence is irrelevant.[2]

---

1. For example, the Mishnah (*Pesachim* 50a-b) addresses the custom of not doing work on *Erev Pesach*. This custom only developed in certain communities, but it is theoretically reasonable to observe such a custom in any geographic location. Accordingly, it is by no means absurd to obligate someone whose community refrains from work on *Erev Pesach* to even refrain from it when visiting a community which does not share his custom. On the other hand, *Yom Tov Sheini* is only a logical custom for communities in the Diaspora.
2. Regarding the general issue of *Yom Tov Sheini* for Israeli visitors to the Diaspora, see *Shulchan Aruch* (*Orach Chaim* 496:3) and *Teshuvot Tzitz Eliezer* (9:30).

GRAY MATTER

The Compromise Approach - Rav Salant and Rav M. Soloveitchik

Some *poskim* are torn between the cogency of the *Chacham Tzvi*'s reasoning and the overwhelming majority of authorities, who side with Rav Yosef Karo, so they adopt a compromise approach.[3] In principle, they accept the view of the *Chacham Tzvi*, ruling that men should don *tefilin* and all should recite weekday prayers. However, they add that one should refrain from forbidden acts on *Yom Tov Sheini* in deference to the view of Rav Yosef Karo. Rav Yechiel Michel Tukachinsky (*Ir Hakodesh V'hamikdash* 19:11) records that Rav Shmuel Salant adopted such an approach. Similarly, Rav Aharon Lichtenstein recounts that when Rav Yosef Dov Soloveitchik visited Israel in 1935, he stayed there during *Shavuot*. He asked his eminent father, Rav Moshe Soloveitchik, what to do for *Yom Tov Sheini*. Rav Moshe Soloveitchik replied that he essentially concurred with the *Chacham Tzvi*'s view, but one should nonetheless avoid doing *melachah* to accommodate the ruling of Rav Yosef Karo.

Rav Tukachinsky provides several practical rules for one who wishes to adopt this approach:

1) After the first night of *Yom Tov*, one should hear *havdalah* from an Israeli and should not recite *kiddush*.
2) On the day after the Israeli *Yom Tov*, one should recite weekday prayers. Nevertheless, one should abstain from *melachah*, just as one would during *Yom Tov Sheini* in the Diaspora.

---

3. These authorities are unable to simply adopt the seemingly stricter view and require the observance of two days of *Yom Tov*, for this seeming stringency is sometimes a leniency. For example, by treating the day as *Yom Tov*, men would not perform the *mitzvah* of *tefilin*. In addition, reciting the holiday prayers would mean losing the opportunity to recite weekday prayers. It is thus essential for these authorities to decide which view they fundamentally accept, despite the fact that they recommend adhering to certain stringent practices of the opposing view. By deciding in favor of the *Chacham Tzvi*, they are only able to accept stringent practices from Rav Karo's view when those practices do not detract from the *mitzvot* of a weekday (such as donning *tefilin* and reciting weekday prayers).

THE SECOND DAY OF YOM TOV FOR VISITORS TO ISRAEL

3) On *Shmini Atzeret*, one should not eat in the *sukkah*.⁴
4) For the *seder* on the second night of *Pesach*, one should eat *matzah* and *maror* without reciting the blessings, recite blessings on only the first and third cups of wine, and recite the Haggadah without the concluding blessing (*asher ge'alanu*). Rav Lichtenstein reports that Rav Yosef Dov Soloveitchik counseled that one should attend a *seder* conducted by one who follows Rav Karo's views and listen to the blessings recited by the host.
5) When *Yom Tov* falls out on a Thursday, the visitor from the Diaspora should avoid doing *melachah* on Friday. Consequently, he should make an *eruv tavshilin* to permit preparing food on Friday for *Shabbat*, but he should not recite a blessing over it.

Determining Da'ato Lachazor

If a visitor follows the opinion of Rav Yosef Karo, he will not necessarily observe two days of *Yom Tov* while in Israel. In each specific case, it must be determined whether or not the visitor plans on staying in Israel, as one should only observe *Yom Tov Sheini* if one plans on returning to the Diaspora (*da'ato lachazor*).

The Radbaz (*Teshuvot* 4:73) writes that *da'ato lachazor* is determined by whether one brings his family with him, because leaving one's family behind indicates that one intends to return to them. The *Mishnah Berurah* (496:13) rules in accordance with the Radbaz. Accordingly, one who travels with his entire family should only observe one day of *Yom Tov*. Today, however, it may be anachronistic to apply such a ruling, as the ability to travel has changed drastically even since the time of the *Mishnah Berurah*. In our time, one who travels with his entire family might well be on a temporary family vacation. Rav Moshe Feinstein (*Teshuvot Igrot Moshe, Orach Chaim* 3:74; also see *Techumin* 10:366-367)

---

4. See *Teshuvot Minchat Shlomo* (1:19), who rules that even those who follow Rav Yosef Karo's approach should not sit in a *sukkah* on *Shmini Atzeret*. It should be noted that although Rav Shlomo Zalman follows Rav Karo's ruling, he uses the *Chacham Tzvi*'s view as a consideration in his rulings regarding *Yom Tov Sheini*.

thus rejects applying the Radbaz's criterion today, whereas Rav Eliezer Waldenberg (*Teshuvot Tzitz Eliezer* 9:30) still considers it relevant.[5]

Other authorities suggest different ways to determine *da'ato lachazor*. The *Aruch Hashulchan* (O.C. 496:5), in addition to citing the Radbaz, also claims that one who intends to stay where he is going for at least a year becomes a resident of his destination (even without bringing his family). Accordingly, one who goes to Israel for a year should observe only one day of *Yom Tov*.

Rav Ovadia Yosef (*Teshuvot Yabia Omer*, vol. 6, O.C. 40, and *Teshuvot Yechaveh Da'at* 1:26) cites and accepts the view of earlier Sephardic rabbis to treat single Yeshivah students of marriageable age as intending to permanently settle in Israel. He explains that a Yeshivah student, even if he is not dating an Israeli at the time and expects to return to the Diaspora, theoretically could marry an Israeli and staying in Israel. A married man, on the other hand, must return to his family and job outside Israel. Rav Ovadia adds, however, that if a single man adamant insists that he will not stay in Israel under any circumstances, such as if he feels that he cannot leave his parents, then he must keep two days of *Yom Tov* even in Israel.[6]

---

5. Rav Waldenberg addresses a practical case involving an Israeli couple that traveled abroad for two years. He instructs the couple to observe two days, like permanent residents of the Diaspora. In addition to the Radbaz's criterion, he also uses the length of the trip as a reason to view it as a more permanent change of residence. It is unclear if he would follow the Radbaz alone, given the other opinions for determining *da'ato lachazor*. At the very least, Rav Waldenberg makes no mention of the Radbaz's opinion being outdated.

6. Rav Ovadia himself clearly rules that even when someone's parents in the Diaspora want him to return permanently to their country, he has the right to defy them, settle in Israel, and only return to the Diaspora for temporary visits. Nonetheless, Rav Ovadia acknowledges that some individuals might hesitate to do this, so he writes that one who feels he will return to the Diaspora regardless must observe two days of *Yom Tov*.

THE SECOND DAY OF YOM TOV FOR VISITORS TO ISRAEL

Rav Moshe Feinstein (*Teshuvot Igrot Moshe*, O.C. 2:101) treats anyone in Israel who is supported by his parents in America as a resident of the Diaspora.

Conclusion

One should try to spend *Yom Tov* in Israel. By visiting Israel for *Yom Tov*, one partially fulfills the *mitzvah* of *yishuv Eretz Yisrael* according to some views (see *Mishnah Berurah* 248:28). In addition, one supports the Israeli economy and deepens his family's connection to *Eretz Yisrael*. However, one must consult a rabbi for a ruling on which of the three views to follow. In addition, many very detailed questions often arise over the course of *Yom Tov Sheini* in Israel, so one must be amply prepared to deal with them.[7] Of course, the best solution to this problem is to move to Israel permanently and avoid this debate altogether.

---

7. For practical examples, see *Teshuvot Minchat Shlomo* (1:19 and 2:58:7-12).

May Women Read the Megillah?

One of the more interesting halachic questions relating to *Purim* is the propriety of a woman reading *Megillat Esther*. This topic has been debated from the time of the earliest *Rishonim* until today, and we will survey the major issues and concerns surrounding it.

Talmudic Background

The Mishnah (*Rosh Hashanah* 29a) states that whoever is not required to fulfill a particular *mitzvah* cannot discharge other people of their obligation to perform it. Thus, a woman cannot blow the *shofar* on behalf of a man, for she is not obligated to blow the *shofar*. Moreover, the Gemara (*Berachot* 20b) explains that the level of obligation of the one performing the *mitzvah* must equal that of the individuals whom he wishes to discharge. For example, the Gemara discusses whether a woman is obligated to recite *birkat hamazon* (grace after meals) on a biblical or rabbinical level. It explains that only if a woman is obligated in *birkat hamazon* on the same level as a man can she recite it on his behalf.

Accordingly, the question of whether a woman can read the *Megillah* on behalf of a man depends upon whether they share the same level of obligation. The Gemara (*Megillah* 4a; also see *Arachin* 3a) seems to clearly obligate women to read the *Megillah* on the same level as men, as it states, "Women are obligated in the reading of the *Megillah*, because they also were involved in the miracle [of *Purim*]."[1]

---

1. See Rashi and *Tosafot* for different explanations of the women's involvement in the miracle.

MAY WOMEN READ THE MEGILLAH?

Tosafot (s.v. *Chayavot*) write that this passage appears to indicate that women may read the *Megillah* on behalf of men. The Rambam (*Hil. Megillah* 1:1) apparently agrees with this assertion of *Tosafot*. He writes, "Everyone is obligated to recite the *Megillah*, including men and women," and makes no distinction between the genders regarding the level of obligation.[2]

However, *Tosafot* (*ibid.* and *Arachin* 3a s.v. *La'atuyei*) quote the opinion of the *Ba'al Halachot Gedolot* (*Behag*) that "a woman may only recite the *Megillah* on behalf of other women, but not on behalf of a man." As a source for this ruling, *Tosafot* cite a passage from the *Tosefta* (*Megillah* 2:4) which rules that an *androginos*[3] may not recite the *Megillah* on behalf of a man. *Tosafot* explain that this restriction stems from the partial female status of the *androginos*. Accordingly, if an *androginos* cannot recite the *Megillah* on behalf of a man, certainly a woman cannot. This view apparently understands that the Gemara in *Masechet Megillah* does not obligate a woman to **read** the *Megillah*; rather, she merely must **hear** it. The Rosh (*Megillah* 1:4) cites a passage from the *Yerushalmi* (*Megillah* 2:5) as proof for the opinion of the *Behag*. The passage records that both Rabi Yehoshua ben Levi and Rabi Yonah, father of Rabi Mana, would make sure to read the *Megillah* on behalf of the women of their families, because women are obligated to **hear** the *Megillah*.[4] It is very significant to note that both *Tosafot* and the Rosh agree that, according to the *Behag*, a woman can read the *Megillah* on behalf of other **women**.

---

2. *Magid Mishnah* and *Or Samei'ach* (both commenting on *Hil. Megillah* 1:1) note that the Rambam appears to permit women to read the *Megillah* on behalf of men. This is also the way that Rav Yosef Dov Soloveitchik explained the Rambam's opinion.

3. This term refers to someone with both male and female features. His status is sometimes parallel to a male and sometimes parallel to a female (see *Encyclopedia Talmudit* 1:55-60).

4. Much of the passage cited by the Rosh does not appear in our editions of the *Yerushalmi*.

GRAY MATTER

Tosafot in *Sukkah* (38a s.v. *Be'emet*) present a different understanding of the *Behag*'s opinion.[5] According to their version, the *Behag* believes that although women, like men, are obligated to *read* the *Megillah*, they cannot discharge a group of others, for it is an inappropriate activity for a woman (perhaps because it is a public activity, which *Tosafot* deem unbecoming for women). The *Korban Netaneil* (*Megillah* 1:40) asserts that when *Tosafot* in *Sukkah* say that a woman should not read on behalf of a group, they include a group of **women**, unlike the Rosh and *Tosafot* in *Masechet Megillah*. The *Korban Netaneil* notes, however, that the *Magen Avraham* (271:2) disagrees with him and believes that even according to *Tosafot* in *Sukkah*, it is only inappropriate when women read for **men**. Indeed, Rav Yehuda Henkin (*Teshuvot Bnei Banim* 2:10 and *Equality Lost*, pp. 57-59) notes that the *Tosafot HaRosh's* parallel passage to the *Tosafot* in *Sukkah* clearly indicates that women are only prevented from reading on behalf of **men**.[6]

Basis of the Behag

Is there a conceptual basis for distinguishing between the obligations of men and women to read the *Megillah*? We will summarize the creative suggestions of some *Acharonim*.[7] The *Marcheshet* (22) writes that according to the *Behag*, *Megillah* reading for men has two aspects: **hearing** the *Megillah* to

---

5. It is not uncommon for *Tosafot* to contradict themselves in different places, because they represent the views of many different Tosafists (see Maharsha, *Pesachim* 27a). In addition, the *Tosafot* that appear in standard editions of the Gemara originate from different authors in different parts of the Gemara.

6. The *Tosafot HaRosh* are a summary of the teachings of the Tosafists similar to the *Tosafot* printed in our Gemara. They often contain additional words, which serve to clarify the intentions of the various Tosafists cited.

7. We have only cited some of the better known explanations of the *Behag's* view. Additional explanations appear in Rav Yosef Dov Soloveitchik's *Reshimot Shiurim* to *Sukkah* (compiled by Rav Hershel Reichman), p. 184, and in the *Marcheshet* (22).

MAY WOMEN READ THE MEGILLAH?

publicize the miracle of *Purim* (*pirsumei nisa*), and remembering the wicked actions of *Amaleik*. The *Marcheshet* posits that the *Behag* exempts women from the *mitzvah* of remembering *Amaleik* (like the opinion of the *Sefer Hachinuch* 603). Hence, women have only one aspect in their obligation to read *Megillah* - hearing the *Megillah* for *pirsumei nisa*. They cannot read the *Megillah* on behalf of men, who have the added dimension of remembering *Amaleik*.[8]

The *Or Samei'ach* (*Hil. Megillah* 1:1) suggests a reason for linking **reading** to the memory of *Amaleik*. He notes that the need to write down the *Megillah* stems from God's commandment to Moshe to commemorate the heinous attack of *Amaleik* in **writing** (*Shemot* 17:14). The *Purim* miracle can be recounted orally for *pirsumei nisa*, but written commemoration of *Amaleik* necessitates reading out of a scroll. Accordingly, women, who are merely obligated to orally recount the miracle, cannot discharge men of their obligation to read out of a *Megillah* scroll and commemorate *Amaleik* in writing. The *Or Samei'ach* thus explains the *Behag*'s intention in writing that men are obligated to read the *Megillah*, while women are only obligated to hear the *Megillah*.

The *Avnei Neizer* (O.C. 511) takes an approach that resembles the *Marcheshet*'s, but with one notable difference. Like the *Marcheshet*, he suggests that the distinction between men and women lies in the *mitzvah* to remember *Amaleik*. He suggests,

---

8. The *Marcheshet* permits women to read the *Megillah* at night even for men, arguing that war is not practiced at night. Since the men's added dimension of obligation is to remember and wage war against *Amaleik*, and this dimension is irrelevant at night, women are thus obligated on the same level as men at night. There is no hint of this distinction between day and night anywhere in the *Behag*, *Shulchan Aruch*, or any of the later prominent authorities (such as the *Mishnah Berurah* and *Aruch Hashulchan*). It would thus appear, even at night, that a woman should not read the *Megillah* for men in practice. As Rav Yitzchak Herzog (*Teshuvot Heichal Yitzchak* 2:43) notes, we do not generally implement fancy "*pilpul*" style explanations against the consensus of the traditionally accepted authorities.

however, that this distinction exists even assuming that women, too, are required to remember *Amaleik* (see *Minchat Chinuch* 689). The *Avnei Neizer* explains that women must remember *Amaleik* in a general sense. However, the rabbinical enactment to remember *Amaleik* specifically by reading the *Megillah* on Purim does not apply to women, as they are not obligated in time-bound *mitzvot*. They must **hear** the *Megillah* due to their involvement in the miracle, but actively **reading** (as men must do) is a separate time-bound obligation. According to all of these approaches, the *Behag* permits women to read the *Megillah* on behalf of other women, for all women share the same level of obligation.

Shulchan Aruch and its Commentaries

Rav Yosef Karo, writing in the *Beit Yosef* (*Orach Chaim* 689), cites various opinions among the *Rishonim* regarding whether the view of the *Behag* is accepted. No consensus on this question emerges. In the *Shulchan Aruch* (O.C. 689:2), Rav Karo presents the opinion that women can read the *Megillah* on behalf of men as the primary view.[9] He subsequently cites the opinion of the *Behag* that women cannot read the *Megillah* on behalf of men. It seems clear from the language of the *Shulchan Aruch* that women can read the *Megillah* for other women according to all opinions.

The Rama, adding to this rule of the *Shulchan Aruch*, cites the Mordechai, who asserts that if a woman reads the *Megillah* for herself, she should recite "to hear the *Megillah*" ("*lishmoa Megillah*"), rather than the conventional blessing of "*al mikra Megillah*." This follows *Tosafot* in *Megillah* and the Rosh's presentation of the *Behag* that women are obligated only to hear the *Megillah*, but not to read it. The Rama does not prohibit the reading of the *Megillah* by women for other women.

---

9. Regarding the applicability of *kol ishah* (the prohibition for men to hear women sing) to *Megillah* reading, see *Nishmat Avraham* (5:76-77) and Rav Moshe Harari's *Mikra'ei Kodesh* (*Hilchot Purim* 6:10 and note 37, and *Hilchot Leil Haseider* 6:15 and note 38).

May Women Read the Megillah?

The *Magen Avraham* (689:6) cites from a *midrash* that a woman should not even read the *Megillah* for herself. Rather, she should be sure to hear the reading from a man. This author and Rav Zvi Grumet heard an explanation of this opinion from Rav Yosef Dov Soloveitchik (later printed in *Har'rei Kedem*, Chapter 200). Rav Soloveitchik suggested that it was based on the previously cited passage from the *Yerushalmi*, which recorded the practice of two *Amoraim* to read the *Megillah* for the women in their families. Rav Soloveitchik explained that the *Yerushalmi* is teaching that women do not have an independent obligation to read the *Megillah*. Instead, it is the obligation of the man of the house to read the *Megillah* to all the family members of that household.

To summarize, there are two possible reasons to preclude women reading the *Megillah* for other women. First is the opinion of the *Korban Netaneil* that it is inappropriate for women to read **in public** for other women. Second, the *Magen Avraham* adopts the approach of the *midrash* that women should not read the *Megillah* even for themselves. While we shall see that many latter day authorities reject both these reasons, it seems clear that women should not read the *Megillah* for men, as the *Shulchan Aruch* cites the *Behag*'s opinion as a viable approach, and the Rama rules in accordance with it. The commentaries to the Rama voice no disagreement with his ruling.

Latter-Day Codifiers

Both the *Chayei Adam* (155:11) and the *Mishnah Berurah* (689:8) present the *Magen Avraham*'s objection to a woman reading herself the *Megillah*. However, the *Chayei Adam* strongly questions the basis of the *Magen Avraham*'s citation and therefore rules that a woman who has no one to read the *Megillah* for her should read it herself. The *Mishnah Berurah* accepts the decision of the *Chayei Adam*. Moreover, the *Mishnah Berurah* (689:7) writes that a woman can even read the *Megillah* for other women. In the *Sha'ar Hatziyun* (689:16), he explains the basis for ruling like the *Chayei Adam*. He notes that the primary opinion in the *Shulchan Aruch* follows the Rambam and the other *Rishonim* who rule that women can read the *Megillah* even for men.

GRAY MATTER

Furthermore, even according to the *Behag*, most authorities understand that women can read the *Megillah* for themselves. Nevertheless, the *Mishnah Berurah* (*Sha'ar Hatziyun* 689:15) rules that a woman should not read for many women because of the *Korban Netaneil*'s interpretation of *Tosafot*, that a public women's reading is inappropriate. The *Aruch Hashulchan* (O.C. 689:5) seems to even permit one woman to read for many others, as he does not cite the opinion of the *Korban Netaneil*.

Other Considerations

Although many authorities permit women to read the *Megillah* for themselves (especially when the reading does not take place in a public setting), several issues can complicate such a reading. It is unclear whether a group of ten or more women constitute a *minyan* (quorum) for the purpose of *Megillah* reading.[10] The presence of a *minyan* is very significant in light of the Rama's ruling (O.C. 692:1) that the blessing recited at the conclusion of *Megillah* reading, "*harav et riveinu*," is only recited in the presence of a *minyan*. While the *Biur Halachah* mentions that some authorities disagree with the Rama, the *Biur Halachah* himself concludes that the Rama's ruling should be followed. A women's *Megillah* reading likely loses the opportunity to recite this blessing.[11] Interestingly, the *Aruch Hashulchan* does not cite this as a reason that women should not read the *Megillah* themselves.

---

10. See Rama (O.C. 690:18) and *Aruch Hashulchan* (O.C. 690:25). For an analysis of whether women can be part of the group of ten to read the *Megillah*, see this author's essay in *Beit Yitzchak* (22:301-304).

11. We have written that it is "likely" lost, as one could theoretically argue in favor of combining two minority opinions to permit reciting this blessing in the presence of ten women. The opinions are those who disagree with the requirement of a *minyan* for *harav et riveinu* and those who permit counting women in a *minyan* for *Megillah* reading. Regarding the ability to recite a blessing when a double doubt (*safeik s'feika*) exists, see the sources cited by Rav Ovadia Yosef (*Taharat Habayit*, vol. 2, p. 486). It should also be noted that we have based ourselves on the opinion of the Rama, whose rulings are authoritative for Ashkenazic Jewry. For Sephardic women, Rav Moshe Harari (*Mikra'ei Kodesh*, *Hil. Purim* 6, footnote 39) reports that Rav Mordechai

MAY WOMEN READ THE MEGILLAH?

Aside from the specific benefit of reciting "*harav et riveinu*," the *Shulchan Aruch* (O.C. 690:18) writes that one must "pursue a *minyan*" for reading the *Megillah*, because reading the *Megillah* with a *minyan* is considered qualitatively better. Furthermore, it is generally preferable to read the *Megillah* in a larger group (*berov am hadrat melech;* see *Magen Avraham* 689:10). Additional *Megillah* readings of any kind detract from this ideal. Of course, practical considerations must always be weighed against this preference. Clearly, if a communal *Megillah* reading is getting so large that people must struggle to properly hear the *Megillah*, it is proper to have more than one reading.

An additional problem arises with certain women hearing the *Megillah* from another woman. The *Mishnah Berurah* (689:15) notes that some authorities do not permit anyone to read the *Megillah* for others without either a *minyan* present (as is the case in most communal *Megillah* readings) or in a situation where the listener does not know how to read the *Megillah* himself. The *Shulchan Aruch* (O.C. 689:5) adopts this position, and the *Mishnah Berurah* appears to favor it, too. Women's readings generally do not have a *minyan* present, so these authorities would likely not permit a woman to read the *Megillah* for women who can read it themselves.[12]

Eliyahu does not permit reciting this blessing without ten men present, while Rav Ovadia Yosef permits its recital, provided that there are ten women present. For greater elaboration on Rav Ovadia's view, see the fifth volume of *Yalkut Yosef* (*Dinei Kri'at Hamegillah* 7 and *Hilchot Mikra Megillah* 39).

12. We have not stated the application to women's readings in an absolute manner, as it is predicated upon the assumption that ten women do not constitute a *minyan* for *Megillah* reading. As we have indicated above, however, this is not entirely clear. In fact, Rav Moshe Harari (*Mikra'ei Kodesh, Hil. Purim* 6, footnote 39) implies that Rav Ovadia Yosef, who considers ten women a *minyan* for reciting "*harav et riveinu*," would permit reading the *Megillah* for a group of ten or more people, regardless of gender, even if some of them could read the *Megillah* themselves. Rav Harari adds that those who reject Rav Ovadia's opinion regarding "*harav et riveinu*" (such as Rav Mordechai Eliyahu) would presumably reject it here, too.

Another relevant factor is the possible inability of women to read the *Megillah* for others once they have fulfilled their own obligation.[13] The *Biur Halachah* (689 s.v. *Venashim*) prohibits a woman who has already heard the *Megillah* to reread it for other women. Rav Moshe Feinstein[14] permits such a reading, but he does not permit the reader to recite the blessings for the *Megillah* reading. According to his opinion, the listener should recite the blessings if the reader has already fulfilled her own obligation.

Finally, the question of deviation from established practice must be considered. Rav Hershel Schachter (*Nefesh Harav*, p. 145) cites Rav Yosef Dov Soloveitchik's opposition to women reading the *Megillah* for other women in a synagogue, out of concern for deviating from established synagogue protocol and practice. Rav Soloveitchik's grandson, Rav Mayer Twersky (*Tradition* 32:3:13), reports that the Rav was also concerned with the opinion of the *Magen Avraham* (cited earlier) that women may not even read the *Megillah* for themselves.[15]

---

13. A man who has already heard the *Megillah* may read it again for others because of the principle of *arvut* (*Berachot* 20b). This principle states that every Jew is responsible to ensure that all other Jews fulfill *mitzvot*. Accordingly, even one who has already performed a *mitzvah* himself (such as *kiddush* or *Megillah* reading) may do it again for another Jew's benefit. There is some dispute regarding the applicability of *arvut* to women, which is why the *Biur Halachah* does not permit a woman to reread the *Megillah* for others. For greater discussion of the applicability of *arvut* to women, see *Dagul Meirvavah* (O.C. 271), Rav Akiva Eiger's gloss to the *Shulchan Aruch* (O.C. 271, commenting on *Magen Avraham* 271:2), and *Nishmat Avraham* (1:9-10).
14. *Teshuvot Igrot Moshe* (O.C. 1:190). Also see Rav Moshe Harari's *Mikra'ei Kodesh* (*Hilchot Purim* 6:8). It is somewhat surprising that Rav Moshe Feinstein does not mention the *Biur Halachah*'s opinion, nor does the *Biur Halachah* refer to the comments of the *Dagul Meirvavah* and Rav Akvia Eiger, which we cited in the previous footnote.
15. Regarding the Rav's approach towards women's *Megillah* readings, Rav J.J. Schachter (*The Torah U-Madda Journal* 8:261) writes, "[Initially,] his answer was a one word 'No'.... We proceeded to engage in a discussion of the issue, the Rav marshalling arguments explaining his position and I arguing with each of them, one by one.... Finally... he said, 'Schechter, if you want, I can give you a *heter*, but you shouldn't do it.'"

MAY WOMEN READ THE MEGILLAH?

Conclusion

It seems clear that it is halachically inappropriate for women to read the *Megillah* for men, as many *Rishonim* agree with the *Behag*, and the Rama rules in accordance with him.[16] The issue of women reading the *Megillah* for other women seems to be unresolved. Rav Yehuda Henkin (*Bnei Banim* 2:10) permits women to read the *Megillah* for other women.[17] This view has also been attributed to Rav Aharon Lichtenstein (cited in *Tradition* 32:2:104-105). On the other hand, Rav Hershel Schachter (*Be'ikvei Hatzon* 5:1,4,5), Rav Shlomo Zalman Auerbach, Rav Mordechai Eliyahu, Rav Avraham Shapira (all cited in *Tradition* 32:2:106-107), and Rav Mordechai Willig (in a public address delivered in Teaneck, New Jersey) oppose such readings.[18]

---

16. This is certainly true for Ashkenazic women, as Ashkenazic Jews follow the Rama's rulings. Regarding Sephardic women reading the *Megillah* for men, see *Yalkut Yosef* (vol. 5, *Dinei Kri'at Hamegillah* 12).
17. Rav Henkin elsewhere affirms that he even permits women's readings when *Purim* falls out on *Shabbat* in Jerusalem, and the *Megillah* is read on Friday (*Bnei Banim* 3:7). By contrast, Rav Aharon Lichtenstein (quoted in *Tradition* 32:2:105) reportedly rules in such a year that women's readings should not be conducted in Jerusalem, as a *minyan* is required when the *Megillah* is not read on its proper date, and it is questionable if ten women qualify as a *minyan*.
18. Those whom we have cited as opposing public women's *Megillah* readings may differ regarding a woman reading the *Megillah* privately for herself or another woman. Rav Mordechai Eliyahu (cited in Rav Moshe Harari's *Mikra'ei Kodesh*, *Hil. Purim* 6:8 and note 29) permits a woman to read the *Megillah* in private *lechatchilah* (even without extenuating circumstances), despite objecting to women reading publicly even *bedieved* (explained by Rav Harari that a woman who attended a women's public *Megillah* reading must reread the *Megillah* without reciting its blessings). It is unclear how the other authorities feel about a woman reading the *Megillah* in private.

Should One Get Drunk on Purim?

Our observance of the famous Talmudic rule (*Megillah* 7b) that one should ingest alcoholic beverages on *Purim* has not always led to optimal results. Hatzoloh (the Jewish volunteer ambulance service in New York) has run educational campaigns imploring us "not to get carried away on *Purim*," both figuratively and literally. We will explore the halachic sources in order to demonstrate that this Halachah need not cause serious health problems.

Introduction

The *Biur Halachah* (695:2 s.v *Chayav* and *Ad*) raises a fundamental question. How can *Chazal* obligate us to drink on *Purim* if we find several incidents in *Tanach* (Noach, Lot, Nadav and Avihu) that demonstrate the great dangers inherent in imbibing too much alcohol. He answers (citing the *Eliah Rabba*) that the miracle of *Purim* came about through parties at which alcohol played a central role. We thus consume alcohol on *Purim* in order to commemorate the great miracle.

The *Biur Halachah* also cites an important comment of the Me'iri about drinking on *Purim*. The Me'iri writes:

> Nevertheless, we are not obligated to become inebriated and degrade ourselves due to our joy. We are not obligated to engage in a *simchah* of frivolity and foolishness, rather [to engage in] a *simchah* of enjoyment which should lead to love of God and thankfulness for the miracles He has performed for us.

SHOULD ONE GET DRUNK ON PURIM?

Talmudic Sources

The Gemara (*Megillah* 7b) presents the rule that one should drink[1] alcoholic beverages on *Purim* until he cannot distinguish between "cursed be Haman" and "blessed be Mordechai."[2] It relates an eye-opening incident related to this obligation. Rabbah and Rabi Zeira made a *seudat Purim* (*Purim* feast) together. As a result of their inebriation, Rabbah arose and "slaughtered" Rabi Zeira.[3] Subsequently, Rabbah prayed on behalf of Rabi Zeira and the latter recovered. The next year Rabbah invited Rabi Zeira for a *seudat Purim*; Rabi Zeira declined the offer and said, "Miracles do not occur all the time."

This passage appears to link drinking on *Purim* with the *seudat Purim*. Apparently, drinking per se is not an obligation; rather, it is part of the *mitzvah* of *seudat Purim*. Perhaps drinking at the *Purim* feast serves to characterize the meal as a *Purim* feast.[4] Indeed the Rambam (*Hilchot Megillah* 2:15), *Tur* (*Orach Chaim* 695), and *Shulchan Aruch* (O.C. 695:2) all present the rule of drinking on *Purim* within the context of the laws of *seudat Purim*. It would seem that there is no halachic obligation fulfilled by drinking on *Purim* unless it is done within the context of the *seudah*. Furthermore, the Gemara (*Megillah* 7b) comments that if one has eaten a *seudah* at night, he has not fulfilled his obligation of *seudat Purim*. Accordingly, little is accomplished from a halachic perspective by drinking alcoholic beverages on *Purim* night.

---

1. Rashi understands that the Gemara is referring to drunkenness. See, however, *Korban Netaneil* (*Megillah* 33b, 1:10).
2. The Gemara never distinguishes between the genders regarding drinking on *Purim*. Nevertheless, Rav Mordechai Eliyahu (cited in Rav Moshe Harari's *Mikrav'ei Kodesh*, *Hilchot Purim*, *Milu'im* to Chapter 13, note 5) exempts women from this obligation, noting that the Gemara (*Ketubot* 65a) discourages women from ever drinking significant quantities of alcohol.
3. Rabbeinu Avraham ben Harambam (letter printed at the beginning of the *Ein Yaakov*) and the Maharsha (*ad. loc.* s.v. *Kam*) claim that Rabbah did not literally slaughter Rabi Zeira. Instead, the Gemara means that Rabbah coaxed him into drinking so much alcohol that it brought Rabi Zeira close to death.
4. See this author's essay in *Beit Yitzchak* (26:595-596).

GRAY MATTER

Rishonim's Approaches

The Gemara might record the incident involving Rabbah and Rabi Zeira to reject or limit the rabbinical decree regarding drinking on *Purim*. The *Baal Hamaor* (*Megillah* 3b in Rif's pages) cites and accepts the opinion of Rabbeinu Ephraim that the Gemara presents the incident to rescind this Halachah, so it is now improper to drink on *Purim*. On the other hand, the Rif (*ibid.*) and the Rosh (*Megillah* 1:8) cite the obligation to drink on *Purim* without any reservations whatsoever. Apparently, they believe that the Gemara presents the story merely as a cautionary note, with no impact on the Halachah.

The *Orchot Chaim* (cited in *Beit Yosef* O.C. 695) objects to getting drunk on *Purim* without specifically mentioning Rabbah and Rabi Zeira's incident. He writes, "[The Gemara] does not mean that one should become drunk, for drunkenness is an absolute prohibition, and there is no greater sin than it - it leads to adultery, murder, and many other sins - rather, one should drink a bit more than usual." The *Orchot Chaim* makes no reference to the story of Rabbah and Rabi Zeira per se; he merely notes that a literal interpretation of the obligation to get drunk on *Purim* is untenable, as it runs counter to Torah values.[5]

The Maharil (*Hilchot Purim* 10) cites a clever explanation of drinking until one cannot distinguish between "cursed be Haman" and "blessed be Mordechai" from the *Agudah*. He notes that the numerical value (*gematria*) of each Hebrew phrases (*arur Haman, baruch Mordechai*) equals 502. Accordingly, he explains that the Gemara obligates drinking until one cannot perform the calculations to reach 502 for the *gematria* of each phrase. This stage requires considerably less wine than the amount required for blurring the distinction between the characters Haman and Mordechai. The Maharil (*ibid.*) and *Magen Avraham* (695:3) accept this opinion.

The Rambam (*Hilchot Megillah* 2:15) presents a middle approach. He states that one should drink until he is inebriated and

---

5. It is unclear how the *Orchot Chaim* fits his opinion into the Gemara; see *Aruch Hashulchan*, O.C. 695:5.

SHOULD ONE GET DRUNK ON PURIM?

sleeps as a result of the alcohol he consumed. The *Aruch Hashulchan* (695:3) explains that, according to the Rambam, the story of Rabbah and Rabi Zeira modifies this Halachah, as the Rambam does not write that one should drink until he cannot distinguish between Haman and Mordechai. Rather, he should only drink to the extent that it causes him to sleep. Indeed, when he is asleep he cannot distinguish between Haman and Mordechai.

Whatever the desired level of drunkenness may be, it should be noted that the *Haghot Maimoniot* (commenting on *Hil. Megillah* 2:15) cites the Raavyah as stating that drinking on *Purim* is *"lemitzvah velo le'ikuva,"* meaning that one does not transgress anything by failing to drink on *Purim*, even assuming that drinking is encouraged.[6] The *Bach* (O.C. 695) codifies this statement.

Shulchan Aruch and Commentaries

The *Tur* and *Shulchan Aruch* adopt the approach of the Rif and Rosh that one should drink on *Purim* until he literally cannot distinguish between Haman and Mordechai. On the other hand, the *Bach* (O.C. 695) rules in accordance with Rabbeinu Ephraim that Rabbah and Rabi Zeira's incident negates any obligation to become extremely drunk. Nevertheless, the *Bach* claims that even this approach requires drinking "more than usual, such that one becomes merry... or even drunk enough that one could not speak before a king, although he will still maintain control of himself." The Rama rules that one should merely drink a bit more than usual and then go to sleep, thus being unable to distinguish between Haman and Mordechai. The Rama concludes by citing the Talmudic teaching, "One can do more or less as long as his intentions are focused on serving God."[7]

Late Codifiers

The *Biur Halachah* (695 s.v. *Ad*) cites the *Chayei Adam*, who limits this Halachah in a manner similar to the *Orchot Chaim*.

---

6. See Maharil, *Teshuvot* 56, where he explains the Raavyah's rationale.
7. See *Berachot* 17a and *Menachot* 110a.

GRAY MATTER

He writes, "If one believes that drinking on *Purim* will interfere with his performing any *mitzvah*, such as *birkat hamazon*, reciting *minchah* or *maariv*, or that he will behave in a boorish manner, it is preferable that he not drink (or become inebriated), as long as his motives are proper." It is obvious that one who is driving after the *seudat Purim* **must** refrain from drinking.[8] In addition, both the *Mishnah Berurah*[9] (695:5) and the *Aruch Hashulchan* (O.C. 695:5) rule that it is proper to merely drink a bit more than usual and then to nap. By following this rule, and avoiding drinking and driving, incidents similar to what happened when Rabbah and Rabi Zeira made a *seudat Purim* will hopefully be avoided.

Liquor

Rashi (*Megillah* 7b s.v. *Livsomei*) and the Rambam (*Hil. Megillah* 2:15) describe the obligation to drink on *Purim* specifically as drinking **wine**.[10] In fact, the *Aruch Hashulchan* (O.C. 695:5) specifically warns against drinking liquor, because it causes one to vomit.

Conclusion

The *Mishnah Berurah* and *Aruch Hashulchan* teach us not to get carried away on *Purim*. Unfortunately, many of us know of friends who have been killed or seriously injured in accidents on *Purim* as a result of excessive drinking. We must remember that Torah commands us to maintain our health and well-being (*Devarim* 4:9; Rambam, *Hil. Rotzeiach* 11:4).

---

8. See Rav Moshe Harari's *Mikra'ei Kodesh* (*Hilchot Purim*, *Milu'im* to Chapter 13, note 5), where Rav Mordechai Eliyahu and Rav Avigdor Neventzall forbid Israeli soldiers to get drunk if they have access to firearms.
9. The *Mishnah Berurah* is the same person as the *Biur Halachah* (Rav Yisrael Meir Hakohein Kagan).
10. See Rashi to *Megillah* 7b and *Korban Netaneil* (*Megillah* 1:10), who also seem to assert that one fulfills this rule only by drinking *wine*. See this author's essay in *Beit Yitzchak* (26:595-596) for an explanation of the significance of specifically requiring wine.

The Minhag of Kitniyot
Part I: General Overview

Over the past millennium, the custom developed in Ashkenazic communities to refrain from eating *Kitniyot*, certain legumes, on *Pesach*. We will base our discussion in part on an essay by Rav Yehudah Pris of Yeshivat Birkat Moshe (Maaleh Adumim) in *Techumin* (13:163-180).

Gemara and Rishonim

The Torah forbids us to eat *chametz* (leaven) on *Pesach*. Something becomes *chametz* when flour and water mix together long enough for the dough to rise. The Mishnah (*Pesachim* 35a) rules that *chametz* can be produced only from certain grains: wheat, barley, rye, spelt, and oats.[1]

---

1. Some question exists regarding the identification of the Gemara's *"shibolet shu'al"* as oats. Rav Yosef Efrati (*Mesorah* 13:66-71) notes Professor Yehudah Felix's claim that *shibolet shu'al* could not possibly be oats, and Rav Efrati vigorously disputes this claim. He cites Rav Yosef Shalom Eliashiv as supporting the view that *shibolet shu'al* is undoubtedly oats (the view accepted by almost all *Rishonim*). Ezra Frazer reports that Rav Aharon Lichtenstein does not flatly reject Professor Felix's claims, but he believes that one should continue to treat oats as *shibolet shu'al*, absent absolute proof that *shibolet shu'al* is something else. Rav Hershel Schachter has told this author that in case of great need one may use oat *matzah* at the *Pesach seder*. In general, Rav Schachter wrote this author that one should try to eat other *mezonot* foods together with oat products to avoid any doubt regarding the *berachot* before and after oats.

GRAY MATTER

Millet and rice are not included in this list, explains the Mishnah, because they spoil and do not ferment. However, Rabi Yochanan Ben Nuri includes rice in the list of grains that can potentially become *chametz*. The Gemara (*Pesachim* 114b) states that Rabi Yochanan Ben Nuri is a lone authority concerning this topic. The *Rishonim* therefore rule in accordance with the majority view, which contends that rice cannot become *chametz*. The Rambam, for example, writes (*Hilchot Chametz U'matzah* 5:1):

> There is no prohibition regarding *chametz* except with respect to the five categories of grain. There are two types of wheat... and three types of barley... but *kitniyot* such as rice... and the like are not included in the prohibition of *chametz*. Even if one were to knead rice flour... with hot water and cover it with a cloth until it rises like fermented dough, it may still be eaten on *Pesach*, for it is not *chametz*; instead it is *sirachon* (decay).[2]

The Rif omits the opinion of Rabi Yochanan Ben Nuri, indicating his acceptance of the majority view as the actual Halachah. Similarly, the Rosh (*Pesachim* 2:12), *Baal Hamaor* (*Pesachim* 26b in Rif's pages), and Ritva (*Pesachim* 35a s.v. *Hanei*) all rule in accordance with the majority view.

The Beginning of the Ashkenazic Custom

Although most *Rishonim* reject Rabi Yochanan Ben Nuri's ruling, some *Rishonim* are nonetheless stringent regarding the consumption of rice and similar foods. The primary authority who espouses this stringency is the *Smak*, who writes (*mitzvah* 222 note 12):

---

2. See *Techumin* (1:97), where Dr. B.P. Munk discusses the chemical difference between *chimutz* and *sirachon*.

THE MINHAG OF KITNIYOT PART I

Regarding *kitniyot*, such as rice and beans, our rabbis have the practice not to eat them on *Pesach*. I believe that I have heard that one should not cook them on *Pesach*, besides in boiling water from the moment they are placed in the pot [this is what the Gemara calls *chalitah* - H.J.]. Many great rabbis are lenient concerning this issue, but it appears very difficult to permit something when the common practice to be strict dates back to the early ages. It is reasonable to say that this stringency did not emerge as a concern for [*kitniyot* being actual] *chametz*, because they would not err on matters familiar even to the youngest of students, and the Gemara explicitly states that only the five species of grain have the potential to become *chametz*... Rather, the reason is an edict to prevent violation of Torah law, since *kitniyot* are cooked in a manner similar to the way that grains are cooked. Had we permitted *kitniyot*, one could have easily become confused [with *chametz*], because they are cooked similarly... In addition, in many locales, *kitniyot* are made into bread, and people who are not well versed in Torah laws might become confused. This is not at all similar to vegetables, which are clearly distinguishable from the five grains. It is a proper *minhag* (custom) to refrain from eating all *kitniyot*, including mustard seed, because of their similarity to grain. Although the Talmud (*Pesachim* 114b) specifically permits rice, this rule applied only in Talmudic times, when all were well versed in Halachah. However, today we should certainly follow the decree that we mentioned... and even to put *kitniyot* in boiling hot water should be forbidden, because one might become confused and permit placing them in cold water.

GRAY MATTER

The *Beit Yosef* (*Orach Chaim* 453) cites a different concern (which appears later in the *Smak*) - that *kitniyot* are mixed with grains that have the ability to become *chametz*. The Ritva (*Pesachim* 35a s.v. *Tana*) alludes to this concern:

> One must carefully inspect [*kitniyot*, such as rice,] because spelt is constantly mixed with rice... Many pious individuals avoid eating these species on *Pesach* if they were cooked, due to concerns regarding these mixtures.

Tur, Shulchan Aruch, Acharonim

The *Tur* (*Orach Chaim* 453) cites the *Smak*'s stringency, but he comments that it is excessive. The *Beit Yosef* adds that only Ashkenazic Jews abide by this stringency. Accordingly, he rules in his *Shulchan Aruch* (O.C. 453:1) that one may cook and consume *kitniyot*, as they cannot become *chametz*. The Rama, (*Darchei Moshe* 453:2) however, writes that Ashkenazic Jews have adopted the strict practice of not eating *kitniyot* on *Pesach*. Similarly, in his gloss to the *Shulchan Aruch*, he rules that Ashkenazic Jewry must not deviate from this custom. The Vilna Gaon notes that a source for this stringency appears the Gemara (*Pesachim* 40b), which records that Rava forbade servants who were not halachically scrupulous to make bread from legumes on *Pesach* (see *Tosafot* s.v. Rava and the Rosh 2:28).

Interestingly, some Ashkenazic authorities expressed serious reservations about the *minhag* of *kitniyot*, and a few even strongly criticized it.[3] Nevertheless, the *Aruch Hashulchan* (O.C. 453:4-5), writing at the dawn of the twentieth century, presents what has become the normative practice of Ashkenazic Jewry:[4]

---

3. See Rav Yaakov Emden (*Mor Uktzi'ah* 453), in the name of his famed father, the *Chacham Tzvi*, and *Encyclopedia Talmudit* (16:104 note 691).
4. The *Chatam Sofer* (*Teshuvot, Orach Chaim* 122) also uses sharp words against Ashkenazic Jews who are lax in observing the *minhag* of *kitniyot*.

THE MINHAG OF KITNIYOT PART I

Our forebears practiced for many years the avoidance of eating rice, etc. This prohibition has been accepted as a protection of our observance of Torah law; it is thus forbidden for us to abandon this practice. Those who question this practice and are lenient concerning it are demonstrating that they have neither fear of God nor fear of sin. They also display a flawed comprehension of the proper ways of Torah observance...

Although there are some countries which have not followed this stringency, all of Germany, France, Russia, and Poland have accepted upon themselves and their descendants this wonderful stringency, which has a good reason, and one who deviates from it should be bitten by a snake.

Kitniyot in Case of Illness and Famine

The practice to avoid eating *kitniyot* on *Pesach* is merely a custom, and not a rabbinical enactment, so there is some flexibility regarding it. For example, the *Mishnah Berurah* (453:7) writes that a seriously ill individual may eat *kitniyot*, even if his life is not in danger. He notes that the *Chatam Sofer* (*Teshuvot, Orach Chaim* 122) states that one should place the *kitniyot* in boiling water, since boiling prevents fermentation. The reasoning behind this leniency is that we assume our ancestors did not accept the stringency *of kitniyot* to apply in a case of illness. Rav Yehuda Amital told this author that it was permissible for this author's family to boil and serve kasha[5] to his father *z"l* on *Pesach* when he was suffering from an advanced stage of lung cancer, and kasha was one of the few food items that he was able to eat.

---

5. Kasha is made from buckwheat, which has the status of *kitniyot*. In situations where kasha must be fed to a sick person on *Pesach*, it is essential to verify that none of the five grains that produce true *chametz* have been mixed into the kasha.

GRAY MATTER

Similarly, the *Aruch Hashulchan* (O.C. 453:5) writes:

> It was explicitly stipulated that in the event of famine or severe economic conditions, the local sages, led by the chief rabbi, are permitted to temporarily suspend the *minhag* of avoiding *kitniyot* on *Pesach*. However, today, when potatoes are so readily available, there is no such need to be lenient.

A number of individuals on very strict diets have asked if they may eat *kitniyot* on *Pesach*. It may be possible to permit such individuals to consume boiled food items that are only questionably *kitniyot*, such as quinoa, soy, peanuts, and string beans, even if their custom is to refrain from these foods. Those for whom this is a relevant concern must seek competent rabbinical guidance.

The Minhag of Kitniyot
Part II: Ashkenazim Eating with Sephardim

In this chapter, we focus on the issue of whether an Ashkenazic Jew may eat non-*kitniyot* products at a Sephardic Jew's home on *Pesach*.

Rav Ovadia Yosef's Responsum

Rav Ovadia Yosef (*Teshuvot Yechaveh Da'at* 5:32) rules that an Ashkenazic Jew may eat non-*kitniyot* food at a Sephardic Jew's home on *Pesach*. He does not require special utensils that have not been used for *kitniyot* for the Ashkenazic guest. He bases his opinion on a similar ruling of the Rama (*Orach Chaim* 453:1): "It is obvious that if *kitniyot* fell into food during *Pesach*, they do not render the food forbidden *b'dieved* (*post facto*)."

Accordingly, Rav Ovadia argues the following:

> It is clear that the food particles of *kitniyot* absorbed into pots in Sephardic homes that are released into non-*kitniyot* food do not forbid the food to Ashkenazim. Even if the utensils have been used within the past twenty-four hours (and are thus emitting a good taste), it is still permissible for Ashkenazim to eat from them, **because there is surely more permissible food than there are *kitniyot* that emerge from the walls of the pot.**

GRAY MATTER

Precedents for Rav Ovadia's Ruling

Rav Ovadia cites several interesting precedents for his ruling. The first is a responsum of the Rama (132:15) regarding those who are strict about the issue of *chadash* (the prohibition against eating grain sown after Pesach, before the following year's sixteenth of Nissan) in the Diaspora. Just as most observant Diaspora Jews today are lenient in this area, most observant Jews in pre-war Europe were lenient (see *Mishnah Berurah* 489:45). The Rama writes that those who adopt the strict position regarding *chadash* may nonetheless eat food that absorbed flavor from the utensils of those who are lenient about *chadash*. He reasons that, in his community, even those who are strict only treat *chadash* as a doubtful rabbinical prohibition (as opposed to the many authorities who consider *chadash* to be an absolute biblical prohibition even in the Diaspora). The Rama thus claims that the light nature of *chadash* facilitates eating food that may have absorbed its flavor from pots. The flavor of the *chadash* is nullified (*bateil berov*) by the non-*chadash* food.

Rav Ovadia equates *kitniyot* to the Rama's case of *chadash*. *Kitniyot* are also an unusually light prohibition, so one may be lenient regarding the flavor in pots that cooked *kitniyot*.

A second precedent cited by Rav Ovadia is a ruling of the Radbaz (*Teshuvot* 4:496). His responsum discusses whether those who did not rely on a particular *shochet* may eat food cooked by those who did rely on him. The Radbaz rules leniently because he claims that the *shochet* in question was probably acceptable. Even those who do not rely on him for their actual meat could at least eat food cooked in utensils that absorbed the flavor of his meat. Again, writes Rav Ovadia, we see that certain prohibitions are treated unusually lightly, so their flavor is permitted. *Kitniyot*, a mere custom of Ashkenazic Jewry, should also be treated this way.[1]

---

1. The Radbaz also mentions other factors in his lenient ruling, which run counter to normative practice today. Nevertheless, Rav Ovadia claims that

THE MINHAG OF KITNIYOT PART II

Rav Ovadia's third precedent is an important ruling of the Rama in his gloss to the *Shulchan Aruch* (Y.D. 64:9). The Rama addresses a type of fat whose permissibility depended upon varying customs among Ashkenazic communities of his time. He permits members of the communities that abide by the strict view to eat food cooked in utensils of people in the lenient communities. The Rama reasons that the lenient communities were following a legitimate ruling of their halachic authorities. Even one who was strict about the actual fat did not need be strict about its flavor, because there is a valid opinion that permits the flavor.[2]

From all of the above precedents, Rav Ovadia concludes that there are certain light prohibitions where flavor is nullified when mixed with permissible food, and he asserts that *kitniyot* are one such prohibition.

---

kitniyot are a lighter prohibition than the meat which the Radbaz addresses, so the flavor of *kitniyot* is permitted even without the additional factors utilized by the Radbaz.

2. This leniency is quite surprising, as those who prohibit the fat in question treat it as a biblical prohibition. Accordingly, even if they think that the biblical prohibition is somewhat debatable (in deference to the lenient view), they should not go so far as to permit the fat's flavor. (Flavor is ordinarily prohibited on a biblical level as long as one can detect it in the food; see *Shulchan Aruch*, *Yoreh De'ah* 98:2; *Shach*, Y.D. 98:7; and *Biur Hagra*, Y.D. 98:10.) Rav Ovadia cites several authorities who address this problem. They explain that not only is the fat's prohibition doubtful (*safeik*), as there are those who permit it, but there is also another doubt involved (*safeik s'feika*). Flavor must enhance another food in order to prohibit it, and it is always doubtful if the flavor emerging from the utensils impacts positively or negatively on the food absorbing it. See *Tosafot* (*Avodah Zarah* 38b s.v. *Iy*), Rosh (*Avodah Zarah* 2:35), *Teshuvot Harashba* (497), and *Sefer Issur V'heter* (33:10). All of these *Rishonim* assert that it is always a *safeik* whether the flavor emerging from a pot imparts a good taste. Between these two doubts, the Rama believes that one may eat food that was cooked in the same pot that was used to cook the questionable fat. Similar doubt about the flavor's impact might also explain the other lenient precedents that Rav Ovadia cites. Otherwise, it remains unclear why flavor is nullified so easily.

GRAY MATTER

Other Authorities

As was noted at the beginning of the chapter, the Rama (O.C. 453:1) writes that there need not be a 60:1 ratio of non-*kitniyot* to *kitniyot* in order to nullify any *kitniyot* that might have fallen into a pot of food. Rather, as long as a majority of non-*kitniyot* exists, one has not violated the *minhag* of not eating *kitniyot*. Later authorities appear to accept this view, including the *Eliah Rabbah* (453:4), *Shulchan Aruch Harav* (O.C. 453:5), *Chok Yaakov* (453:5), *Chayei Adam* (127:1), and *Mishnah Berurah* (453:9). The *Chok Yaakov* explains that, although it appears from the *Terumat Hadeshen* that a 60:1 ratio is necessary to nullify the *kitniyot*, the Halachah follows the Rama, who states that only a majority of the food must not be *kitniyot*. The reason for this Halachah is that refraining from *kitniyot* is merely a custom, so it is not treated with the same severity as biblical and rabbinical laws.

The flavor of food is no stricter than the food itself. Accordingly, if the aforementioned authorities rule that the non-*kitniyot* majority nullifies a minority of actual *kitniyot* food, undoubtedly they agree that the non-*kitniyot* food cooked in the pot nullifies the flavor of *kitniyot* that emerges from the pot.[3] Indeed, the *Zera Emet* (vol. 3, O.C. 48) rules that the *minhag* to refrain from *kitniyot* does not include refraining from their flavor. Rav Ovadia thus notes that all of these Ashkenazic authorities agree with his ruling and permit an Ashkenazic Jew to eat food cooked in a Sephardic Jew's dishes on *Pesach*.

Limitations

When discussing pots in which *kitniyot* were cooked, the distinction between *lechatchilah* (*ab initio*, before the occurrence) and *b'dieved* (*post facto*, after the occurrence) must be stressed. The above-cited lenient rulings only permit a *b'dieved* situation,

---

3. In this case, it might suffice to ascertain that the food's volume is greater than that of the absorbed flavor, while the thickness of the walls containing the flavor might not matter (see the Radbaz's responsum cited above).

when food was **already** cooked in a pot that previously cooked *kitniyot*. However, Rav Ovadia Yosef (*Teshuvot Yechaveh Daat* 1:9) and Rav Yehoshua Neuwirth (*Shemirat Shabbat Kehilchatah* 40:80) rule that an Ashkenazic Jew who must cook *kitniyot* on *Pesach* (such as for a sick person) may not **lechatchilah** cook non-*kitniyot* food for healthy Ashkenazic Jews in the same pot. Similarly, Rav Efraim Greenblatt told this author that an Ashkenazic Jew who wishes to visit a Sephardic home on *Pesach* should arrange for food that was not cooked in a pot that previously cooked *kitniyot*.

Beyond the custom of *kitniyot*, some Ashkenazic Jews altogether avoid eating at other people's homes during *Pesach*. Their concern is that different people observe divergent practices and customs regarding *Pesach*, so the guests might not be permitted to eat from the food cooked in the utensils of their hosts. Rav Elazar Meyer Teitz told this author that Rav Michel Feinstein told him that he heard a story about this practice involving Rav Chaim Soloveitchik and the *Chafetz Chaim*. Rav Chaim visited the *Chafetz Chaim* on *Pesach*, and the *Chafetz Chaim*, who was known for his warm hospitality, did not even offer his guest a cup of tea, due to this practice. Apparently, this stringency was very common in many European circles.

Conclusion

If an Ashkenazic Jew finds himself in a Sephardic Jew's home on *Pesach*, he may eat food that was already cooked in pots that previously cooked *kitniyot*. However, an Ashkenazic Jew may not cook food for himself on dishes that were used to cook *kitniyot*. If an Ashkenazic Jew plans in advance to visit a Sephardic Jew on *Pesach*, Rav Ovadia Yosef indicates that he permits the Sephardic Jew to cook in his own pots for the visitor, while Rav Efraim Greenblatt requires the host and visitors to make alternative arrangements. In addition, some Ashkenazic Jews have the custom of not eating anything outside their own homes on *Pesach*.

The Minhag of Kitniyot
Part III: Scope of the Practice

To conclude our discussion of the Ashkenazic practice of not eating *kitniyot* on *Pesach*, we will focus on the scope of this prohibition, as well as addressing which items are included in it.

Owning and Benefiting from Kitniyot

The laws condemning *chametz* are far stricter than nearly all other Torah prohibitions (see *Tosafot, Pesachim* 2a s.v. *Or*). The Torah forbids owning *chametz*, and the Halachah follows the majority view in the Talmud, forbidding any benefit from *chametz*. In this area, we treat *kitniyot* far more leniently. The Rama (*Orach Chaim* 453:1) and *Mishnah Berurah* (453:12) rule that the Ashkenazic *minhag* to avoid *kitniyot* precludes neither owning nor benefiting from them.[1] Consequently, one may keep *kitniyot* in one's home, a particularly relevant concern for families with sick individuals, young children, and pets. A rabbi should be consulted for guidance in determining that a product is merely *kitniyot* and not actual *chametz*.

Oils and Syrups of Kitniyot - Rav Kook and the Badatz

In the year 5669 (1909), a great controversy erupted between Rav Avraham Yitzchak Kook and the Jerusalem Badatz regarding the permissibility of sesame seed oil on *Pesach*. Rav Kook published a short work (summarized in *Yesodei Yeshurun*

---

1. See *Encyclopedia Talmudit* (16:105 notes 703 and 705) for those who rule strictly against the Rama.

THE MINHAG OF KITNIYOT PART III

6:424 and *Hamo'adim Bahalachah*, p.259) outlining why he permitted this item for *Pesach* consumption. Although sesame seeds are *kitniyot*, he notes that their form has changed into oil. No oil can ever become *chametz* even if it contacts water, so the *minhag* to avoid *kitniyot* does not include sesame seed oil. Similarly, the concern of confusing *kitniyot* with grain does not apply once the sesame seeds are no longer in grain form. Furthermore, Rav Kook addresses sesame seeds that were watched to ensure that they would not be exposed to water. The machine producing the oil needed to be completely dry in order to function, further ensuring that there was no concern for *chametz*. Finally, the sesame seeds in question were cooked during their processing, and once something is cooked, it can no longer become *chametz*. Thus, the sesame seed oil in question was so far removed from concern of *chametz* that, according to Rav Kook, the *minhag* of *kitniyot* did not apply to it.

The Jerusalem Badatz strongly rejected Rav Kook's lenient ruling. They argued that the Rama (*Orach Chaim* 453:1) clearly includes oils derived from *kitniyot* in the custom of avoiding *kitniyot*, as noted by the *Chayei Adam* (*Nishmat Adam* 33).

Rav Kook responded that the Rama only intends to prohibit oil from *kitniyot* that were not carefully inspected for other grains or oil from *kitniyot* that were not already cooked or boiled. Several of his contemporaries accepted Rav Kook's understanding of the Rama and his subsequent ruling, including the Maharsham (*Teshuvot* 1:183), the *Marcheshet* (Chapter 3), and Rav Yitzchak Elchanan Spektor (*Teshuvot Be'er Yitzchak*, *Orach Chaim* 11).

Despite the cogency of Rav Kook's arguments and the many great authorities that support it, common practice is to prohibit oil made from *kitniyot*. For example, Coca-Cola changes its formula from corn syrup to sugar for its kosher-for-*Pesach* colas. In spite of our stringency, some authorities do permit oil of products whose *kitniyot* status is questionable, such as peanut oil (Rav Tzvi Pesach Frank's *Mikra'ei Kodesh* p.205-206 and *Teshuvot Chelkat Yaakov* 1:97).

GRAY MATTER

Today many food products contain *kitniyot* that have been manufactured and metamorphosed into a new product, such as ascorbic acid (made from corn syrup). Rav Hershel Schachter (*B'ikvei Hatzon* 27:9) permits transformed *kitniyot* for *Pesach* use, whereas the Star-K (*Kashrus Kurrents*, Passover 1998) does not permit them in *Pesach* foods.

Items Defined as Kitniyot

Much has been written about which items to include in the *minhag* of *kitniyot*. Four issues are generally explored regarding this issue. Is the item defined as *kitniyot* (legumes, such as beans and lentils), or is it at least similar to *kitniyot* (see Rambam, *Hilchot Kilayim* 1:8-9)? Can the item be ground into flour in the same manner as grain? Was the item historically included in the custom of *kitniyot*? Does the item grow near fields of grain (see *Mishnah Berurah* 453:13)?

Historically, the *Semak* (thirteenth century) mentions rice, beans, lentils, chickpeas, sesame, and mustard. The *Chok Yaakov* (453:1) and *Aruch Hashulchan* (O.C. 453:3) include corn in this category, most likely because it is ground into flour. While these foods have undoubtedly been included in the *minhag* of *kitniyot*, there are other foods whose status as *kitniyot* is more controversial.

Potatoes

Although it appears surprising, there are authorities who include potatoes in the *minhag* of *kitniyot*, as they are ground into flour and can be confused with grain flour. The *Chayei Adam* includes potatoes in the category of *kitniyot*, although he notes that in 5531 (1771) rabbis permitted their use on *Pesach* due to famine (see *Nishmat Adam* 20).

Obviously, this ruling is not accepted today (see *Aruch Hashulchan*, O.C. 453:5). Rav Moshe Feinstein (*Teshuvot Igrot Moshe*, O.C. 3:63) explains why we do not regard potatoes as

THE MINHAG OF KITNIYOT PART III

kitniyot despite the fact that they are ground into flour. Noting that *kitniyot* were prohibited as a custom and not through rabbinical legislation, Rav Moshe asserts that we only define something as *kitniyot* if there is a custom to regard it as *kitniyot*. The early Ashkenazic rabbis did not forbid anything that can be ground into flour;[2] rather, they forbade eating certain products. Thus, although there is logical reason to include potatoes in the category of *kitniyot*, they were not historically included. Perhaps, Rav Moshe suggests, the great need for them kept them from being prohibited; perhaps the list of *kitniyot* was kept short because the reasons for prohibiting any *kitniyot* are weak. Whatever the reason, Rav Moshe rules that only things customarily avoided may not be eaten on *Pesach*.

Peanuts

Both Rav Tzvi Pesach Frank (*Mikraei Kodesh* 2:105) and Rav David Tzvi Hoffman (*Teshuvot Melameid Leho'il* 1:88) note that the practice in Jerusalem is to regard peanuts as *kitniyot*. However, Rav Moshe reaches the same conclusion regarding peanuts that he reached regarding potatoes:

> Peanuts were not regarded as *kitniyot* in many places. Thus, in a place where there does not exist a *minhag* to forbid peanuts, they should not be forbidden, for regarding these matters one should not be excessively strict, as the Chok Yaakov writes [453:9]. Peanuts indeed are forbidden for those whose *minhag* is to avoid them, although even they may be lenient in cases of doubt. One may give *kashrut* certification to peanut oil that has no *chametz*, and those who do not follow the strict *minhag* may partake of it.

Rav Moshe recorded in this responsum (written in 1966) the accepted practice of *kashrut* organizations of that time.

---

2. Contrast this statement to *Chayei Adam* 127:1.

GRAY MATTER

However, today it seems that the practice among the major *kashrut* organizations has changed, and they now treat peanuts, and even peanut oil, as *kitniyot*. The general practice to be very strict about *kashrut* on *Pesach* seems to have taken hold with *kitniyot*, despite the rulings of such eminent authorities as Rav Kook and Rav Moshe.

Soybeans

Although the generally accepted practice today is to regard soybeans as *kitniyot*, Rav Yehudah Pris cites Rav Dov Lior as permitting soybeans for *Pesach* consumption (*Techumin* 13:176-178). Rav Pris explains that Rav Moshe's reasoning regarding peanuts applies equally to soybeans, as they were not known to the earlier generations that adopted the *minhag* of prohibiting *kitniyot*. Quinoa may have the same status as peanuts and soybeans in this regard. [3]

Conclusion

The general practice today is to permit eating potatoes on *Pesach*. On the other hand, it is accepted to prohibit syrups and oils produced from *kitniyot*, as well as soybeans and peanuts. Nonetheless, a Rav may consider permitting caraway, cumin, fennel, fenugreek, coriander, soybeans, peanuts, or quinoa for people with restricted diets. He may be similarly lenient regarding syrups and oils produced from *kitniyot* for such individuals.[4] Competent halachic guidance must be sought in such situations. All *kitniyot* are permitted for a seriously ill individual (even if the illness is not life-threatening) or a young child who must eat *kitniyot* (*Chayei Adam* 127:6). This often arises today, as many pills contain cornstarch binders.

---

3. See *Kashrus Kurrents* of the Star-K Kosher Certification (Passover 1998) for a discussion of caraway, cumin, fennel, fenugreek, and coriander. *Kashrus Kurrents* addresses quinoa in the Passover 1997 issue.

4. Of course, care must be taken to ensure that no actual *chametz* is mixed in.

BIOGRAPHY LIST

Biography List

Aaronberg, Rav Yehoshua - The late author of *Teshuvot Devar Yehoshua* who served as a *dayan* on the Tel Aviv Beit Din.

Acharonim - Great rabbinical authorities of the sixteenth century to the present.

Achiezer - Responsa of Rav Chaim Ozer Grodzinsky, a halachic authority who resided in Vilna (1863 - 1940).

Adler, Rav Yosef - Principal of the Torah Academy of Bergen County and Rav of Congregation Rinat Yisrael in Teaneck, New Jersey. Student of Rav Yosef Dov Soloveitchik.

Ahavat Chessed - A halachic work on the laws regarding acts of kindness by Rav Yisrael Meir Kagan. See **Mishnah Berurah**.

Amital, Rav Yehuda - Rosh Yeshivat Har Etzion, Israel, former Minister in the Israeli government, and author of *Hama'alot Mima'amakim*

Ariel, Rav Yaakov - Rav of Ramat Gan, Israel.

Aruch Hashulchan - A halachic work on the *Shulchan Aruch* authored by Rav Yechiel Michel Epstein (1829 - 1908), Rav of Novardok, Russia. The *Aruch Hashulchan He'atid* is a halachic work on the areas of Halachah not discussed in the *Shulchan Aruch*.

Aseih Lecha Rav - Responsa of Rav Chaim David Halevi, Rav of Tel Aviv -Yafo and author of *Mekor Chaim* (Died 1998).

Auerbach, Rav Avraham Dov - Rav of Tiberias, Israel and son of Rav Shlomo Zalman.

Auerbach, Rav Shlomo Zalman - A renowned halachic authority and the author of *Teshuvot Minchat Shlomo*. He resided in Jerusalem and served as Rosh Yeshiva of Yeshivat Kol Torah. He died in 1995.

GRAY MATTER

Aviasaf - Work by Rav Eliezer ben Yoel Halevi (Raavyah), Ashkenazic *Rishon* of the early thirteenth century. The book has not survived, although parts of it are cited in other sources.

Avkat Rocheil - Responsa authored by Rav Yosef Karo of Safed (1488 -1575), who also wrote *Shulchan Aruch*, *Kesef Mishneh*, and *Beit Yosef*.

Avnei Neizer - Responsa by Rav Avraham Bornstein, Rav of Sochaczov, Poland (1839 - 1910). He also wrote the *Eglei Tal*.

Az Nidberu - Responsa of Rav Binyamin Yehoshua Silber, Rav in Bnei Brak, Israel.

Badei Hashulchan - Halachic work discussing various sections of *Yoreh De'ah* by Rav Feivel Cohen, Rav in Brooklyn, New York. He also wrote *Kuntres Midor Ledor*.

Basri, Rav Ezra - Sephardic *dayan* who resides in Jerusalem and is the author of *Teshuvot Shaarei Ezra*.

Bakshi-Doron, Rav Eliyahu - Sephardic Chief Rabbi of Israel.

Be'er Heitiv - Commentary to *Shulchan Aruch* by Rav Zechariah Mendel of Belz, Ukraine (died 1706).

Be'er Yitzchak - Responsa of Rav Yitzchak Elchanan Spektor. See **Ein Yitzchak**.

Beit Efraim - Responsa of Rav Ephraim Zalman Margolies (1760-1828).

Beit Halevi - Responsa and Bible commentary of Rav Yosef Dov Soloveitchik, Rav of Brisk, Lithuania (1820 -1892). The Rosh Yeshiva at Yeshiva University bearing his name is his great-grandson.

Beit Shmuel - Commentary to the *Even Ha'ezer* section of the *Shulchan Aruch* and authored by Rav Shmuel ben Uri Shraga Feivish (Poland, 17th Century).

Beit Yitzchak - A halachic journal published annually by Yeshiva University.

Beit Yitzchak - Responsa of Rav Yitzchak Shmelkes, a prominent authority in nineteenth-century Galicia (1828-1906).

Beit Yosef - Commentary of Rav Yosef Karo to the *Tur*. See **Avkat Rocheil**.

Berlin, Rav Naftali Tzvi Yehudah (Netziv) - Head of Yeshivat Volozhin in Russia and the author of *Teshuvot Meishiv Davar*, *Ha'eimek Davar* on the Torah, *Meromei Sadeh* on the Talmud, and *Ha'eimek She'eilah* on the *She'iltot* of Rav Achai Gaon. The Netziv lived from 1817 to 1893.

BIOGRAPHY LIST

Between Civil and Religious Law: The Plight of the Agunah in American Society - Discussion of the relationship between various Jewish and American divorce laws by Rav Yitzchak (Irving) Breitowitz, Rav in Silver Spring, Maryland.

Bintivot Hahalachah - Responsa of Rav J. David Bleich; see **Bleich, Rav J. David**.

Birurim B'hilchot Hareiah - A halachic compendium devoted to analysis of Rav A. Y. Kook's halachic rulings.

Biur Hagra - Commentary of the Vilna Gaon (1720 - 1797), Rav Eliyahu Kramer of Vilna, to the *Shulchan Aruch*.

Biur Halachah - Analytical commentary to the *Orach Chaim* section of the *Shulchan Aruch* by Rav Yisrael Meir Kagan; see **Mishnah Berurah**.

Blau, Rav Yaakov – Contemporary halachic authority who resides in Jerusalem who authored the *Netivot Shabbat* and *Pitchei Choshen*.

Bleich, Rav J. David - Rosh Yeshiva at Yeshiva University in New York and the author of *Bintivot Hahalachah* and *Contemporary Halakhic Problems*.

Bleich, Rav Moshe - Rav in the Lower East Side of Manhattan, New York.

Bnei Banim - Responsa of Rav Yehuda Henkin. See **Henkin, Rav Yehuda**.

Chacham Tzvi - Responsa of Rav Tzvi Ashkenazi of Amsterdam (1660 -1718).

Charlop, Rav Yaakov Moshe - Rosh Yeshivat Merkaz Harav, Jerusalem, who died in 1952.

Chatam Sofer - Responsa of Rav Moshe Sofer (1763 - 1839), Rav of Pressburg, Hungary.

Chavatzelet Hasharon - Responsa of Rav David Menachem Manish Babad, Rav of Chernobyl in the early 20th century.

Chavot Yair - Responsa of Rav Yair Chaim Bachrach (1638 - 1702), Rav of Worms, Germany.

Chazon Ish - Halachic work by Rav Avraham Yeshayah Karelitz of Bnei Brak, Israel (1878 - 1953). While being highly respected in all areas of Halachah, his views are especially authoritative in the area of *eruvin*.

Chelkat Yaakov - Responsa of Rav Yaakov Breisch, Rav in Zurich, Switzerland. He died in 1977.

Chok Yaakov - Commentary to the laws of Passover of the *Shulchan Aruch*, by Rav Yaakov Reisher (Germany 1670 - 1733).

GRAY MATTER

Choshen Mishpat - The section of *Shulchan Aruch* that deals with monetary laws.

Contemporary Halakhic Problems - A review of contemporary responsa literature by Rav J. David Bleich, Rosh Yeshiva at Yeshiva University in New York.

The Contemporary Eruv - Discussion of the laws of *eruvin* by Rav Yosef Gavriel Bechhofer of Chicago with an emphasis on *eruvin* in modern cities.

Daf Kesher - Weekly publication of Yeshivat Har Etzion that contains *divrei Torah* and Yeshiva news. Every few years, these publications are combined into a book.

Darchei Moshe - The Rama's commentary to the *Tur*. See **Rama**

Darchei Teshuva - A compilation of the responsa literature to the *Yoreh Deah* section of the *Shulchan Aruch*. By Rav Tzvi Hirsch Shapira (1850-1913).

Dasberg, Rav Uri - An editor of *Techumin* who resides in Alon Shvut, Israel.

David, Rav Shmuel - Rav of Afula, Israel, who is a student of Rav Aharon Lichtenstein and the author of *Sheilot Uteshuvot Meirosh Tzurim*. He is a former rabbi of Kibbutz Rosh Tzurim.

Devar Avraham - Responsa of Rav Avraham Shapira, Rav of Kovno in the early 20th century. He died in 1939.

Dichovsky, Rav Shlomo - Member of the *Beit Din Hagadol* of the Chief Rabbinate of Israel.

Divrei Malkiel - Responsa of Rav Malkiel Tannenbaum of Lomza (late 19th and early 20th centuries).

Doveiv Meisharim - Responsa of Rav Dov Berish Weidenfeld of Trzebin (1881-1965).

Eglei Tal - Discussion of many laws of *Shabbat* by Rav Avraham Bornstein, Rav of Sochaczov, Poland (1839 - 1910). He also wrote the *Avnei Neizer*.

Eider, Rav Shimon - The author of numerous halachic works in English who resides in Lakewood, New Jersey.

Eiger, Rav Akiva - Author of many responsa and a commentary to the *Shulchan Aruch* (1761 - 1837). He served as Rav of Posen, Poland.

Ein Yitzchak - Reponsa of Rav Yitzchak Elchanan Spektor, Rav of Kovno, Lithuania (1817 - 1896). He also wrote *Be'er Yitzchak*.

BIOGRAPHY LIST

Eliashiv, Rav Yosef Shalom - Halachic authority who resides in Jerusalem.

Eliyahu, Rav Mordechai - Halachic authority who resides in Jerusalem. He served as Israel's Sephardic Chief Rabbi from 1983 to 1992.

Encyclopedia Talmudit - Encyclopedia of Talmudic concepts published as an ongoing project of *Yad Harav Herzog*.

Even Ha'ezer - The section of the *Shulchan Aruch* that deals with family law.

Feinstein, Rav Reuven - Son of Rav Moshe and Rosh Yeshiva of Mesivta Tifereth Jerusalem in Staten Island, New York.

Feinstein, Rav Moshe - A renowned halachic authority who authored *Teshuvot Igrot Moshe* and served as Rosh Yeshiva of Mesivta Tifereth Jerusalem in New York (Died 1986).

Frank, Rav Tzvi Pesach - Rav of Jerusalem who authored *Teshuvot Har Tzvi*. and *Mikra'ei Kodesh*, a discussion of laws of festivals (Died 1960).

Free Enterprise and Jewish Law - Discussion of certain aspects of Jewish civil law by Rav Aaron Levine, Rav of the Young Israel of Avenue J in Brooklyn, New York, and Professor of Economics at Yeshiva University.

Gevurat Anashim - A work about laws of coercing a husband to give a *get*. See **Shach**.

Goldberg, Rav Zalman Nechemia - A son-in-law of Rav Shlomo Zalman Auerbach who serves on the *Beit Din Hagadol* of Israel's Chief Rabbinate and resides in Jerusalem

Goldwicht, Rav Meir - Rosh Yeshiva at Yeshiva University.

Goren, Rav Shlomo - Israel's Ashkenazic Chief Rabbi from 1972 - 1982 (Died 1994).

Gra - Gaon Rabbeinu Eliyahu, acronym for the Vilna Gaon. See **Biur Hagra**.

Greenblatt, Rav Efraim - Rav in Memphis, Tennessee and author of *Teshuvot Rivevot Ephraim*.

Greenblatt, Rav Nata - Rav in Memphis, Tennessee.

Grumet, Rav Zvi - Associate Principal of the Torah Academy of Bergen County.

Ha'elef Lecha Shlomo - Responsa of Rav Shlomo Kluger (1785-1869).

GRAY MATTER

Halevi, Rav Chaim David - Rav of Tel-Aviv-Yafo, author of *Aseih Lecha Rav* and *Mekor Chaim* (died 1998).

Hama'a lot Mima'amakim - Essays on Religious Zionism by Rav Yehuda Amital, written in the wake of the Yom Kippur War. See **Amital, Rav Yehuda**.

Hamo'adim Behalachah - Discussion of the laws of holidays by Rav Shlomo Yosef Zevin, editor of the *Encyclopedia Talmudit* (died 1978).

Ha'oz Veha'ahavah - discussion of war in the Rambam's thought by Rav Yehoshua Hagar-Lau, Rosh Yeshiva of the Military Prepratory Yeshiva in Beit Yatir, Israel and nephew of Israeli Chief Rabbi Yisrael Meir Lau.

Har Tzvi - Responsa of Rav Tzvi Pesach Frank, Rav of Jerusalem (Died 1960).

Hatznei'a Lechet - Summary of the laws of modesty by the late Rav Elyakim (Getsel) Ellinson (late 20th century), printed in English as *The Modest Way*.

Heichal Yitzchak - Responsa of Rav Yitzchak Isaac Herzog, Ashkenazic Chief Rabbi of Israel at the time of its independence. He also wrote *Techukah Leyisrael Al Pi Hatorah*.

Henkin, Rav Yosef Eliyahu - A halachic authority who resided much of his life in New York (Died 1973). Author of *Teshuvot Ibra* and *Peirushei Ibra*..

Henkin, Rav Yehuda - A halachic authority who has authored *Teshuvot Bnei Banim* and *Equality Lost* and is the grandson of Rav Yosef Eliyahu Henkin. He resides in Jerusalem.

Hilchot Medinah - Discussion of laws pertaining to the State of Israel by Rav Eliezer Waldenberg. See **Tzitz Eliezer**.

Hutner, Rav Yitzchak - Rosh Yeshivas Chaim Berlin in Brooklyn, New York (Died 1980).

Igrot Moshe - responsa of Rav Moshe Feinstein. See **Feinstein, Rav Moshe**.

Ir Hakodesh V'hamikdash - A work about issues pertaining to Jerusalem authored by Rav Yechiel Michel Tukachinsky, Rav of Jerusalem (died 1955).

Issur V'heter - Halachic compendium by Rav Yonah ben Yisrael (late fifteenth century).

Imrei Yosher - Responsa of Rav Meir Arik, Rav in Tarnow, Galicia (1855-1926).

The Journal of Halacha and Contemporary Society - A halachic journal published semi-annually by the Rabbi Jacob Joseph Yeshiva in Staten Island, New York.

BIOGRAPHY LIST

Kahane, Rav Shlomo David - Rav of Warsaw, Poland and later of the Old City of Jerusalem.

Kaminetsky, Rav Yaakov - Rosh Yeshiva of Torah Vodaath. He died in 1986.

Kasher, Rav Menachem - Late author of *Torah Sheleimah* and editor of *Noam* (mid-20th century).

Kefiyah B'get - Comprehensive discussion of the laws of coercing a husband to divorce his wife by Rav Tzvi Gartner of Jerusalem, Israel.

Keren Orah - Commentary on the Talmud by Rav Yitzchak of Karlin, younger brother of the *Mishkenot Yaakov* (mid-19th century).

Kol Mevaser - Responsa of Rav Meshulam Roth, a member of the council of the Israeli Chief Rabbinate. He died in 1962.

Kook, Rav Avraham Yitzchak Hakohen - Ashkenazic Chief Rabbi in Israel from 1921 through 1935 and the author of numerous halachic and philisophical works, including *Teshuvot Orach Mishpat*.

Kook, Rav Tzvi Yehuda - Son of Rav Avraham Yitzchak Hakohen Kook who served as Rosh Yeshivat Merkaz Harav (Died 1982).

Korban Netaneil - Commentary on the Rosh by Rav Netaneil Weil (1687-1969).

Kuntres Midor Ledor - Discussion of the laws of inheritance by Rav Feivel Cohen. See **Badei Hashulchan**.

Kulitz, Rav Yitzchak - Ashkenazic Chief Rabbi of Jerusalem.

Kuzari - Basic work of Jewish philosophy by Rav Yehudah Halevi, an early 11th century Spanish *Rishon*.

Lange, Rav Elimelech - Author of *Hilchot Eruvin*, alumnus of Yeshivat Kerem B'Yavneh.

Lechem Mishneh - Commentary on Rambam's *Mishneh Torah* by Rav Avraham Boton, Rav in 16th century Salonika.

Lev Aryeh - Responsa of Rav Aryeh Grossnass, late *dayan* of the London Beth Din (mid-20th century).

Lichtenstein, Rav Aharon - Rosh Yeshivat Har Etzion in Alon Shvut, Israel and son-in-law of Rav Yosef Dov Soloveitchik.

Liebes, Rav Yitzchak Isaac – late Av Beit Din of the Iggud Harabannim of America and author of *Teshuvot Beit Avi* (died 1999).

GRAY MATTER

Lifshitz, Rav David - Rav of Suwalk, later Rosh Yeshiva at Yeshiva University. He died in 1993.

Lior, Rav Dov - Rav of Kiryat Arba and Rosh Yeshiva of Yeshivat Kiryat Arba, Israel.

Mabit - Rav Moshe ben Yosef Trani, younger contemporary of Rav Yosef Karo in sixteenth-century Safed, Israel.

Magen Avraham - Commentary to the *Orach Chaim* section of the *Shulchan Aruch*, authored by Rav Avraham Gombiner (c. 1634 - 1682).

Maggid Mishneh - Commentary to the Rambam's *Mishneh Torah* by Rav Vidal of Tolosa (14th century Spain).

Maharam Lublin - Acronym for Moreinu Harav Meir of Lublin, a Polish authority who wrote responsa and a commentary on the Gemara (1558-1616).

Maharam of Rothenburg - Rav Meir ben Baruch Halevy of Rothenburg. He authored numerous responsa. The Mordechai and the Rosh are his disciples (1320 - 1390)

Maharil - Rav Yaakov ben Moshe, German Rav in the late 14th and early 15th centuries.

Maharit - Acronym for Moreinu Harav Yosef of Trani, son of the Mabit, Rav in early 17th century Safed, Israel.

Maharsha - Acronym for Moreinu Harav Shmuel Eidels. He authored a commentary to the Talmud and the commentaries of Rashi and Tosafot to the Talmud (c. 1555 - 1632).

Maharsham - Acronym for Moreinu Harav Shlomo Mordechai Schwadron, author of responsa who served as Rav in Berzan, Galicia (1835 - 1911).

Mas'at Binyamin - Responsa of Rav Binyamin Solnik, student of the Rama and Maharshal. He died around 1620.

Meidan, Rav Yaakov - A Rebbe at Yeshivat Har Etzion, Alon Shvut, Israel, known for his colorful insights to Bible, Talmud, and Halachah study.

Meiri - Commentary to the Talmud by Rav Menachem Hameiri (c. 1249 - c. 1306), mostly entitled *Beit Habechirah*.

Meishiv Davar - Responsa of the Netziv. See **Berlin, Rav Naftali Tzvi Yehudah**.

BIOGRAPHY LIST

Mekor Chaim - Discussion of the laws of *Pesach* by Rav Yaakov of Lissa. It contains a section which discusses some laws of *eruvin*. See **Netivot Hamishpat**.

Melamed Leho'il - Responsa of Rav David Tzvi Hoffman, a halachic authority who headed the Orthodox Rabbinical Seminary of Berlin and wrote a Bible commentary to refute Bible critics (1843 -1921).

Melamed, Rav Zalman - Rosh Yeshivat Beit El, Israel.

Miller, Rav Shlomo - Head of the Kolel Avrechim (Institute for Advanced Talmudic Study) of Toronto.

Mikraei Kodesh - Discussion of the laws of festivals by Rav Tzvi Pesach Frank. See **Frank, Rav Tzvi Pesach**.

Mikraei Kodesh - Discussion of the laws of festivals by Rav Moshe Harari, Yeshivat Merkaz Harav, Jerusalem, including many rulings which Rav Harari heard from contemporary Israeli authorities.

Minchat Chinuch - Commentary on the *Sefer Hachinuch* authored by Rav Yosef Babad, who served as Rav of Tarnipol in the Ukraine (1800 - 1875).

Minchat Elazar - Responsa of Rav Chaim Zev Elazar Shapiro, Chassdic Rebbe of Munkacz.

Minchat Shlomo - Responsa of Rav Shlomo Zalman Auerbach. See **Auerbach, Rav Shlomo Zalman**.

Minchat Yitzchak - Responsa of Rav Yitzchak Yaakov Weisz, *dayan* of the Eidah Chareidit of Jerusalem (died 1989).

Mishkenot Yaakov - Responsa of Rav Yaakov of Karlin, older brother of the *Keren Orah*. He died in 1845.

Mishnah Berurah - Commentary to the *Orach Chaim* section of the *Shulchan Aruch* authored by Rav Yisrael Meir Hakohen Kagan (1893 - 1933), who lived in Radin, Poland. He is commonly known as the *Chafetz Chaim*, the title of his work on the laws of slander, and also wrote the *Biur Halachah*, *Shaar Hatziyun*, and *Ahavat Chessed*.

Mishnat Rabbi Aharon - Responsa of Rav Aharon Kotler, Rosh Yeshiva of Lakewood, New Jersey (Died 1962).

Mishpetei Uzziel - Responsa of Rav Ben-Zion Uzziel, Israel's Sephardic Chief Rabbi from 1939 to 1953. He lived from 1880 to 1953.

GRAY MATTER

Mordechai - Halachic compendium on most tractates of the Talmud authored by Rav Mordechai ben Hillel (c. 1240 - 1298).

Moznei Tzedek - Responsa of Rav Menachem Silber, currently a *dayan* on the Satmar Beit Din of Brooklyn, New York.

Nachalat Tzvi - Discussion of laws of conversion and divorce by Rav Gedalia Felder (died 1992), who resided in Toronto, Canada and also wrote *Yesodei Yeshurun*.

Netivot Hamishpat - Commentary on the *Choshen Mishpat* section of *Shulchan Aruch* by Rav Yaakov of Lissa. He also wrote the *Torat Gittin* on the laws of Jewish divorce and the *Mekor Chaim* on the laws of *Pesach*. He died in 1832.

Netivot Shabbat - Discussion of the laws of *eruvin* by Rav Yaakov Blau of Jerusalem. He also wrote *Pitchei Choshen*.

Netziv - See **Berlin, Rav Naftali Tzvi Yehudah**.

Neuwirth, Rav Yehoshua - Halachic authority who resides in Jerusalem.; author of *Shemirat Shabbat Kehilchatah*.

Neventzall, Rav Avigdor - Rav of the Old City of Jerusalem.

Nishmat Avraham - Discussion of *halachot* pertaining to medicine by Dr. Avraham S. Avraham, a physician who resides in Jerusalem, Israel.

Nissim, Rav Yitzchak - Israel's Sephardic Chief Rabbi from 1955 - 1972.

Noam - Halachah journal edited by Rav Menachem Kasher in the mid 20th century.

Noda Biy'hudah - Responsa of Rav Yechezkel Landau, who served as Rav of Prague (1713 - 1793).

Orach Chaim - The section of the *Shulchan Aruch* which deals with the laws of daily living.

Orach Mishpat - Responsa of Rav Avraham Yitzchak Hakohen Kook. See **Kook, Rav Avraham Yitzchak Hakohen**.

Orchot Chaim - Halachic work that gathers opinions of various *Rishonim* by Rav Aharon of Lunel (late 13th and early 14th century Provence).

Orchot Chaim - Summary of the responsa literature on the *Orach Chaim* section of *Shulchan Aruch* by Rav Nachman Kahane of Spinka (early 20th century).

BIOGRAPHY LIST

Oshry, Rav Ephraim - author of *Teshuvot Mima'amakim*, former Rav of Kovno who serves as a Rav in New York.

Otzar Haposkim - Compilation of responsa literature on the *Even Ha'ezer* section of *Shulchan Aruch* published by an institute in Jerusalem.

Pitchei Choshen – Authoritative discussion of business laws by Rav Yaakov Blau of Jerusalem. He also wrote *Netivot Shabbat*.

Pitchei Teshuvah - Summary of the responsa literature from the seventeenth century to the early nineteenth century presented as a commentary to the *Shulchan Aruch*. It was written by Rav Tzvi Hirsh Eisenstadt, Rav of Utian, Russia (1812 - 1868).

Pri Megadim - Commentary on the *Shulchan Aruch* by Rav Yosef Te'omim, Rav of Frankfurt (1727-1792).

Pris, Rav Yehudah - Rebbe at Yeshivat Birkat Moshe, Maaleh Adumim, Israel.

Raavad - Acronym for Rabbeinu Avraham ben David of Posquieres, France, who wrote many works, including critical comments to Rambam's *Mishneh Torah* (c. 1120 - c. 1197)

Raavyah - Acronyom for Rav Eliezer ben Yoel Halevi, Ashkenazic *Rishon* of the early thirteenth century. He wrote *Aviasaf*.

Rabbeinu Chananeil - 11th century author of a commentary to the Talmud and Rav in Kairouan (Tunisia).

Rabbeinu Tam - Rabbeinu Yaakov ben Meir, Rashi's grandson who lived in France and was the most prominent of the Tosafists (1100 - 1171).

Rabinowitz, Rav Nachum - Rosh Yeshivat Birkat Moshe, Maaleh Adumim, Israel.

Radak - Acronym for Rabbeinu David Kimchi author, of a Bible commentary (1160 - 1235).

Radbaz - Acronym for Rabbeinu David ben Zimra, who authored numerous responsa and a commentary on parts of the Rambam's *Mishneh Torah* and served as Chief Rabbi of Egypt (c. 1480 -1573).

Rama - Acronym of Rav Moshe Isserles. He authored glosses to the *Shulchan Aruch*, most of which are considered authoritative by Ashkenazic Jewry. He served as Rav in Cracow, Poland and wrote other works such as the *Darchei Moshe* commentary to the *Tur* and responsa.

GRAY MATTER

Rambam - Acronym for Rabbeinu Moshe ben Maimon, also known as Maimonides. He authored a halachic code called the *Mishneh Torah*, a commentary to the Mishnah (*Peirush Hamishnayot*), and a philosophical work, *Moreh Nevuchim* (*Guide to the Perplexed*). He was born and raised in Spain and later moved to Egypt (c. 1135 -1204).

Ramban - Acronym for Rabbeinu Moshe ben Nachman, also known as Nachmanides. He authored major commentaries to the Torah and Talmud. He lived in Spain and Israel (1194 -1270).

Ran - Acronym for Rabbeinu Nissim, who authored a commentary to the Talmud (c. 1290 - 1375)

Raphael, Rav Shilo - Late *dayan* on the Jerusalem Beit Din (died 1994).

Rashba - Acronym for Rabbeinu Shlomo ben Avraham Aderet, who served as Rav of Barcelona, Spain and authored a commentary to the Talmud and numerous responsa (1235 - 1310).

Rashbam - Acronym for Rabbeinu Shlomo ben Meir. He authored a commentary to the Torah and certain tractates of the Talmud. He was the grandson of Rashi and the older brother of Rabbeinu Tam and lived in France (c. 1085 - 1174).

Rashi - Acronym for Rabbeinu Shlomo Yitzchaki, author of the premier commentaries to the Bible and the Talmud, who lived in Troyes, France (1040 - 1105).

Rav Pe'alim - Responsa of Rav Yosef Chaim of 19th century Baghdad. He also wrote *Ben Ish Chai*.

Ri - Acronym for Rabbeinu Yitzchak, 12th century Tosafist and nephew of Rabbeinu Tam.

Rif - Acronym for Rabbeinu Yitzchak al-Fasi of Fez, Morocco who wrote an abridged version of the Talmud that elucidates the Talmud and issues rulings regarding matters disputed in the Talmud (1013 - 1103).

Rishonim - Great rabbinical authorities of the eleventh century to the fifteenth century.

Ritva - Acronym for Rabbeinu Yom Tov ben Avraham ibn Asevilli who wrote a commentary to the Talmud and lived in Spain during the fourteenth century.

Rivash - Acronym for Rabbeinu Yitzchak ben Sheishet who authored many responsa. He was born in Barcelona in 1326 and died in Algiers in 1408.

Rosenfeld, Rav Shlomo - Rosh Yeshiva of Yeshivat Shedeimot Neiriyah, Israel.

BIOGRAPHY LIST

Rosh - Acronym for Rabbeinu Asher ben Yechiel, who lived in Germany and Spain. He wrote a halachic commentary to the Talmud and responsa and edited an edition of *Tosafot* known as *Tosafot Harosh* (c. 1250 - 1327).

Salant, Rav Shmuel - Rav of Jerusalem, Israel, he lived from 1816 to 1909.

Schachter, Rav Hershel - Rosh Kollel of Yeshiva University and author of *B'ikvei Hatzion*, *Eretz Hatzvi*, and *Nefesh Harav*.

Schachter, Rav JJ - Rav in Boston and former editor of *The Torah U-Madda Journal*.

Schochetman, Professor Eliav - Professor of Jewish Law at Hebrew University, Jerusalem.

Schwartz, Rav Gedalia - Av Beit Din of the Beth Din of America (the Beth Din of the Orthodox Union and the Rabbinical Council of America).

Sefer Hachinuch - Enumeration and discussion of the 613 *mitzvot* written in the thirteenth century by an unknown author (mistakenly attributed to the Ra'ah, Rabbeinu Aharon Halevi).

Seforno - Commentary to the Torah authored by Rav Ovadia Seforno of Italy (1470 - 1550).

Sema - Acronym for *Sefer Me'irat Einayim*, commentary of the *Choshen Mishpat* section of *Shulchan Aruch* by Rav Yehoshua Falk (Poland, 1555-1614).

Semag - Acronym for the *Sefer Mitzvot Gadol*, written by Rav Moshe ben Yaakov of Coucy, France, in the thirteenth century.

Semak - Acronym for the *Sefer Mitzvot Katan*, written by Rav Yitzchak ben Yosef of Corbeil, France (died 1280).

Shaar Hatziyun - Footnotes to the **Mishnah Berurah**.

Shaarei Ezra - Responsa of Rav Ezra Basri, Sephardic *dayan* in Jerusalem, Israel.

Shach - Acronym for *Siftei Kohen*, the premier commentary to the *Yoreh Deah* and *Choshen Mishpat* sections of the *Shulchan Aruch*, authored by Rav Shabtai Hakohen of Vilna, Lithuania (1622 - 1663). He also wrote *Gevurat Anashim*.

The Shame Borne in Silence: Spouse Abuse in the Jewish Community - A discussion of spouse abuse from the perspective of a Torah scholar and psychiatrist, Rav Dr. Abraham Twerski, Associate Professor of Psychiatry at the University of Pittsburgh School of Medicine.

GRAY MATTER

Shapira, Rav Avraham - Rosh Yeshiva of Yeshivat Merkaz Harav who served as Israel's Chief Rabbi from 1983 -1992.

Shaviv, Rav Yehudah - A Rebbe at Yeshivat Har Etzion and an editor of *Techumin*.

Shemirat Shabbat Kehichatah - A presentation of the laws of *Shabbat* by Rav Yehoshua Neuwirth. He resides in Jerusalem.

Sherman, Rav Avraham - Member of the *Beit Din Hagadol* of the Israeli Chief Rabbinate.

Sho'ell Umeishiv - Responsa of Rav Yosef Shaul Nathanson, who served as Rav of Lemberg, Ukraine (1810 -1875).

Shulchan Aruch - The authoritative halachic work authored by Rav Yosef Karo; see **Avkat Rocheil**.

Shulchan Aruch Harav - Halachic work written by Rav Shneur Zalman of Liadi (1745 - 1813).

Sidrei Taharah - Discussion of the laws of *nidah* by Rav Elchanan Ashkenazi (late 18th century).

Singer, Rav Yosef - Rav in the Lower East Side of Manhattan, served as Rav in Pilzno, Galicia before World War II.

Solnica, Rav Hershel - Rav in Queens, New York and Rebbe in the Torah Academy of Bergen County.

Soloveitchik, Rav Aharon - Son of Rav Moshe Soloveitchik who serves as a Rosh Yeshiva at Yeshiva University and Yeshivas Brisk in Chicago.

Soloveitchik, Rav Chaim - Succeeded his father (the *Beit Halevi*) as the Rav of Brisk and authored commentaries to Rambam's *Mishneh Torah* and parts of the Talmud (1853 - 1918).

Soloveitchik, Rav Moshe - Son of Rav Chaim who served as a Rosh Yeshiva at Yeshiva University (1876 -1941).

Soloveitchik, Rav Yitzchak Zev - Succeeded his father (Rav Chaim) as Rav of Brisk, moved to Jerusalem in 1941, and authored a commentary to Rambam's *Mishneh Torah* (1886 -1959).

Soloveitchik, Rav Yosef Dov - Great grandson of the *Beit Halevi* and son of Rav Moshe who was a Rav in Boston, Massachusetts, and the Rosh Yeshiva of Yeshiva University (1903 - 1993). His students refer to him simply as "the Rav."

BIOGRAPHY LIST

Taharat Habayit - Rav Ovadia Yosef's two volume work on *Hilchot Nidah*. It includes an abridged version entitled *Taharat Habayit Hakatzar*. See **Yabia Omer**.

Tashbetz - Responsa of Rav Shimon bar Tzemach Duran, a late Sephardic *Rishon* who served as a *dayan* in Algeria (1361-1444).

Taz - Acronym for the *Turei Zahav*, a major commentary to the *Shulchan Aruch* authored by Rav David Haleivi of Poland (1586 - 1667).

Techukah Leyisrael Al Pi Hatorah - Discussion of laws pertaining to the State of Israel by Rav Yitzchak Herzog. See **Heichal Yitzchak**.

Techumin - A halachic compendium published annually by the Zomet Institute in Alon Shvut, Israel.

Teitz, Rav Elazar Meyer - Rav of Elizabeth, New Jersey and head of its *beit din*; son of Rav Pinchas.

Teiz, Rav Eliyahu - Rav and Member of Beth Din of Elizabeth, New Jersey and son of Rav Elazar Meyer.

Teitz, Rav Pinchas - Rav of Elizabeth, New Jersey (died 1995).

Tendler, Rav Dr. Moshe David - Rosh Yeshiva and Professor of Biology at Yeshiva University; son-in-law of Rav Moshe Feinstein.

Terumat Hadeshen -Responsa of Rav Yisrael Isserlein of Germany (1390 - 1460).

Teshuvot Vehanhagot - Responsa of Rav Moshe Shternbuch, member of the Eidah Chareidit's *Badatz* (rabbinical court).

The Torah U-Madda Journal - A publication of Yeshiva University.

Torat Gittin - Work on the laws of Jewish divorce by Rav Yaakov of Lissa. See **Netivot Hamishpat**.

Tosafot - Talmudic commentaries of the Tosafists, Talmudic scholars in France and Germany in the twelfth and thirteenth centuries.

Tradition - A journal of Orthodox thought published by the Rabbinical Council of America.

Tukachinsky, Rav Yechiel Michel - Rav in Jerusalem who authored the *Gesher Hachaim* and *Ir Hakodesh V'hamikdash* (died 1955).

Twersky, Rav Mayer - Rosh Yeshiva at Yeshiva University, grandson of Rav Yosef Dov Soloveitchik.

GRAY MATTER

Tur - A code of Halachah which served as the prototype of the *Shulchan Aruch*. It was authored by Rabbeinu Yaakov *Baal Haturim*, son of the Rosh (c. 1275 - c. 1340). He also wrote a commentary to the Torah.

Tzitz Eliezer - Responsa authored by Rav Eliezer Waldenberg, member of the *Beit Din Hagadol* of the Israeli Chief Rabbinate, also authored *Hilchot Medinah*.

Waldman, Rav Menachem - Head of the Shvut Ami Institute, who has written extensively on halachic issues relating to Ethiopian Jewry.

Whitman, Rav Zev - Rav of Tenuva (milk production company), Israel.

Willig, Rav Mordechai - Rosh Yeshiva at Yeshiva University and Rav of the Young Israel of Riverdale, New York.

Yabia Omer - Long responsa authored by Rav Ovadia Yosef, Sephardic halachic authority in Jerusalem and former Sephardic Chief Rabbi of Israel. He has also written *Teshuvot Yechaveh Daat*, *Taharat Habayit*, and countless other works.

Yalkut Yosef - Expansive halachic code written by Rav Yitzchak Yosef, Rosh Kollel of Chazon Ovadia and son of Rav Ovadia Yosef.

Yam Shel Shlomo.- A commentary to the Talmud by the Maharshal, acronym for Moreinu Harav Shlomo Luria, who also authored responsa.

Yechaveh Daat - Short responsa authored by Rav Ovadia Yosef. See **Yabia Omer**.

Yesodei Yeshurun - Discussion of laws of *Shabbat* and *Yom Tov* by Rav Gedalia Felder who resided in Toronto, Canada, and also wrote *Nachalat Tzvi* (Died 1992)

Yisraeli, Rav Shaul - Rosh Yeshivat Merkaz Harav, Rosh Kollel of Eretz Chemdah, and member of the Israeli Chief Rabbinate's *Beit Din Hagadol*; author of *Eretz Chemdah*, *Amud Hayemini*, and other works (died 1995).

Yoreh Deah - One of the four sections of the *Shulchan Aruch*, which discusses the laws of kashrut, family purity, mourning, and other laws.

Yosef, Rav Ovadia - see **Yabia Omer**.

Zaks, Rav Mendel - Late son-in-law of Rav Yisrael Meir Kagan (see **Mishnah Berurah**) and *Mashgiach Ruchani* at Yeshiva University.

Zekan Aharon - Responsa of Rav Aharon Walkin, Lithuanian Rav who was murdered in the Holocaust (1865-1942).

Zimbalist, Rav Chaim - Member of the Israeli Chief Rabbinate's *Beit Din Hagadol*.

APPENDIX

A Heartfelt Plea To Agunos

We the undersigned wish to state that we sympathize and empathize with the plight of women who are having difficulty obtaining *gittin* and are trapped in dead marriages by unscrupulous or cruel husbands. There is no *halachic* justification for husbands to engage in this type of activity, and we condemn it with every fiber of our beings.

It is our concern for these women that motivates us to speak out at this time about a potential danger to these women that can have serious and tragic consequences for them and for their entire community.

Recently, an individual by the name of Rabbi Moshe Morgenstern, who heretofore has had no affiliation with any recognized *Beth Din*, nor has recently served in the active rabbinate, has advertised the ability of his "*Beth Din*" to annul Jewish marriages. He claims to be supported by *Gedolai Yisroel* in general, and in particular by the eminent *Posek,* Rav Ovadia Yosef, *shlita*.

Please be aware that his so-called Beth Din does not follow proper *Get* procedure. The annulments and/or *heterim* to remarry issued by his so-called Beth Din are carried out in halachically illegitimate ways. We are certain that virtually no Orthodox rabbi would be willing to officiate at weddings of women who wish to remarry based upon Rabbi Morgenstern's *heterim*. His claim that he follows the teachings of Rabbi Moshe Feinstein, *zt"l*, is **false and misleading**. The prohibition of adultery and the stigma of *mamzerus* for their offspring loom ominously before women who would indeed remarry by virtue of these heterim.

GRAY MATTER

Rav Ovadia Yosef has issued an unusually strong public statement denouncing Rabbi Morgenstern's actions, denying ever having supported him. Furthermore, Rav Yosef requests that the American rabbinate inform the public of the damage that can be done by this type of irresponsible behavior, and to urge women in the strongest terms possible to refrain from going to this so-called Beth Din.

In conclusion we beseech the public to seek out competent *Batei Din* for the resolution of these matters, and we implore *Hashem* to hearken to the tears of anguished women throughout the world and bring about their redemption as well as the redemption of the entire Jewish nation.

Yosef Adler
Rabbi, Cong. Rinat Yisrael, Teaneck, NJ
Shimon Alouf
Rabbi, Cong. Ahaba VeAhva, Bklyn, NY
Kenneth Auman
Rabbi, Young Israel of Flatbush, Bklyn, NY
Hershel Billet
Rabbi, Young Israel of Woodmere, Woodmere, NY
Binyamin Blau
Rabbi, Community & Beth Din, Elizabeth, NJ
Alfred Cohen
Rabbi, Cong. Ohave Yisroel, Monsey, NY
Reuven Fink
Rabbi, Young Israel of New Rochelle, New Rochelle, NY
Menachem Genack
Rabbi, Cong. Shomrei Emunah, Englewood, NJ
Shmuel Goldin
Rabbi, Cong. Ahavath Torah, Englewood, NJ
Baruch Ben Haim
Chacham, Cong. Shaare Zion, Bklyn, NY
Shlomo Hochberg
Rabbi, Young Israel of Jamaica Estates, Jamaica Est., NY
Avraham Kanarek
Rabbi, Cong. Beth Tefilla, Paramus, NJ

Appendix

Efraim Kanarfogel
Rabbi, Beth Aaron Cong., Teaneck, NJ
Simcha Krauss
Rabbi, Young Israel of Hillcest, Flushing, NY
Yaakov Lerner
Rabbi, Young Israel of Great Neck, Great Neck, NY
Milton Polin
Rabbi Emeritus, Kingsway Jewish Center, Bklyn, NY
Steven Pruzansky
Rabbi, Cong. Bnai Yeshurun, Teaneck, NJ
Jonathan Rosenblatt
Riverdale Jewish Center, Riverdale, NY
Asher Schechter
Rabbi, Cong. Ahavas Achim, Fairlawn, NJ
Fabian Schonfeld
Rabbi, Young Israel of Kew Gardens Hills, NY
Max Schreier
Rabbi, Avenue N Jewish Center, Bklyn, NY
Peretz Steinberg
Rabbi, Young Israel Queens Valley, Kew Gardens Hills, NY
Michael Taubes
Rabbi, Kehilas Tzemach Dovid, Teaneck, NJ
Moshe Tendler
Rabbi, Community Synagogue, Monsey, NY
Elazar Mayer Teitz
Rabbi, Community and Beth Din, Elizabeth, NJ
Eliyahu Teitz
Rabbi, Community and Beth Din, Elizabeth, NJ
Feivel Wagner
Rabbi, Young Israel of Forest Hills, Forest Hills, NY
Herschel Welcher
Rabbi, Cong. Ahavas Yisroel, Kew Gardens Hills, NY
Mordechai Willig
Rabbi, Young Israel of Riverdale, Riverdale, NY
Neil Winkler
Rabbi, Young Israel of Fort Lee, NJ, Fort Lee, NJ
Benjamin Yudin
Rabbi, Cong. Shomrei Torah, Fairlawn, NJ